DIALECTICS
OF FAITH-CULTURE
INTEGRATION

DIALECTICS
OF FAITH-CULTURE
INTEGRATION

Inculturation or Syncretism

Michael Muonwe

To order additional copies of this book, contact:
Xlibris
1663 Liberty Drive
Bloomington, IN 47403
1-888-795-4274
www.Xlibris.com
Orders@Xlibris.com
552479

TABLE OF CONTENTS

FOREWORD

"He who comes to me and hears my words and puts them into practice is like a man building a house, who dug deep and laid the foundation on rock—but the one who hears my words and does not put them into practice is like a man who built a house on the ground without a foundation." (Lk 6,47f)

It has rightly been said, and not only in the Gospel, that practice without a sound theory is like a house without foundations, while on the other hand a mere theory remains a foundation without a proper dwelling, as long as it stands on its own as a goal in itself without any ensuing practice. Both are correlative, and need each other. What is the use of music theory if one can never hear a composition based on it? I like to put this point forward, because I think it touches one of the most conspicuous features of Michael Muonwe's work. The author of this book has always understood the indissoluble tie between digging deep into the realm of theory—since only abstract conceptualization can universalize the communication of ideas and ideals—and the urgency of translating the gained insights into practice. In his case, this means that theological, philosophical and sociological concepts need good theoretical clarification, in order to build practicable roads and bridges towards a tangible improvement of the situation of men and women who may still live in dire need of deeper human appreciation and more social justice.

I had the honour and the great satisfaction of being a guiding companion and fellow-traveller on Michael's path to academic fulfilment at the Catholic University of Leuven, Belgium. From the very beginning, I was impressed by his intelligence in grasping problems and dealing with them; I admired his broadness of scope and mind, the clarity of his reasoning, and his eagerness to learn from criticism. But for all his theoretical dedication and hard work, he never lost sight of the calling which lays at the basis of his academic research, namely his relentless concern for a pastoral commitment that truly cares about an unmitigated inculturation of the Christian faith into his native Igbo culture.

The present book deals with general and often problematic concepts such as culture, inculturation and syncretism; it is about translation, adaptation, indigenisation, contextualisation—all very debatable theoretical issues indeed. And the work must be done! But I am quite confident that the attentive reader will easily see how both critical appraisal of these variety of concepts and concrete pastoral care are closely interwoven. I am very happy with the publication of this book and sincerely hope it gets the attention it deserves. Above all, may it reach the people it is intended to in Europe, Nigeria and beyond, in fact, in every continent or region where the Gospel is still struggling with the complex relationship between inculturation and syncretism.

Bellem, Christmas 2013,
Prof. dr. Peter Schmidt

ACKNOWLEDGEMENTS

This work is the fruit of a research that began some years back at the Catholic University of Leuven, Belgium. I am very grateful to the university for providing the enabling environment for such a critically enriching research as this. I thank in a special way Prof. Dr. Peter Schmidt who has been a very helpful guide and friend during the period of its composition. His critical remarks and candid suggestions were significant assets for me. I am delighted that he is the one that composed the forward.

My deep sentiments of gratitude also go to my bishops—Most Rev. Dr. Simon Okafor (now retired) and Most Rev. Dr. Paulinus Ezeokafor. I would not have been able to initiate and complete this research without their permission and continued support. The encouragement and friendship I received from the presbyterium of Awka diocese, Nigeria, my family and friends have been tremendous. May the Incarnate Word, whose taking of the flesh has remained the ultimate paradigm for all inculturation, continue to enlighten us all, even as we endeavour to make his message a living possession for all men and women in all corners of the globe.

This book is dedicated to the loving memory of my sister, Christiana Ekene Nwagbo.

GENERAL INTRODUCTION

Reservations concerning the relevance of Christian faith in addressing the recurring challenges of life faced by people in different cultures cannot be reasonably ignored in our today's society. The situation has surely become a thing of worry for the church, especially as it realises that it is gradually losing grounds in some societies. In the West, before the transformation brought about by secularisation, Christianity seemed to be the only story in town. It remained somehow ensconced within the culture and enjoyed, more or less, unquestioned authority and normativity. With modernity and secularisation, however, and emergence of pluralised and detraditionalised western society, things never remained the same. Christian faith becomes more challenged than ever to show its plausibility and credibility within the emerging culture. Besides, with the contemporary (postmodern) critical consciousness, people no longer become Christians as a matter of course as it used to be in the past. They tend to radicalise in a more concrete and outstanding manner the awareness of their historicity as inaugurated by modernity. In this context, as tradition loses its normativity, people see themselves as architects of their own destinies and masters of their own affairs. Likewise, the presence of other religions and many other basic life possibilities has provided many more alternatives from which choices can be made. More than ever, people now see the responsibility as basically theirs, of making religious and faith choices that best suit their personal 'life-plans.' The situation is such that some even go to the point of combining elements from the various options available as if to make sure none is missed.

This seems to be the case with the New Age movement. This kind of situation invariably sends a note of warning to Christianity not only to find better ways of expressing its truth, but more importantly to be more aware and respectful of the "other" with regard to truth claims.[1]

Similar situations are experienced in other parts of the globe. In Asia, Africa, South America and many islands in the Caribbean, the issue of Christianity being regarded as a foreign religion has always been on the front burner, especially in recent years. In these places, it is a question of Christianity versus the traditional religions and cultures of the natives or the former slaves, as the case may be, which have been part of the people's life for ages before Christianity. In some instances, Christianity becomes syncretised with some of these other alternatives. The challenging nature of the situation has contributed in no small measure in jolting Christianity from its complacency to fashion out ways to "compete" favourably with these religions as far as offering meaning that is fundamental to the people's aspirations is concerned. The church is bound to ask questions concerning how it can so effectively permeate these societies in order to engage in an intimate encounter with the innermost symbols mobilising the peoples' cultures. These issues cannot just be glossed over. They rather demand deep theological reflection and ecclesiastical action.

To give some instances of the complex nature of the situation, some years back, I met with two priests of Igbo traditional religion (southeast Nigeria). In the course of a brief discussion that followed, it was revealed that both of them were previously among the leading members of their local parish community. According to them, they found it necessary to revert to the traditional religion from where they were previously converted to Christianity because the new religion had failed to give meaning to their lives. It had failed to meet their aspirations. The answers that Christianity provided, they argued, were never genuine responses to their questions. They maintained that the God which Christianity proclaimed was not at home with their

---

[1]   For more on this, see See Lieven Boeve, *God Interrupts History: Theology in a Time of Upheaval*, trans. Brian Doyle (New York: Continuum, 2007), 203-206. See also Terrence Merrigan, "What's in a Word? Revelation and Tradition in Vatican II and in Contemporary Theology," in *Vatican II and Its Legacy*, BETL, no. 166, ed. Mathijs Lamberigts and Leo Kenis (Leuven: Leuven University Press, 2002), 59-61.

environment. For them, he was a foreign (western) God, which made it difficult for him to understand them when they talked or prayed to him. On the contrary, their own Igbo Supreme Being, they reasoned, because he knew them to their very root, understood their plights even before they presented their supplications to him.

There was also a case of another man in one of the parishes in Awka diocese in Nigeria who vowed never to go near the church again as long as he lived. Before then, he was the vice chairman of the local parish pastoral council. He lamented that the indigenous priests posted to the parish had successively continued to drag the parish down. According to him, since the western missionary priests previously in-charge of the parish left, the local priests posted there had been introducing "pagan" drums and dances into the liturgy. According to him, people were no longer serious with the Mass. The solemnity and decorum necessary for the Mass had been lost to the extent that people always clapped their hands during liturgical celebrations. The priests also encouraged the lay associations in the parish to learn traditional dances and organised competitions for the youths on the traditional proverbs. But the man in question said he could not be a party to such a polluted form of Christianity. Moreover, the Sunday Masses were rarely sung in the melodious Latin, which, for him, was one of the major marks of the unity and universality of the church. If people could do things their own way, he questioned, where then lay the highly priced oneness of the church? For him, everything had fallen apart. He reasoned that, since the priests had started introducing into the church the things he left behind to be a Christian, it was better for him to go back to the traditional religion and not be involved in such an admixture that might bring two "Gods" into conflict. He maintained that religion was better appreciated when things remained mysterious and less understood. He asked: "If the solemnity of the Mass is trivialised this way, from where comes the sense of awe one should experience before God?"

Doubtless, these two separate instances represent, as it were, two different attitudes or reactions to similar theological, pastoral and cultural problems. The first case may be said to be an unambiguous offshoot of lack of effective utilisation of the wisdom, philosophy and general cultural riches of the people in communicating the message of Christianity. As a result, the church's organisation and general pastoral planning could simply be described as "pale imitations of Western church patterns of thought and structures."[2] Being so, the faith stood apart as a stranger to the people's culture. This was why the two men regarded the local Christian community as worshiping a western God. For them, being a Christian in this context entailed alienation from their cultural roots. This made them see no reason in continuing to identify with this faith, which they perceived as addressing western issues, while those questions and problems most relevant to their situation were little attended to. They preferred rather going back to their former traditional religion which they felt was intricately interwoven with their entire culture, and being so, was able to reach them where it really pinched.

The second case portrays a man who could be said to have a wrong conception of the proper relationship that should exist between religion, especially Christianity, and culture. Sequel to that, he understood Christian faith as pure and abstract essence, which could be polluted by its contact with the local culture. He was yet to be convinced that the Christian faith itself could not have existed apart from culture. It may never have occurred to him that what he was defending as pure Christian faith already bore undeniable stamp of western culture with which it had been in contact for centuries, and that its existence did not preclude the existence of other forms manifesting the peculiarities of other cultures. This really serves as a pointer to the method of evangelisation used by western missionaries in the region by which almost everything belonging to the local culture was regarded as devilish. Consequently, the local people (including this particular man, of course) were meant to believe that using them to convey the Christian faith might portend an assault to the Christian God. This does not rule out the fact that the priests concerned may have indiscriminately introduced the traditional cultural elements into the parish liturgy and life without appropriate catechesis, or without actually studying the culture deeply to know the symbolic suitability of those elements in communicating the specific Christian message. If this was the case, it could have led to a situation where conflicting messages were conveyed to the people, which might be difficult for them to reconcile. But this may be reading too much into the situation, especially as the man was not objecting to inappropriate use of those elements, but their employment in the first place.

---

[2]   Luke Fashole, "What is African Christian Theology," *AFER* 16, no. 4 (1974): 383.

Whereas in the first instance, the two men reacted seriously against what they perceived as cultural alienation occasioned by lack of effective and creative engagement of the faith with their local culture, in the second instance, the man never welcomed the employment of the local culture. Both reactions show that Christianity is yet to be properly received by the people concerned. It is actually against this background that the present research finds its motivation.

One thing is clear: some people are yet to come to sufficient acknowledgment of the role or place of religion in a culture or the extent of influence of culture on religion. This has sometimes led to wrong ideas concerning Christian faith and reflections on it. This is somehow manifest in the sometimes-unfriendly attitude towards cultural pluriformity of Christianity, thus, restricting vibrant possibilities for its creative engagement with different cultural contexts. Sometimes the attitudes of some church authorities seem to suggest that they understand their own presentation of the Christian truth to be universal, timeless and unchanging. Consequently, it is assumed that all are to understand, appreciate and value it the same way. By this very fact, the cultural potentials of various people are to a great extent under-utilised in the process of proclamation of the gospel. When this is the case, it becomes sometimes difficult for the people to see the relevance of their continued identification with Christianity in their personal lives.

But we are aware of the simple rule in human communication that, for one to be well understood, he or she must adapt his message to the level or the thought pattern of the receiver. The Thomistic thought has the principle that "whatever is received is received according to the mode of the receiver."[3] If this maxim is anything to go by, then, one must acknowledge the fact that, for Christian faith to make any meaning for the people, it must be proclaimed and lived through their culture, which is their way of life and the carrier of their identity. We cannot escape the fact that our actions are to some extent conditioned by our culture; that we look at reality from the point of view of our culture, because it helps to fashion our mind-sets. It forms part of the basis from which we evaluate the messages that come our way and the way we make selections and choices of actions. In effect, to reach us where we are, this reality cannot be reasonably neglected.

---

[3]   Thomas Aquinas, *Summa Theologiae* I, q. 76, a. 1, obj. 3.

Musimbi Kanyoro has made it clear that every form of understanding one may have "of the gospel in any culture is situation-variable."[4] No meaningful evangelisation can be achieved without the medium of culture. No one can evangelise in a cultural vacuum, nor can the faith be considered as culture-free. God's communication to mankind has always been done through people's cultures. He has always addressed us in our particularities. In the Old Testament, God communicated himself to the Israelites through the medium of their culture. In the New Testament, the Word of God actually became flesh. He became one of us. Jesus was born into the first-century Palestinian Jewish community. He communicated his message of the kingdom of God through the linguistic imageries, cultural symbols, proverbs and other cultural riches of the Jews.

The church is called upon to continue this practice of making the message of the kingdom reach people in their different circumstances and cultures (cf. Mt 28:19). Indeed, one needs to acknowledge that the church has made some efforts for the greater part of its history to live up to the demands of this command, though not without regrettable shortcomings. In recent years, especially beginning from the second half of the last century, it has taken this challenge rather more seriously. Both theologians and the church's hierarchy have tried, in one way or the other, to address the issue of the need for a better relationship between Christian faith and different cultures. It is a challenge that faces the church world-over and which cannot be ignored.

As a contribution to this all-important endeavour, this research is designed in such a way that it brings to the fore the overall significance of culture both in the reflections on, communication, and living out of Christian faith. Its end is to fashion out a better approach for making the meaning conveyed by Christian faith be properly received and appreciated by each culture, especially given the circumstances of today's society. It is also directed towards highlighting the enormity of challenges that the approach portends for the church and its theologians as well as proposing better ways of meeting them head-on.

In a nutshell, the research addresses these questions: To what extent can the understanding of culture influence the relationship between

---

4   Musini Kanyoro, "Called to One Hope: The Gospel in Diverse Cultures,"
     in *Called to One Hope: The Gospel in Diverse Cultures*, ed. Christopher
     Duraisingh (Geneva: WCC, 1998), 103.

it and Christian faith? How can culture be properly understood in order to allow for its maximum appreciation and utilisation in the actualisation of the church's missionary mandate? How is Christian faith to be proclaimed or integrated into a given culture in order to make sure it is made meaningful to the people? Which model of relationship between Christian faith and culture best manages the "continuous tension between the centrifugal pull of diverse cultures away from uniformity and the centripetal pull of church leaders to unity and orthodoxy[?]"[5] Or, rather, how are we to conceive of the relationship between Christian faith and culture that best respects the demands of cultural pluralism in our contemporary society? What is the limit of the engagement of Christian faith with different cultural and religious traditions that will be able to guard against compromise or loss of its own identity? Or clearer still, how is the faith to engage different cultures without being religiously syncretic?

In order to do justice to the above questions, I have divided the work into four chapters. The first chapter is committed to examining two broad understandings of culture. It is intended to explore how the church's understanding of culture can make some significant difference in its disposition towards variety and diversity discernible among the various people to whom it ministers. Also to be examined in the chapter is how the church has tried to respond to the challenges posed by the progressive change in the understanding of culture, especially as it concerns its appreciation of the centrality of culture in any attempt to comprehend, dialogue with, or transmit the faith.

The second chapter focuses on the landmark achievement of the Second Vatican Council in its reconceptualization of culture. It investigates the basic orientations of the council and how its greater appreciation of the church's historicity, cultural pluralism and their implications influenced the shift it made in the magisterial teaching on culture. Also discussed is how the shift helped the council to articulate a better understanding of theological mediation between Christian faith and culture. The short-comings of the council's ideas on culture is likewise examined.

The third chapter appraises and theologically legitimates the theology and practice of inculturation as a viable and inevitable option

---

[5] Walter Principe, *Faith, History and Cultures: Stability and Change in Church Teachings*, The Pere Marquette Theology Lectures, no. 22 (Milwaukee, WI: Marquette University Press, 1991), 44-45.

for the church in order to meet up with the challenge of making Christianity much more relevant to people. The chapter is structured in such a way that the meaning of inculturation will first be explored. To make its meaning clearer, inculturation will be delineated from other approaches taken in trying to relate the faith to culture. This leads to the examination of whether or not commitment to the process of inculturation poses a threat to the unity and catholicity of the church. Important to the discussion in the chapter is the examination of some assumptions, wrong conceptions and attitudes that have constituted some obstacles to authentic inculturation. Having done this, I will then discuss the theological basis for inculturation.

Study of the challenges posed by religious syncretism to inculturation is my central concern in the fourth chapter. It involves a critical analysis of the various ways syncretism has been understood, especially in recent scholarship, by experts from various fields of study. Special place will be given to the theological articulation of the concept. It is within this context that I will distinguish syncretism from genuine inculturation as well as figure out situations that can favour the emergence of syncretism as far as Christianity is concerned. Better ways of addressing such situations will also be examined. This chapter will be followed by the general conclusion, which summarises the fruits of the research.

The research incorporates descriptive, historical, analytical and hermeneutic-critical methods in the study of relevant literature. This is pursued within the basic framework of interdisciplinary openness and cross-fertilisation of ideas. This is considered important given the nature of the problem at hand and the research objectives. The problems being addressed manifest such a complexity that cuts across borders of disciplines. It is, therefore, exigent to note at the onset that the choice of literature is not restricted to theology. Since the research concerns discussions on faith and culture, I will enter into dialogue with anthropologists, sociologists, historians of religion, philosophers, etc. I believe that this kind of cross-pollination of ideas among dialogue partners from different relevant fields of study will help in no small measure in addressing the subject matter from a more critically-balanced perspective, thus, contributing to making the research more fruitful and more pastorally relevant.

1

CHURCH, THEOLOGY AND CONCEPTUALISATION OF CULTURE

INTRODUCTION

The way the church understands culture makes a whole lot of difference as regards how it appreciates its position and responsibility in relation to its evangelising mission in the world. This bears some significant implications for the theological and the practical aspects of the church's life. The influence that the understanding of culture exerts on theology is necessitated by the mediative role the latter plays between culture and the Christian faith. The people who are objects of the church's mission are also affected by it because they are not merely the architects of culture but are also themselves shaped by culture. As architects of culture, they influence the direction of cultural growth and development. But culture also moulds their perception of reality in general and their evaluation and appreciation of the Christian faith in particular. In effect, this first chapter addresses the different conceptions of culture and how the interplay of Christian faith, theology and culture is to be construed. It also addresses questions concerning how the theological mediation between faith and culture can better facilitate effective evangelisation.

Taking the above into consideration, the different conceptions of culture will first be examined. The relevance of these conceptions to the church's relation to people of varied cultural backgrounds will also be studied. This entails a critical assessment of how the church and its theologians have been able to manage the challenges posed by cultural dynamism and variances as the church steps forward to spread the gospel to all nations. This assessment will be done in the light of the goal of making the Christian faith well received by people of different cultures. This is especially important in today's theological reflection where cultural criticism is not only important but also inevitable for authentic reception, development and practice of the faith.

UNDERSTANDING CULTURE

Culture is a commonly used term. However, as many scholars have observed, its meaning remains evasive. The British cultural and political analyst, Raymond Williams, has described it as "one of the two or three most complicated words in the English Language."[1] He attributes this to the intricacy of its development through history and the fact that it is used by scholars across different academic disciplines and ideological persuasions.[2] For the American professor of law, Nomi Stolzenberg, it is "an exceedingly vague and ambiguous term."[3] The Irish theologian, Michael Gallagher, describes it as a "chameleon term" the scope of which seems so inclusive that it can easily be manipulated by authors to serve their own specific ends.[4] This has made some scholars avoid any form of association with

---

[1]   Raymond Williams, *Keywords: A Vocabulary of Culture and Society* (London: Fontana, 1976), 76.

[2]   Ibid., 76-77. See also Ary Crollius, "The Meaning of Culture in Theological Anthropology," in *Inculturation: Its Meaning and Urgency*, ed. John Walligo *et al.* (Nairobi: St. Paul, 1986), 47-48; Kwame Bediako, "Culture," in *New Dictionary of Theology*, ed. Sindair Ferguson and David Wright (England: Inter-varsity, 1988), 183-184. Robert Borofsky argues that people conceive it differently in our contemporary society depending on the political, nationalistic, or ethnocentric end they may like it to serve. See Robert Borofsky, "Introduction," *American Anthropologist* 103, no. 2 (2001): 433.

[3]   Nomi Stolzenberg, "What We Talk about When We Talk about Culture," *American Anthropologist* 103, no. 2 (2001): 443.

[4]   Michael Gallagher, *Clashing of Symbols: An Introduction to Faith and Culture*, Revised and Expanded ed. (London: Darton, Longman and Todd, 2003), 13.

it, while some others move for its exclusion in academic discourse.[5] That notwithstanding, the term is still very much in use in the social sciences and humanities. According to the American anthropologist, Roger Lohmann, it is so "central" in these fields of study "because of its pervasive relevance to everything that human beings think, feel, and do."[6] He maintains that its centrality is "not only in spite of, but also because of, its multiple meanings and ambiguity."[7] In short, the concept has undergone a whole lot of revisions, reformulations, and even rejections throughout its history. In view of this, it seems perfectly in order to trace its development as well as examine how it is understood today. This will perhaps lead to a fuller appreciation of its meaning and significance in the society, and show why it cannot be reasonably bypassed in any meaningful attempt to understand, dialogue with, or communicate any message, Christian or otherwise, to any group of people.

DIALECTICS OF NATURE AND CULTURE: CULTURE AS HUSBANDRY

According to Williams, when the term, culture, originally appeared in English language, it was used as "a noun of process," denoting "the tending of something, basically *of* crops or animals."[8] In order words, it describes the human intervention in the natural growth of plants and animals. This original meaning bears some significant implications, especially with regard to the conception of how culture is related to nature and vice versa. The most basic is that there is already

---

5 Leopold von Weise, a German sociologist, for one, has argued that it should "be avoided entirely in descriptive sociology." See Leopold von Weise, "Review of Six Essays on Culture by Albert Blumenthal," *American Sociological Review* 4, no. 4 (1939): 594; Lila Abu-Lughod suggests that the term, culture, be entirely dropped in favour of 'discourse,' as used by Michel Foucault, and 'practice,' as it is employed by Pierre Bourdieu. See Lila Abu-Lughod, "Writing against Culture," in *Recapturing Anthropology: Working in the Present*, ed. Richard Fox (Santa Fe, NM: School of American Research, 1991), 137-162.

6 Roger Lohmann, "Culture," *Encyclopedia of Religion* 3 (2005): 2087.

7 Ibid., 2089.

8 Williams, *Keywords*, 77. See also Terry Eagleton, *The Idea of Culture* (Oxford: Blackwell, 2003), 1; Kathryn Tanner, *Theories of Culture: A New Agenda for Theology* (Minneapolis, MN: Ausburg Fortress, 1997), 3.

a natural given (crop or animal) on which human beings intervene culturally. Put differently, to be cultural implies not a flight from the natural. Thus, even when humans strive to transform or transcend nature, they employ tools and means which are either natural or derived from it. Culture could then be said to be produced by nature which it in turn manipulates.[9]

This change exerted on nature by culture does not entail annihilation or arbitrary manipulation of nature, for nature does resist exploitation or manipulation beyond certain limits. That is why it still persists in one way or the other in what we perceive as cultural. Indeed, it seems beyond question that there is nothing cultural that one could assume to be entirely unnatural.[10] This challenges the dichotomous thinking that usually sets culture at odds with nature. One can use the influence of human biological constitution on human culture as an instance of how nature sets limit to culture. Human culture will certainly be different, if, for instance, those human organs (like breasts or eyes) located in front of human beings were at their back, or if humans lacked hands, feet or eyes. Humans are able to do as much as they do in their relationships, friendships, sexuality, technological and scientific breakthroughs simply because of their specific natural endowments. If these had been different, we would have witnessed a different direction in human culture.[11] The theory of evolution has clearly shown how the development of limbs and brains in humans exerted significant effects on the direction of the development of humankind and its culture. This original idea of culture, therefore, contains within it a rejection of determinism or reductionism on the part of nature, on one hand, and on the part of culture, on the other. As the British literary theorist and critic, Terry Eagleton, puts it, it incorporates "a tension between making and being made, rationality and spontaneity, which upbraids the disembodied intellect of the Enlightenment as much as it defies the cultural reductionism of so much contemporary thought."[12] In this sense, then, he continues, we do not need to deconstruct any opposition between nature and culture, because the very notion of culture already contains such

---

9   Eagleton, *The Idea of Culture*, 3.
10   Ibid., 4.
11   James Downs, *Cultures in Crisis* (Beverly Hills, CA: Glencoe, 1971), 40-53.
12   Eagleton, *The Idea of Culture*, 5.

a deconstruction.[13] This original meaning is very important and fundamental to other developments of the concept in history.

NORMATIVE-CLASSICIST UNDERSTANDING OF CULTURE

When culture is understood in the normative-classicist sense, it denotes the process of refinement and development of humans in accordance with the values (especially the intellectual) considered ideal and exemplary. Its first usage in this sense is sometimes attributed to the Roman Philosopher, Marcus Cicero (103BC-43BC), who, in his *Tusculan Disputations*, employs it to qualify the process of refinement of the soul attained through philosophical reasoning, and posits this as the ideal achievement for all human beings.[14] Many authors who used the term in the sixteenth and the seventeenth centuries understood it in this sense, even though they may not have all agreed that such intellectual refinement was only achieved through philosophy. It was in this sense that Francis Bacon (1605) speaks of "the culture and manurance of minds,"[15] and Thomas Hobbes (1651) of "a culture of their minds."[16] In this newer usage, a cultured or cultivated person was a gentleman or lady, a good-mannered and civilised person, an urban dweller who had fine taste. To be cultured one needed to possess those things valued as the refined, appropriate and superior tastes in life. Hence, culture was not what people automatically possessed as members of a given society.[17] It was rather "a matter of good manners and good taste, of grace and style, of virtue and character, of models and ideals, of eternal verities and inviolable laws."[18] In the words of the Canadian theologian, Hervé Carrier, when

---

[13] Ibid., 2.

[14] See Cicero, *Tusculanes*, II, 13.

[15] Williams, *Keywords*, 77

[16] Ibid.

[17] See Gertrude Jaeger and Philip Selznick, "A Normative Theory of Culture," *American Sociological Review* 29, no. 5 (1964): 654.

[18] Bernard Lonergan, *A Second Collection*, ed. William Ryan and Bernard Tyrrell (London: Darton, Longman & Todd, 1974), 92. Describing further this notion of culture, Lonergan writes: "culture was conceived not empirically but normatively. It was the opposite of barbarism. It was a matter of acquiring and assimilating the tastes and skills, the ideals, virtues and ideas that were pressed

construed this way, culture denotes "fine arts, humanism, science, instruction, and education."[19] It not only refers to these processes of refinement of the mind but also to their products. In this sense, culture becomes an elite possession, and to be cultured means to belong to the elite class, which not only determine what it is to be cultured, but also disseminate it to those it considers deficient in it.[20] This view of culture has not been completely superseded today. At least, at the mention today of the word, culture, many think immediately of great works of art, artefacts, literature and other monuments and momentous achievements deposited in museums, libraries and archives.[21]

When this idea of culture was applied in the sixteenth and the seventeenth centuries to the society in general, it became synonymous with civilisation such that only those societies thought to be civilised were, more or less, also believed to possess culture. Every society was valued against a certain standard of intellectual progress and techno-scientific advancement. Judging with these parameters, some societies were valued as superior and paradigmatic as far as culture was concerned, while others were regarded as cultureless, or at best, low cultured. Two American sociologists, Gertrude Jaeger and Philip Selznick, observe that this view of culture is largely associated with the humanists, with their distinction between "high" and "low" cultures.[22]

---

upon one in a good home and through a curriculum in the liberal arts. It stressed not facts but values. It could not but claim to be universalistic. Its classics were immortal works of art, its philosophy was the perennial philosophy, its laws and structures were the deposit of the wisdom and the prudence of mankind. Classicist education was a matter of model to be imitated, of ideal characters to be emulated, of eternal verities and universal laws. It sought to produce not mere specialist but uomo universale that could turn his hand to anything and do it brilliantly." See Bernard Lonergan, *Method in Theology* (New York: Seabury, 1979), 301.

[19] Hervé Carrier, "Understanding Culture: The Ultimate Challenge of the World-Church," in *The Church and Culture since Vatican II: The Experience of North and Latin America*, ed. Joseph Gremillion (Notre Dame, IN: University of Notre Dame Press, 1996), 13.

[20] Rosamund Brillington *et al.*, *Culture and Society: A Sociology of Culture* (London: Macmillan, 1991), 9.

[21] See Gerald Arbuckle, *Culture, Inculturation, Theologians: A Postmodern Critique* (Collegeville, MN: Liturgical, 2010), 2.

[22] Jaeger and Selznick, "A Normative Theory of Culture," 654. These authors distinguish this view from the anthropological view, which, according to them, is

When this notion of culture held sway, the West, who then thought of themselves as the only civilised group of people, assumed that they alone possessed culture; others did not.[23] To be cultured, therefore, one needed to conform to the western norm for civilisation. This mentality became re-enforced in the process of colonisation and Christianisation when the non-western other was literally forced to adhere to the ways of the West. How the colonised Africans, for instance, felt concerning the effect of this understanding of culture could be gleaned from the words of the first president of Tanzania, Julius Nyerere, who writes: "Of all crimes of colonialism there is none worse than the attempt to make us believe we had no indigenous culture of our own, or that what we have was worthless—something of which we should be ashamed, instead of a source of pride."[24]

In the nineteenth century Britain, this conception of culture found its outstanding representation in the work, *Culture and Anarchy* (1869), by the British poet and cultural critic, Matthew Arnold. For him, culture should be understood as "the study and pursuit of perfection."[25] It has to do with an all-round development of a person in a harmonious fashion, "which consists in becoming something rather than in having something, in an inward condition of the mind and spirit, not in an outward set of circumstances."[26] People of culture, he notes, are those who have achieved greatness in the field of classical learning and "noble" achievements, and thus have reached a certain level of refinement:

> The great men of culture are those who have had a passion for diffusing, for making prevail, for carrying from one end of society to the other, the best knowledge, the best ideas of their time; who have laboured to divest knowledge of all that was harsh, uncouth,

---

rather non-selective and does not take an evaluative or normative stance. This is the view we describe in this work as pluralist (we shall come to that shortly), and which in their estimation is the dominant view held by many experts during their own time.

[23] See Lohmann, "Culture," 2087. See also See Eagleton, *The Idea of Culture*, 9-10; Stolzenberg, "What We Talk about," 442.

[24] Julius Nyerere, *Ujamaa* (London: Oxford University Press, 1974), 66.

[25] Matthew Arnold, *Culture and Anarchy: An Essay in Political and Social Criticism* (London: Smith and Elder, 1909), 7.

[26] Ibid., 9-10.

difficult, abstract, professional, exclusive; to humanize it, to make it efficient outside the clique of the cultivated and learned, yet still remaining the *best* knowledge and thought of the time, and a true source, therefore, of sweetness and light.[27]

He, thus, understands culture as the best that humans have ever achieved in the world, which should be made available not only to a few but to all. Culture, he argues, tries "to make the best that has been thought and known in the world current everywhere; to make all men live in an atmosphere of sweetness and light, where they may use ideas, as it uses them itself, freely,—nourished, and not bound by them."[28] Inherent in this idea is the selective attribution of the term, culture, to some individuals and societies and exclusion of others. Here lies the danger spotted out by Jaeger and Selznick in the normative conception of culture—it easily lends itself to ethnocentrism.[29]

During the period under study, the people regarded as not yet cultured or "low" cultured were disparagingly referred to as barbarians or savages. Culture became a value shared by people "to a greater or lesser extent and, in the measure they did so, they ceased to be barbarians."[30] Daniel Wilson, the Canada's first anthropologist, having been influenced by Charles Darwin's evolutionary theory, argues that culture evolves from its crudest form to the height of civilisation. This means that a time was when human societies lacked culture. He uses the term "savage" to refer to those who, according to him, are not yet civilised and are, thus, still under the lowest level of cultural evolution. Though he admits they are all human beings, he maintains that their level of cultural appropriation differs significantly from those he considers as higher societies. This difference, he points out, is in degree and not in kind.[31] Having denied such people of anything that could be described as genuine culture, and religion being a constituent of culture, they are also invariably denied of any genuine religion. If they had religion, it could best be described as animism: ". . . there is

---

27   Ibid., 31. Emphasis in the original.
28   Ibid., 31.
29   Jaeger and Selznick, "A Normative Theory of Culture," 654.
30   Lonergan, *A Second Collection*, 92.
31   Wilson Daniel, *Anthropology*, The Humbolt Library Series (New York: Humboldt, 1885), 29.

usually discerned among such *lower races* a belief in unseen powers pervading the universe, this belief shaping itself into an animistic or spiritualistic theology, most resulting in a kind of worship."[32]

So, we now see, as noted by the Canadian theologian, Bernard Lambert, that such an understanding of culture ends up splitting the human race into two groups—"those who are fully human and those who are not,"[33] and as such someone "is always in danger of having another man regard him as a non-man or an under-man."[34] In short, underlying all this is the belief that there is only one (best) way of doing things, a way of acting and a system of meaning that is universally applicable and valid at any point in time. It represents a mono-cultural view of the world, which is an impoverishment of the idea of culture itself.[35] Instead of being pluralistic, culture is rather seen as monolithic and universalistic. In an unambiguous fashion, Kathryn Tanner, an American theologian, captures this conception of culture when she says: "The word *culture* when used in a high culture or evaluative sense is, therefore, found in the singular rather than the plural: there is *a* high culture to be shared in varying degrees by cultured persons, but no high cultures."[36] Another implication of this understanding of culture is that it encourages a romantic view of the way of life of a people. By concentrating solely on the intellectual achievements, it also entails a neglect of the people's feelings regarding their way of life.[37]

---

[32] Ibid., 29. Emphasis is mine. From the tone of his assertion, it seems their being described as religious is a kind of concession. This can be gleaned from the phrase, "a kind of worship." In fact, Wilson had an evolutionist notion of culture. Accordingly, he argues further that the ancestors of the civilised races were at a point in history on that level of cultural development where those he refers to as savage tribes are.

[33] Bernard Lambert, "*Gaudium et Spes* and the Travail of Today's Ecclesial Conception," in *The Church and Culture since Vatican II: The Experience of North and Latin America*, ed. Joseph Gremillion (Notre Dame, IN: University of Notre Dame Press, 1985), 41.

[34] Ibid.

[35] Aylward Shorter, *Towards a Theology of Inculturation* (MaryKnoll, NY: Orbis, 1994), 25; Eagleton, *The Idea of Culture*, 16.

[36] Tanner, *Theories of Culture*, 5. Emphas is mine.

[37] Arbuckle, *Culture, Inculturation, Theologians*, 2.

Church and Classicist Assumptions

The influence exerted on the church by the Roman Empire in its early stages of expansion cannot be so easily glossed over. Being a strong force to reckon with during the first centuries of Christianity, its understanding of culture had much influence on the church's theology and practice. For the Romans at the time, culture meant "a universal system of values and laws that could be elicited through philosophical reflection and imposed through education."[38] They, like other ancient civilisations,[39] arrogated the possession of culture exclusively to themselves. To be cultured, therefore, entailed imbibing Roman ideas, its education and mannerism. With such classicist mindset, they believed that not being a Roman citizen was equivalent to not having any culture. In effect, through military conquests and corollary expansion of the Empire, they strove hard to impose their cultural ideal to the whole world.[40]

By the fourth century, Christianity's fortune changed in the Empire with Constantine's edict of Milan in 313. By this edict, Christianity became legalised.[41] It later became the official religion of the Empire in 380, during the reign of Theodosius (379-395).[42] It was as a result of the church's romance with the Empire at this period,

---

[38]   Shorter, *Towards a Theology of Inculturation*, 18. It is they (the Romans) who determined what these values were.

[39]   One can mention here the Hellenisation campaign, which began with Alexander the Great, by which Greek culture was, more or less, exported to the captured states. Some scholars believe that it is more likely that Alexander adopted the policy merely out of pragmatic concerns of having a better grip at, and exerting effective control over, his vast Empire in order to ensure smoother governance. See Peter Green, *Alexander the Great and the Hellenistic Age: A Short History* (London: Orion, 2008), 21.

[40]   Leonardo Mercado, *Inculturation and Filipino Theology* (Manila: Divine Word, 1992), 18-19.

[41]   Paul Maier, *Eusebius—The Church History: A New Translation with Commentary* (Grand Rapids, MI: Kregel, 1999), 343. See also Adrian Hastings, "150-550," in *A World History of the Church*, ed. Adrian Hastings (Grand Rapids, MI: Eerdmans, 1999), 36.

[42]   Ibid., 41. Hastings writes that Theodosius not only declared Christianity the official religion of the Empire, but also forbade all 'pagan' religions in the year 391. This marks a further development from Constantine's edict of religious tolerance. It also paved the way for the binding of the State and Christianity.

which saw its bonding with the State into a strong religio-political system, that the church came to adopt this view of culture.[43] A century latter, when the eastern (Byzantine) part of the Empire severed itself more and more from the West and the Roman pontiff successfully inherited the defunct line of emperors in the West, this view of culture became more consolidated within the church.[44] It impinged so much upon its understanding of, and relationship to, people of different nations of the world, especially those beyond the precincts of the ancient Christendom. We will examine in detail how this has influenced missionaries in their practical apostolate, and how it became manifest in some official magisterial documents as well as among theologians.

Missionaries and Cultures

There is no naysaying the fact that, for about two thousand years of its existence, especially from the fourth century C.E, Christianity had mostly adopted a triumphalist and exclusivist posture in its relationship with other religions and cultures. Accordingly, its missionaries, though with some notable exceptions,[45] consistently exhibited significant levels of highhandedness in their various missionary fields leading to the denigration of the local people together with their traditional religions and cultures. They had always sought to present the gospel to people in different parts of the globe in exactly the same way it was developed and practised within Europe.[46] Time and energy were expended for centuries trying

---

[43] Shorter, *Towards a Theology of Inculturation*, 18.

[44] Ibid. See also Johann-Baptist Metz, "Unity and Diversity: Problems and Prospects for Inculturation," *Concilium* 204, no. 4 (1989): 79.

[45] Such exceptions include the Jesuit missionaries, like Roberto de Nobili in India and Matteo Ricci in China, who sacrificed a lot in order to show some respect to the local cultures of these nations, even against stiff oppositions from some ecclesiastical authorities. For the pastoral work of de Nobili among the Indians, see Peter Schineller, *A Handbook on Inculturation* (Mahwah, NJ: Paulist, 1990), 35-37; Paul Collins, "The Praxis of Inculturation for Mission: Roberto de Nobili's Example and Legacy," *Ecclesiology* 3, no. 3 (2007): 323-342.

[46] Wilbert Shenk, "Missionary Encounter with Culture," *International Bulletin of Missionary Research* 15, no. 3 (1991): 108. Because most of the missionaries

to convert people not merely to the Christian religion but also to the supposed superior culture thought to be universal and exemplary. Conversion to Christianity entailed conversion from one's culture to the "ideal" culture of the West.[47] Neither was the contingency of human knowledge and experience as a result of which they are heavily influenced by the environment given adequate attention, nor the legitimacy of people's autochthonous values given any serious thought. All that mattered most was their conversion to Christianity and their involvement in the Christian rituals of initiation and other sacramental practices in a particular predetermined manner. Analysing this method of missionary expansion and conversion, Karl Rahner observes:

> [T]he concrete, real activity of the Church—despite the contradiction to its own nature involved in its attitude to the world outside Europe—was what we might venture to describe as that of an export firm, exporting to the whole world a European religion along other elements of this supposedly superior culture and civilization, and not really attempting to change the commodity.[48]

According to the American theologian, Peter Shineller, this happens because people assume "that Christianity must be accepted in the form in which it is offered, whether that be Irish, French, or

---

were Europeans, the European culture was regarded as normative for all societies and enjoyed the exclusive right to existence and export to others. Others were merely allowed to accept and assimilate them irrespective of the implications. It is true these missionaries could be said to have had genuine intentions, but their strategies seemed heavily influenced by the mentality prevalent at their time. In certain instances the indigenous or local cultures seem to be completely destroyed in favour of the "better" alternative. This does not, however, mean there were no exceptional instances where genuine effort was made to take people's cultures seriously.

[47]   Eugene Hillman, *Toward an African Christianity* (Mahwah, NJ: Paulist, 1993), 8, 11. See also Aylward Shorter, *Evangelization and Culture* (New York: Geoffrey Chapman, 1994), 30.

[48]   Karl Rahner, *Theological Investigations*, vol. 20, trans. Edward Quinn (London: Darton, Longman and Todd, 1981), 78; Peter Schineller, *A Handbook on Inculturation* (Mahwah, NJ: Paulist, 1990), 15. Schineller further likens this attitude to that of the colonial powers who saw little or nothing of value in the culture of the colonised.

German Catholicism."[49] It was a prevalent idea that presenting the gospel in another way might constitute an offence to the ecclesial unity and apostolicity of the church. Catholicity was, thus, conceived in terms of uniformity.[50] Eugene Hillman, an American theologian and missionary who has had long years of experience in Africa, argues that at times such an attitude of cultural superiority, or what he describes as "cultural arrogance"[51] was even presented to the people as part of the divine ordinance. He notes:

> Western culture, owing much to its Greco-Roman antecedent, was uncritically assumed to be normative for the entire human family. Christians from other cultural worlds were expected, indeed required, sometimes in the name of 'divine law,' to abandon their own traditional ways of being human and religious. They were then morally coerced into embracing the 'superior' ways of Europe, uncritically imagined to be somehow more compatible with Christianity.[52]

Many a time, the cultures of other races were judged as not fit for communicating the Christian message because they were thought as pervaded by evil spirits and demonic forces, which Christianity had come to wrestle, conquer, expunge and exorcise.[53] Such an approach to missionary activity left much to be desired. It seriously hindered the effectiveness of the missionary work in so many places, the vestiges of which still remain today. Articulating its implications, Lonergan notes:

> In so far as one preaches the gospel as it has been developed within one's own culture, one is preaching not only the gospel but also one's own culture. In so far as one is preaching one's own culture,

---

[49]   Schineller, *A Handbook on Inculturation*, 15.

[50]   See Walter Principe, *Faith, History and Cultures: Stability and Change in Church Teachings*, The Pere Marquette Theology Lectures, no. 22 (Wisconsin, WI: Marquette University Press, 1991), 42.

[51]   Hillman, *Toward an African Christianity*, 37.

[52]   Ibid., 36.

[53]   Cf. Giancarlo Collet, "From Theological Vandalism to Theological Romanticism? Questions about a Multicultural Identity of Christianity," *Concilium*, no. 2 (1994): 31.

one is asking others not only to accept the gospel but also renounce their own culture and accept one's own.[54]

The missionary work in many parts of Africa in the nineteenth century and the greater part of the twentieth century testifies to this. Equipped with the classicist mentality, Africa largely represented in the minds of some of the missionaries a land of savages, where the conception of God was never present. Hence, missionary work was, to a large extent, meant to teach the people how to conceive and worship God. A remark made regarding the missionary work in Africa by a renowned German biographer, Emil Ludwig, can help us have a better understanding of the issue. Edwin Smith, a South African missionary and anthropologist, recounts in one of his works his conversation with Ludwig in which he narrated to Ludwig the work the missionaries were doing in Africa, and how they *taught* Africans about God. According to him, Ludwig was surprised how the people could understand them and responded: "How can the untutored African conceive God? . . . How can this be? Deity is a philosophical concept which *savages* are incapable of framing."[55] His remark is very much similar to what was written in 1867 about the northern Nilotic tribe by the British explorer, Samuel Baker, who once served as the Governor-General of the Equatorial Nile Basin (today's Southern Sudan and Northern Uganda) from 1869 to 1873. He writes: "Without any exception, they are without a belief in a Supreme-Being, neither have they any form of worship or idolatry, nor is the darkness of their minds enlightened by even a ray of superstition."[56] One can imagine the kind of missionary strategy to be adopted by such people, like Ludwig and Baker, if they were missionaries and were deployed in the mission field to evangelise the so-called "untutored savages" with "darkened" minds.

It is indeed observed that in the missionary field the controlling image of Christ was that of the conqueror king and a mighty ruler who had come to unleash deadening blow to the people's cultural past. In

---

[54] Lonergan, *Method in Theology*, 362.
[55] Edwin Smith, *African Ideas of God* (London: Edinburgh House, 1961), 1. Emphasis mine.
[56] Samuel Baker, "The Races of the Nile Basin," in *Transactions of the Ethnological Society of London* (London: John Murray, 1867), 231.

many African societies, this image of Christ, some have argued, "fitted into the colonial ambiance of the propagation of Christianity as well as the missionary's self-image of a benevolent paternal figure who knows what is best for African converts." [57] Little wonder that African music, dances and modes of worship were initially excluded from liturgical celebrations. They were all seen as unworthy of the Christian God. This was also the case with the native personal names that were usually not allowed for christening. Missionaries imbued with the classicist mindset would insist on saints' names, which, sometimes, parents knew next to nothing about.[58] A similar missionary method is said to have also been adopted by Francis Xavier and his fellow Jesuit missionaries in the sixteenth century among the Goa of India. Here the natives were made to denounce their indigenous names and adopt in their place even the family names of Portuguese or Spanish origins.[59] They were meant to believe that these foreign names offered superior status. In the regions of Goa, Bacaim and Macao, the Portuguese Jesuit missionaries employed force to convert the natives; a development that made many of the natives flee their homeland. The situation was worse in Goa and Bacaim than in Macao because the former were completely under the Portuguese control. There was hardly any separation between the secular and religious affairs. The king of Portugal had authority over the missionaries who were from his territory. That was why the missionaries implemented a legislation enacted at Lisbon in 1559 that

---

[57]   See Elizabeth Amoah and Mercy Oduyoye, "Christ for African Women," in *With Passion and Compassion: Third World Women Doing Theology*, ed. Virginia Fabella and Mercy Oduyoye (Maryknoll, NY: Orbis, 1988), 37. See also Teresa Hinga, "Jesus Christ and the Liberation of Women in Africa," in *Feminist Theology from the Third World Perspective*, ed. Ursula King (Maryknoll, NY: Orbis, 1994), 263.

[58]   Augustine Nebechukwu, "Third World Theology and the Recovery of African Identity," *Journal of Inculturation Theology* 2, no. 1 (1995): 19; Hillman, *Toward an African Christianity*, 12. According to Chukwudi Njoku, this attitude of the missionaries to the African culture within the period was inspired by the cultural triumphalism, resulting from the achievements of the age of enlightenment in Europe. He, therefore, describes their activity as a "civilizing mission." See Chukwudi Njoku, "The Missionary Factor in African Christianity, 1884-1914," in *African Christianity: An African Story*, ed. Ogbu Kalu (Pretoria: Department of Church History, University of Pretoria, 2005), 227-229.

[59]   Hillman, *Toward an African Christianity*, 37.

authorised that all orphaned children be forcefully taken from their relatives, baptised and brought up in the Christian way.[60]

For most of the missionaries, the traditional religions of the natives were of little or no value, devilish, and without any genuine theology. Dialogue with them was thus considered pointless and unwarranted.[61] To dialogue with them, it was feared, might result in some form of compromise with the "heathen" environment perceived as completely anti-Christian and dangerous. What rather prevailed was a sustained effort to assert the supremacy of Christianity, as it was practised in Europe, and to present it as the sole bastion of unchanging and unchangeable truths that ought to be swallowed the way they were. Hendrik Kraemer, writing for the International Protestant Council in 1938, expresses his conviction that the adoption of such attitude to the other cultures was best suited for Christian evangelisation. According to him, an ideal "missionary is a revolutionary and he has to be so, for to preach and plant Christianity means to make a frontal attack on the beliefs, customs, the apprehensions of life and the world . . . on the social structure and the basis of the society."[62] This way of thinking presupposes that no other culture outside the Christian Europe has a genuine knowledge of God. James Bashford cautions against this way of thinking when he notes: "Surely, we belittle God if we imagine that he has left the majority of the human without any light and without any help for century after century until we Christians in our benevolence come to their relief."[63]

In the early days of the Christian missionary activities among the Igbos of Southeast Nigeria, the missionaries mainly saw their mission as a battle "against the forces of paganism, which endangers the

---

[60] Charles Boxer, "A Note on Portuguese Missionary Methods in the East: Sixteenth to Eighteenth Centuries," in *Christianity and Missions, 1450-1800*, ed. James Cummins (Aldershot: Variorum, 1997), 81-85.

[61] Elizabeth Isichei, "Seven Varieties of Ambiguity: Some Patterns of Igbo Response to Christian Missions," *Journal of Religion in Africa* 3, no. 3 (1970): 211; Njoku, "The Missionary Factor in African Christianity, 226-227.

[62] Hendrik Kraemer, *The Christian Message in a Non-Christian World* (London: The Edinburgh House, 1938), 34.

[63] James Bashford, "Adaptation of Modern Christianity to the People of the Orient," *American Journal of Theology* 17, no. 3 (1913): 390.

soul."[64] Their work was primarily understood as a fight against the evil forces which they claimed pervaded the region and posed a menace to the souls of humans. This mentality was also seen among the first indigenous clergy that worked under the supervision of the western missionaries. Little wonder that Samuel Crowther (who later became the first African Aglican bishop in Nigeria), in his letter to Henry Venn of the C.M.S. in Fernando Po, shortly before the establishment of the C.M.S. permanent station in Igbo society (precisely, in Onitsha) in July 1857, had this to say: "many a heart burns to see the day when the Gospel of liberty to the captives of Satan shall be proclaimed on the banks of the Niger."[65] When eventually the C.M.S. permanent station became a reality and the missionaries settled for their work, one of Crowther's colleagues in the 'battlefield,' J. C. Taylor, writes thus concerning the Igbo society and the need for more missionaries: "May many come willingly to labour in pulling down the strongholds of Satan's kingdom, for the whole of the Ibo district is his citadel."[66] In a similar vein, one of the Catholic missionaries from the congregation of the Holy Ghost Fathers warns his nephew, in these words, regarding the danger of coming to Africa: "All those who go to Africa as missionaries must be thoroughly penetrated with the thought that the *Dark Continent* is a *cursed land*, almost entirely in the power of the devil."[67] Quite the reverse, Fr. Joseph Shanahan (later bishop), an Irish

---

[64] Elizabeth Isichei, "Seven Varieties of Ambiguity," 210. See Christopher Ubah, "Religious Change among the Igbo during the Colonial Period," *Journal of Religion in Africa* 18, no. 1 (1988): 75-78. For a discussion on how such conversions have fared among the Igbos of Nigeria, see Martin Asiegbu, "Inculturation: Creating Maps of Christianity as One Understands It?," *Bigard Theological Studies* 25, no. 2 (2005): 93-110.

[65] Crowther to H. Venn, Fernando Po, 29 May, 1857, cited in Samuel Nwabara, *Iboland: A Century of Contact with Britain, 1860-1960* (London: Hodder and Stoughton, 1977), 48.

[66] Samuel Crowther and J. C. Taylor, *The Gospel on the Banks of the Niger* (London: Dawsons of Pall Mall, 1869), 325.

[67] Holy Ghost Fathers Archives, Paris, 191/A/5, cited in Isichei, "Seven Varieties of Ambiguity," 210. Emphasis mine. That is why Mbefo remarks, concerning the purpose of the missionary school apostolate in this region: "Their purpose was primarily to train christians who would help in fighting the royal battle. That battle was being waged on the banks of the Niger 'against the citadel of Satan', whereby Christ himself was the 'Commander-in-Chief of the apostolic army." Luke Mbefo. "Tensions between Christianity and African Traditional Religion:

missionary to the Igbo society, writes about Europe that it "has been the chosen Continent, the chosen nation of God."[68]

According to Isichei, even after their long stay and work among the Igbo people, these missionaries never underwent any substantial change in their perception of the Igbo mission land. Hence, their toughness on the new converts they were able to make, probably to purge them of the pagan defilement that spiritually threatened the soul.[69] The natives were threatened with hell fire should they not abandon their supposed "devilish" ways and cultures and embrace the "missionary model." This threat, it is true, led to some conversions to the new religion, but one really wonders to what extent such could go.[70] Tough public penances were readily imposed on the converts. One immediately recalls the attitude of Fr. Lejeune, who has been described as very rigid, strict and uncompromising in character. His stiffness was not only directed to Igbo people generally but more importantly to his closest collaborators—the catechists—which made them write a protest letter, jointly signed by about seventy of them, to the Holy Ghost Congregation headquarters in Paris demanding his removal.[71] Another protest letter was also written and signed by someone who identified himself as Bernard O. Oyo to Paris. The author writes: "since one year and a half the Christians are dropping their faith through the bad example of Mr Lejeune who has no patience or courage ... who is that whip? We hope he will be sent away, he is not a 'Father' but a man who never has pity even unto a dog and who always thinks he is right in everything he does."[72]

In Tanzania, cases were reported where mission schools had to be temporarily closed. The students were sent home due to recurring mental breakdowns, resulting from their inability to cope with and reconcile their traditional worldview with the indoctrination coming

---

The Igbo Case" in *Yearbook of Contextual Theologies*, vol. 93 (Frankfurt: Verlag, 1994), 127.

[68]   See Isichei, Elizabeth Isichei, *A History of the Igbo People* (London: Macmillan, 1976), 192.

[69]   Isichei, "Seven Varieties of Ambiguity," 210.

[70]   Ibid., 217-218.

[71]   Peter Clarke, "The Methods and Ideology of the Holy Ghost Fathers in Eastern Nigeria 1885-1905," *Journal of Religion in Africa* 6, no 2 (1974): 96-97, 104.

[72]   C.S.Sp Archives, Paris, Boite 193, Dossier B, Vol. II, cited in Clarke, "The Method of the Holy Ghost Fathers," 97.

from the new Christian religion. Though one may have reasonable grounds to doubt such a conclusion, Knud Ochsner maintains that the psychiatric report following the incident traced the cause to "conversion hysteria" resulting from the students' inability to reconcile the two worlds.[73] For those students coming from communities where Christianity's presence had lasted for over one generation, Ochsner notes that the situation was even worse, because they became victims of a clash not just between two but of three worlds—"the traditional animistic view of life; the distinct cultural pattern of the village congregation with its frequently antagonistic attitude to the traditional religion, to other Christian communities and the modern 'godless' world, and the secular society with its emphasis on science and technology."[74]

The situation of the missionary activity in the so-called third world countries was, indeed, worsened by the fact that, in many of these places, missionary work went side by side with colonialism. This has made some writers from these regions so reactional that they tend to write off the whole activity as if the missionaries did not in any way have good intentions for the people. Even non-religious commentators offer significant evaluation of the faith-culture encounter in African setting. The assertion of the first president of Kenya, Jomo Kenyatta, concerning how the missionaries denigrated and vilified the Africans and their culture is useful here. According to him,

the African was regarded as a clean slate on which anything could be written . . . The Europeans based their assumption on the conviction that everything that the African did or thought was evil.

---

[73] Knud Ochsner, "Church, School and the Clash of Cultures: Examples from North-West Tanzania," *Journal of Religion in Africa* 4, no. 2 (1971): 98. In this article, Knud gives a detailed analysis of a survey he conducted among 300 students from three different schools: one government school and two mission schools. He attempted to find out the students' attitude towards the reconcilability of the different worldviews. In the final analysis, he is of the opinion that the tension created by such a situation could only be mellowed down when the students are made to feel more at home in their environment; and the school, instead of being alienating, aims at becoming more integrated into the life of the people. See Ibid., 114. See also Isichei, "Seven Varieties of Ambiguity," 212.

[74] Ochsner, "Church, School and Clash of Cultures," 99.

The missionaries endeavoured to rescue the depraved souls of the African from 'eternal fire'; they set out to uproot the African body and soul, from his old customs and beliefs, put him in a class by himself, with all his tribal traditions shattered and his institutions trampled upon. The African after having been detached from his family and tribe, was expected to follow the white man's religion without questioning whether it was suited for his condition of life or not.[75]

Chinua Achebe's novel, *Things Fall Apart,* also portrays the conflict that erupted at the encounter between the culture of the missionaries and the local culture of Africans, especially the Igbo of southeast Nigeria.[76] Without prejudice to the above observations, one should also recognise the fact that these missionaries were coming from a culture, which has a very different way of looking at the world and reality. So, it may not have been easy, even for those with the best of intentions among them, to adapt to the "strange" ways of life of the people and be able to value them objectively.[77]

The experience of the American Indians at the hands of the missionaries is not different from what we have so far described. Describing the missionary work of the Jesuits among the Anishnaabeg of Manitoulin Island, Theresa Smith maintains that the missionaries not only succeeded in spreading Christianity but also in eroding the cultural and traditional heritage of the natives. The "beliefs, practices and symbols were not only replaced by Christian ones,"[78] she notes, "but were denounced as demonic in origin."[79] They also employed intimidation tactics whereby the natives were threatened with hell fire should they not give up their original ways of being human and embrace that of the missionaries. Smith admits, however, that through this method, conversions were made but they were mainly nominal and

---

[75]   Jomo Kenyatta, *Facing Mount Kenya* (London: Heinemann, 1979), 269-270.

[76]   Chinua Achebe, *Things Fall Apart* (London: Heinemann, 1981).

[77]   See, for example Walbert Bühlmann, *The Mission on Trial, Addis Ababa 1980: A Moral for the Future from the Archives of Today* (Middlegreen: St. Paul, 1978), 74-75.

[78]   Theresa Smith, "The Church of the Immaculate Conception: Inculturation and Identity among the Anishnaabeg of Manitoulin Island," *American Indian Quarterly* 20, no. 4 (1996): 515.

[79]   Ibid.

"did not always entail the transformation of consciousness for which the Jesuits had hoped."[80] No wonder, then, Theodore Zuern, who worked as a missionary among the American Indians, recounting the attitude of some older missionaries before him, states:

> At the end of the fifteenth century when the Catholic missionaries of Europe came to convert the native peoples of America, they brought Christ wrapped in the cultural traditions of Europe. They established local Churches cluttered with practices and rituals more attune to Western European nations than to Native American societies.[81]

He also observes the use of such derogatory terms as "low Indians" and abusive appellations as "savage pagans," which, he says, continued to be employed in much of the literature from the American society even up to the 19th century. Zuern describes this as a manifestation of cultural arrogance and cautions against uncritical judgment of other people's culture *solely* from one's own perspective.[82]

---

[80] Ibid.

[81] Theodore Zuern, "The Preservation of Native Identity in the Process of Inculturation, as Experienced in American Indian Cultures," in *On Being the Church in a Modern Society*, Inculturation: Working Papers on Living Faith and Cultures, ed. Ary Crollius (Rome: Pontifical Gregorian University Press, 1983), 7. Obviously, Zuern's statement was inspired by his pastoral experience among the American Indians. He expresses his surprise at how these missionaries denigrated the peoples' culture, which was regarded as being on the initial stages of cultural development; thus, should be relinquished to embrace the "perfect" European culture, which served as the model. Acccording to him: "Such an approach ignored the fact that all cultures are gifts from God and that in the finite human family cultural diversity reveals the infinity of the creator of that family." Ibid., 1. According to Leonardo Boff, the experience of such missionary strategy was also witnessed among the Latin Americans. According to his description, it involved, among other things, imposition, cultural denigration, seizure of people's material possessions and enslavement. For more on this, see Leonardo Boff, *New Evangelization* (Maryknoll, NY: Orbis, 1991), 99-101.

[82] Zuern, "The Preservation of Native Identity," 3. The situation has changed in recent years. Writing in 1983, Zuern says it was only within ten years before then that Lakota men were opportune to have permanent deacons from among their folk.

Roman Pontiffs and Theologians

One needs not stretch too far into history to detect how the Eurocetric monoculturalism permeated and influenced the outlook of the church's official documents and pronouncements. A critical look at some papal documents in the last two centuries immediately confirms this. During the last quarter of the 19th century, for instance, when the missionary activity in many parts of Africa was at its peak, Pope Leo XIII, in the encyclical, *Inscrutabili*, argues in favour of possession by the bishop of Rome of the immutable laws and principles applicable to all. In the Roman pontiff, he argues, "the abiding and unchangeable principles of right and good find their earthly guardian and champion."[83] That is why the church, according to him, has been a bearer of the light (of the gospel) to various cultures of the world, raised people from their savagery, degradation and superstition unto the "original dignity of their noble nature."[84] Hervé Carrier has no doubt that Leo understands culture in its classical sense, and consequently equates it with higher civilisation.[85]

The same thought runs through the writings of Benedict XV, who describes unbelievers as blind, without the knowledge of God, and yet to be saved from the dominion of Satan.[86] According to him, such non-Christian people are under the shadow of death. He identifies their conversion to Christianity as elevation to the light of civilization and "high culture."[87] Similarly, Pius XI, in the encyclical letter, *Rerum Ecclesiae*, also speaks of those pagans and unhappy beings to whom the church owes it as a duty to elevate from their low status and superstition unto salvation.[88] He states that it is only "the gospel and the benefits of [western] Christian culture and civilization"

---

[83] Leo XIII, "Encyclical Letter, On the Evils Affecting Modern Society: Their Causes and Remedies, *Inscrutabili*, 21 April 1878," in *The Church Speaks to the Modern World: The Social Teachings of Leo XIII*, ed. Etienne Gilson (Garden City, NY: Image, 1954), no.3.

[84] Leo XIII, "*Inscrutabili*," 5.

[85] Carrier, "Understanding Culture," 17.

[86] Benedict XV, "An Encyclical Letter, On the Propagation of the Faith throughout the World, *Maximum Illud*, 30 November 1919," *AAS* 11 (1919): 451.

[87] Ibid., 442, 446.

[88] Pius XI, "Encyclical Letter, On Catholic Missions, *Rerum Ecclesiae*, 28 February, 1926," *AAS* 18 (1928): 67.

that will bring them to the light.[89] It is, however, significant to note that he cautions against European missionaries looking down on the local missionaries as of inferior race and intelligence. But even at that, he notes that, if in any way one is to see such backwardness of mind among those living in those remotest *barbarous* races, one should be able to understand that such is caused by the limitedness of their living conditions which does not pressure them to make maximum use of their intelligence.[90] His employment of words, such as "barbarians" and "savages" to refer to those outside the frontiers of the western Christian culture is also noteworthy.[91]

Even more noteworthy is the fact that some of the pontiffs found nothing wrong in forceful invasion and enslavement of people simply because they were outside the purportedly universal, western culture.[92] This is true of the papal bull, *Romanus Pontifex* (1455), of Nicholas V. In the bull, the pontiff grants to the king of Portugal, Alfonso V, "free and ample faculty . . . to invade, search out, capture, vanquish, and subdue all Saracens and pagans whatsoever . . . to reduce their persons to perpetual slavery, and to apply and appropriate to himself and successors the kingdoms . . . and to convert them to his and their use and profit."[93] Even though the historical context of the above bull is significant here,[94] one wonders what could have been the fate of those people in the hands of the king given such a faculty without reservation. This clearly shows that the church at the time was yet to

---

[89] Ibid., 65.

[90] Ibid., 77.

[91] Ibid., 70.

[92] Shorter, *Towards a Theology of Inculturation*, 21.

[93] Nicholas V, "Bull, *Romanus Pontifex*, 8 January 1455," in *European Treaties Bearing on the History of the United States and Its Dependencies*, ed. Gardiner Davenport (Washington, DC: Carnegie Institute of Washington, 1917), 23. For the original Latin version of the bull, see pp. 13-20.

[94] This was a period when Portugal and Castile were laying conflicting claims to sovereignty over the newly discovered worlds. The above bull came specifically as a response to an appeal made to the Pope by King Alfonso V of Portugal as he struggled with Henry IV of Castile over the ownership of Morocco, Guinea and Guinea trade. With *Dum Diversas* (18 June 1452), Nicholas V conceded the territory to Portugal, thereby giving Alfonso V full right over the whole area. What we read in *Romanus Pontifex*, which he issued three years later, is a confirmation of the earlier decision. See Ibid., 9-12.

give adequate attention and consideration to the implications of the diversity of cultures and peoples.

This was also the case on the theological sphere. Theologians with classicist mindset sought to produce a uniform theology that could be equally relevant and valid at all times and in all situations. They assumed there were abstract universals in the manner of Plato's forms on which was founded any valid knowledge. These universals or unities lay beyond spatio-temporal limitations. Any claim to knowledge was seen as a participation in it. Alterations and differences were perceived as accidental and tangential. The result was gross neglect of cultural differences and historical peculiarities and their influences on the knowing subject, the manner of knowing and the object of knowledge. Thus, local theologies developed out of the exigencies of the western culture were thought to be universal and applicable to every other society. When this was applied to the Christian doctrine, the conclusion was that the diversity of cultures and social conditions of people could not necessitate a change in the doctrine itself. If any change was allowed, it merely addressed the outward expressions. This way of thinking, granted it acknowledges that there is substantial commonality among human beings, is utterly inadequate to the extent that it ignores the significance of the differences among humans occasioned by differences in cultures, indiosyncracies and mentalities, which are also subject to change over time.[95]

This theological disposition ultimately influenced the method of evangelisation whereby immersion into the Christian doctrine meant no more than the recitation of the Catechism as found in the books, even if one never understood them and the categories with which they were formulated or expressed. In many instances, the Catechism offered answers to questions the people knew next to nothing about, while the questions coming from their situations were left unattended to.[96] The major theological themes developed in the schools were taught that way, and the people, in spite of their literary and cultural backgrounds, were expected to understand them just the same way and

---

[95]   See John Thiel, "Pluralism in Theological Truth," *Concilium*, no. 6 (1994): 58-59; Lonergan, *Method in Theology*, 301, 302.

[96]   See Robert Schreiter, *Constructing Local Theologies* (Maryknoll, NY: Orbis, 2004), 3.

to follow suit.[97] A similar logic influenced the universal imposition of Latin on all the Christian people as the uniform language of liturgy and theology, following the promulgation of the Roman Missal of 1570 by Pius V.[98]

Another significant line of thought among theologians that sustained the classicist theological thinking was founded on the understanding of the nature of the church and its origin. The argument was that, since the church was believed to have its origin in God, it also followed that its truth derived from the mystery of God's being. Since God is unchangeable as well as beyond space and time, the teaching of the church should also enjoy unchangeable, universal validity and applicability. This being the case, whatever was endorsed in the Vatican had to be applied the same way without modifications world over.[99] This reinforced the claim that the church's centralised hierarchy possessed the knowledge of the best ways of promoting God's kingdom and saving souls in any part of the world.[100]

PLURALIST NOTION OF CULTURE

Scholars have identified what could be judged to be the first challenge to the normative understanding of culture in the thoughts of the German theologian and philosopher, Johann Herder, about the end of the eighteenth century.[101] Herder has persuasively argued in his unfinished work, *Ideas towards a Philosophy of the History*

---

[97] One can easily recall the effect of the imposition of Bellarmine catechism in Asia about the year 1632 by the missionaries. According to Emilio Alberich, this contributed so much in undermining Christianity's impact on the continent, especially as regards its perception by indigenes as a foreign import. Emilio Alberich, "Is the Universal Catechism an Obstacle or a Catalyst in the Process of Inculturation?," *Concilium* 204, no. 4 (1989): 89.

[98] Cf. Ibid., 80; Hillman, *Toward an African Christianity*, 13. See also Patrick Chibuko, "The Structures of Rituals: Rules and Creativity," in *The Mission to Proclaim and to Celebrate Christian Existence*, ed. Peter De Mey, Jacques Haers and Jozef Lamberts (Leuven: Peeters, 2005), 295-297.

[99] Thiel, "Pluralism in Theological Truth," 60; Michael Angrosino, "The Culture Concept and the Mission of the Roman Catholic Church," *American Anthropologist* 96, no. 4 (1994): 824.

[100] Rahner, *Theological Investigations*, 79.

[101] See, for instance, Eagleton, *The Idea of Culture*, 12-13; Williams, *Keywords*, 78-79.

of Man (1784-1791), that there is no society in the globe that has not got a culture, which is their own distinctive set of values and ways of life reflecting their specificity as a people with peculiar circumstances and experiences at a given time. In this sense, he argues, one can comfortably talk about plurality of cultures, for it is not a property that can only be claimed by a specific group of people but one possessed by all societies.[102] Herder distinguishes culture from civilisation. According to him, unlike culture, which identifies a people, civilisation can cut across nations and has to do with intellectual and techno-scientific achievements.[103] He criticises the notion of linear progression of culture from the barbaric non-European other to the European ideal of civilisation.[104] On the idea of presumed superiority and normativity of the European culture prevalent at his time, he makes the following remarks: "Men of all the quarters of the globe, who perished over the years, have not lived solely to manure the earth with your ashes, so that at the end of time your posterity should be made happy by the Europeans. The very thought of a superior European culture is a blatant insult to the majesty of Nature."[105]

The English anthropologist, Edward Tylor (1832-1917), is often mentioned as one of those whose contribution is very significant for the development of the modern pluralist notion of culture. Just like Herder, he believes that all societies possess culture and none should be regarded as bereft of it. He, nevertheless, worked within the evolutionist understanding of culture by which it is argued that there is a progression of culture from the lowest, most inferior, primitive, and savagery stage to the most complex, advanced and rationalistic form. One implication of this is the conclusion that some societies are more cultured than others.[106] His definition of culture, which helped to

---

[102] Johann Herder, "Ideas towards a Philosophy of the History of Man," in *Theories of History*, ed. Patrick Gardiner (Glencoe, IL: The Free Press, 1959), 31-51. See also Williams, *Keywords*, 79.

[103] See Roger Scruton, *Modern Culture* (London: Continuum, 2007), 1.

[104] Herder, "Ideas towards a Philosophy," 34-51.

[105] Cited in Williams, *Keywords*, 79.

[106] See Martinez Hewlett, "Evolution: Evolutionism," *Encyclopedia of Religion* (2005): 2914-2915. Sure, not all aspects or products of culture are equally valuable. Each society has its own values and disvalues, but none of these can make its culture less a culture or more a culture than any other. For an anthropologist, as Luzbetak points out, every culture enjoys an essential

broaden the concept beyond mere ideas and intellectual achievements, runs thus: "that complex whole which includes knowledge, beliefs, art, morals, law, custom, and any other capabilities and habits acquired by man as a member of society."[107] For Browns, this definition is possibly "as good a definition as any"[108] among anthropologists. According to him, one of its merits is its holistic view of culture by which the different aspects of the human person is understood as a unit.[109] Lohmann mentions four major accomplishments of the definition. First, it makes it impossible to regard a people as lacking a culture simply because one sees their way of life as different from one's own. Next, with it, scholars are able to talk about cultural differentiations as one moves from one society to the other. Third, each culture is seen as having something unique to contribute to the overall progress of the human society as a whole. Lastly, it portrays culture as a common property of any given society and not simply that of the individuals *per*

---

completeness. Louis Luzbetak, *The Church and Culture: An Applied Anthropology for the Religious Worker* (Techny, IL: Divine Word, 1970), 62. 'Completeness,' as he uses it, neither implies that cultures are closed systems that are not open to growth and mutual enrichment, nor should it lead to the denial of the fact that some aspects or products of particular culture are really not geared towards human upliftment, nor that some of the products cannot be said to be better equipped to help humanity than others. To imply this is to run the risk of falling into extreme forms of cultural relativism with its own problems. It means, instead, that each culture should be accorded an inalienable integrity and wholeness. For more on the implications of cultural relativism, see Grace de Laguna, "Cultural Relativism and Science," *The Philosophical Review* 51, no. 2 (1942): 141-166; Paul Schmidt, "Some Criticisms of Cultural Relativism," *The Journal of Philosophy* 52, no. 25 (1955): 780-791. Kathryn Tanner puts it this way: "no people has any more culture than any other." See Tanner, *Theories of Culture*, 36.

[107] Edward Tylor, *Primitive Culture: Researches into the Development of Mythology, Philosophy, Religion, Language, Art, and Custom*, vol. 1 (London: Murray, 1871), 1. According to Kroeber and Kluckhohn, Tylor's usage of the concept of culture in this modern sense can be traced back to the influence exerted on him by the work of Gustav Kelmn, *Allgemeine Culturgeschichte der Menschheit*, the first volume of which appeared in 1843. It was from this German author, they argue, that Tylor got the meaning which he introduced into English. See Alfred Kroeber and Clyde Kluckhohn, *Culture: A Critical Review of Concepts and Definitions* (New York: Vintage, 1963), 13-14.

[108] Downs, *Cultures in Crisis*, 34.

[109] Ibid.

se that make up the society.[110] Another significance of the definition that is worth noting is its account of culture as something not genetically inherited but transmitted through learning and education.[111]

Despite the merits of this definition, some scholars see it as too broad and as falling short of the kind of precision needed in the social sciences.[112] In the quest to arrive at such a precision, many other definitions have been proffered by anthropologists since the time of Tylor. In 1952, two American anthropologists, Alfred Kroeber and Clyde Kluckhohn, made a critical review of the concept and compiled more than 60 different definitions of it by social scientists. After such a detailed research, they offered a definition, by which they hoped to unify the various aspects of culture covered by other authors:

> Culture consists of patterns, explicit and implicit, of and for behaviour acquired and transmitted by symbols, constituting the distinctive achievement of human groups, including their embodiments in artifacts; the essential core of culture consists of traditional (i.e., historically derived and selected) ideas and especially their attached values; culture systems may, on the one hand, be considered as products of action, on the other as conditioning elements for further action.[113]

According to Robert Borofsky, these two authorities must have thought that, by giving such a definition after their extensive research, they would have succeeded in offering an authoritative definition that might somehow quell the contestation surrounding the concept among anthropologists. Unfortunately, this never happened. Borofsky regards their efforts as "a political agenda of sorts,"[114] which never worked because the "definition never really caught on within the discipline."[115]

---

[110]   Lohmann, "Culture," 2087-2088}

[111]   See Arbuckle, *Culture, Inculturation, Theologians*, 2.

[112]   Wendy Griswold, *Cultures and Societies in a Changing World*, 3rd ed. (Thousand Oaks, CA: Pine Forge, 2008), 8.

[113]   Kroeber and Kluckhohn, *Culture*, 357.

[114]   Borofsky, "Introduction," 433.

[115]   See Ibid.

What one notices in more recent definitions of culture, although with some notable exceptions,[116] is the greater tendency to see it as having primarily to do with the mind and only secondarily with behaviour. This shift (which is evident even in the definition offered above by Kroeber and Kluckhohn) is occasioned by the belief that human actions, or better still, "learned behaviour is, in the final analysis, a product of how we think about things—our cognition."[117] Culture is, therefore, seen as a kind of 'mental or cognitive map' that directs people's interaction with their environment. Some anthropologists, like Albert Blumenthal, would even go to the extent of contending that culture consists only of ideas existing in the mind, which has nothing to do with perceptible or observable phenomena.[118] Some others try to link culture as ideas with culture as observable phenomena and behaviour. This is the basic idea behind its description by the American cultural anthropologist, Richard Shweder, as "community-specific ideas about what is true, good, beautiful and efficient. To be 'cultural,' those ideas . . . must be socially inherited and customary, and they must be constitutive of different ways of life."[119]

This view is also expressed by Tanner and Luzbetak. Luzbetak argues that, although culture is manifestly embodied in artefacts, concrete behaviours, material objects, rituals and events, these are not culture, *per se*. He is of the view that, while some anthropologists regard these as essential components of culture, they are only mere expressions of the underlying "ideational code"—the inner core of

---

[116]   See, for instance, Gary Ferraro and Susan Andreatta, for whom culture essentially consists of three equally relevant components, which include: what people possess, the way they think and how they behave as members of a given society. Their definition of culture runs thus: "everything that people have, think, and do as members of a society." They stress on the interconnectedness of all these three areas, and argue that none is more important than the other. Gary Ferraro and Susan Andreatta, *Cultural Anthropology: An Applied Perspective*, 8th ed. (Belmont, CA: Wadsworth, 2010), 28.

[117]   Downs, *Cultures in Crisis*, 35.

[118]   See Albert Blumenthal, *The Relations between Culture, Human Social Interaction, Personality and History* (Marietta, OH: Marietta College, 1938), 7.

[119]   Richard Shweder, "Rethinking the Object of Anthropology and Ending up Where Kroeber and Kluckhohn Began," *American Anthropologist* 103, no. 2 (2001): 437.

culture—consisting of symbols, values, concepts, meanings, beliefs, attitudes, and so forth. As he argues, essentially speaking, culture is the fundamental "ideational code" that gives rise to the external expressions.[120] He defines it as "a plan or blueprint . . . according to which a society is to adapt itself to its *physical, social* and *ideational* environment."[121] Luzbetak notes, however, that such codes cannot exist fully detached from reality, that is, from the concrete lives of the people. In other words, to talk about culture is not only to talk about its inner core but also of its outward expressions.[122] For Tanner, culture refers to *"the meaning dimension of social life."*[123] She argues that anthropologists today tend to see culture simply as constituted by the ideas, symbols, meanings and beliefs that lie behind social behaviour. Though she argues that culture understood this way could be analysed independently of social behaviours, she believes that both are usually interconnected in practice.[124]

Bernard Lonergan's view comes close to those of the last three authors discussed above when he conceives culture as "a set of meanings and values informing a common way of life."[125] In another place, he speaks of it as "the meaning we find in our present way of life, the value we place upon it."[126] This (common) way of life, according to him, exhibits rich diversity corresponding to the diversity of the "distinct sets of such meanings and values."[127] Meanings (and values), for him, constitute the core components of culture. But they are not just free-floating. They are made manifest in symbolic, artistic, philosophical, historical, and linguistic expressions, as well as in human behaviour and interactions. These constitute the extrinsic components of culture, the external embodiments of its inner, deeper level, both of which are inseparably connected.[128] What Lonergan

---

[120]   Louis Luzbetak, *The Church and Cultures: New Perspectives in Missiological Anthropology* (Maryknoll, NY: Orbis, 1988), 156-157.

[121]   Ibid., 157. Emphasis in the original.

[122]   Ibid., 167-168.

[123]   Tanner, *Theories of Culture*, 31. Emphasis in the original.

[124]   Ibid., 31.

[125]   Lonergan, *Method in Theology*, 301.

[126]   Lonergan, *A Second Collection*, 91.

[127]   Lonergan, *Method in Theology*, 301.

[128]   Ibid., 57, 78. See Gallagher's comment on Lonergan's position: Gallagher, *Clashing of Symbols*, 21.

wants to put across here is that culture comprises two different dimensions, one of which is more visible than the other, but both of which interact continuously: "There is constant interaction between the more hidden sets of assumptions (meanings and values) and the more manifest field of observable social patterns (common ways of life) and of conscious interpretations (philosophies, etc.)."[129]

One thing that is easily observed in most of the postmodern conceptions of culture is the tendency to lay less emphasis on homogeneity of culture within societies because it seems to present culture as a well-organised, seamless, and innocuous reality devoid of struggles and tensions. Such a homogenous approach, it is argued, also tends to visualise culture more as a product, thereby undermining the ongoing historical and social process behind cultural formation. Postmodern approach places more emphasis on contestations, strains, conflicts, power struggles, differences and fragmentations through which the culture of a particular group is shaped and sustained. It calls attention to the fact that what usually counts as people's culture often turns out to be the ideas, beliefs, assumptions and customs shaped by the dominant few (who could either be members of the society in question or foreigners) who usually determine the course of history in different societies as against the often marginalised majority. This is clear, for instance, in the poststructuralist analysis of culture, especially their stress on the process of cultural formation, and how culture is ideologically manipulated by those advantageously placed in the power structure in different societies.[130] This has helped to expose and critique the metanarratives behind cultural formation. It has also drawn attention to individual reflexivity, the consequent diversity and plurality of narratives operative in the production of culture within societies.[131]

In sum, one can affirm that culture is the way of life of a people, which comprises basically learned ideas, symbols, and meanings, but also their mode of production and their expressions in behaviour, arts, languages, and other human capabilities, by which the people are able to confront the different challenges posed by their environment.

---

[129]   Ibid.

[130]   For a brief summary, see Arbuckle, *Culture, Inculturation, Theologians*, 5-10; Tanner, *Theories of Culture*, 38-60.

[131]   Arbuckle, *Culture, Inculturation, Theologians*, 13.

Whether the stress is placed more on ideas or less so, the most important realisation from our discussion is that culture is the key to understanding any particular society because it is central to their life. Further, there can be no society without a culture. Through it, each society is able to preserve its inherited tradition as well as deal with the present challenges and problems. Being a way of life that a particular people has developed over a long period of time, sometimes stretching back to centuries, it often serves as a source of cohesion, stability, meaning, and sense of purpose for them as they adapt to new and often challenging conditions of life.[132] But it can as well become oppressive and serve as a tool for victimisation and marginalisation of some people within the society. Being like a lens through which the members of a given society visualise reality, culture should not be neglected once one wants his or her message, be it Christian or non-Christian, to get across to them.

SOME BASIC CHARACTERISTICS OF CULTURE

The first characteristic of culture, which seems evident in our discussion above, is that it is the possession of a given society and not that of individuals. "It is an attribute, then, of a particular social group."[133] That is why it is able to unite all the members of the society in spite of the uniqueness of each individual and the differences among them. Even within larger societies where subgroups exist with their respective subcultures, the general culture of the society still serves as the focal point of unity. In the United States of America, for instance, where many of such subgroups exist (like the Hispanics, the black Americans), though each of them possesses its own subculture by which its members organise their lives, being part of the wider American society, all of them also share the common American

---

132 Luzbetak, *Church and Cultures: New Perspectives*, 158.

133 Tanner, *Theories of Culture*, 26. Luzbetak argues that, though culture, strictly speaking, corresponds to the boundaries of "social groups speaking the same or related language and having more or less similar economic, social, and ideological systems," it is also loosely applied in anthropology to refer to the way of life of a number of societies with closely related and very similar ways of life. It is in this sense that one can talk about western culture, oriental culture, or African culture. See Luzbetak, *Church and Cultures: New Perspectives*, 171.

culture. They are not conceived as totally separate or apart from this wider culture to which they all belong.[134]

Authors usually differentiate between culture and idiosyncrasy. While the former belongs to the society as a whole, the latter is said to belong to individuals that make up the society. According to Luzbetak, idiosyncrasy, as used in anthropology, refers to the ways of life specific to the individual members of a society which are not transmitted as a possession of the society, that is, as its culture. That it refers to the individual ways of life within the society, Luzbetak further demonstrates, does not necessarily make it odd. It exists simply because of differences in the ways individuals visualise reality, their situations in life and the challenges they face within the society. Besides, while individual members and their idiosyncrasies come and go, the society and its culture persist.[135] It is this persistence that allows the transmission of culture from one generation to the next as a traditional or social inheritance.

This brings us to another important characteristic of culture: its transmissibility and continuity from parents to offspring generation after generation.[136] Its passage from the parents to the newly born members of the society happens through the process of enculturation or socialisation. Through it, the new members learn, many a time unconsciously, the cultural patterns specific to their people and assimilate their cultural practices and values. This is one of the features of culture that has been an object of criticisms for some scholars. It is argued that understanding culture as an inherited tradition undermines and even denies individual agency and free choice, because the traditions being received or assimilated by the new members are not, so to say, of their own making.[137] But the point needs to be made that culture, being a social heredity, does not necessarily make the

---

[134]   Tanner, *Theories of Culture*, 27. See also Luzbetak, *Church and Cultures: New perspectives*, 171-172; Shorter, *Towards a Theology of Inculturation*, 17.

[135]   Luzbetak, *Church and Cultures: New Perspectives*, 169, 172-173. See also Tanner, *Theories of Culture*, 26-27.

[136]   See Bronislaw Malinowski, "Review of Six Essays on Culture by Albert Blumenthal," *American Sociological Review* 4, no. 4 (1939): 591.

[137]   Shweder shows how some anthropologists have debunked the idea of seeing culture as an inherited tradition based on this claim. See Shweder, "Rethinking the Object of Anthropology," 439. See also Lohmann, "Culture," 2088.

members of the society mere passive recipients of past traditions.[138] Adhering to certain traditional wisdom or value, Richard Shweder notes, does not necessarily mean there is no agency, or that culture influences people's actions in a deterministic way. It does not imply absence of questioning, argumentation or disputes concerning meanings, values, beliefs or practices. According to Shweder, even fundamentalists with their strict adherence to tradition are no less "agentic" than those considered liberationists, "and neither stands outside some tradition of meaning and value."[139] It is true, however, to say that, at birth and during childhood, human beings may be said to be somehow passive receptacles for their culture through learning and enculturation. But, it is also a fact that this does not continue throughout life; one reaches a point where one can positively contribute in a significant way, knowingly or unknowingly, to the growth and development of one's culture.[140] Probably to highlight the human agency involved both in its transmission and reception, Edward Shorter has described culture as "a tradition of accumulated choices."[141] Tanner has also made the all-important point that "there is nothing to human life with any definite form or shape of its own that might exist outside culture so as to be so regulated or repressed. Culture makes human life from the first; it is in that sense its constitutive medium and not some secondary influence."[142]

The point is that, just as culture is central in shaping people's behaviour so also is human actions, through which culture is expressed, central in shaping culture. Tanner articulates it this way: "Human beings may be made by culture but they also make it."[143] Some other authors have also tried to underscore this mutual interaction. Luzbetak states that, though through culture people are able to be guided towards what a society considers valuable, noble and beautiful, it does not deny individual freedom, differentiations, and variations in behaviour and actions. Inasmuch as the members of a given society have some basic commonalities among them, they

---

[138] See Tanner, *Theories of Culture*, 28-29.

[139] Shweder, "Rethinking the Object of Anthropology," 439.

[140] See Tanner, *Theories of Culture*, 29.

[141] Shorter, *Toward a Theology of Inculturation*, 45.

[142] Tanner, *Theories of Culture*, 27.

[143] Ibid., 28.

neither appropriate their cultural riches in exactly the same way, nor relegate their individuality by being members of the group. On the contrary, within societies, there are always struggles and conflicts as regards values, beliefs and customs, as well as how these influence social action. This is precisely where individual idiosyncrasies, group affiliations and orientations within a social group play significant roles. Indeed, people can freely choose to act in accordance with the cultural norms of their society, or choose to act against it in specific situations.[144] It is through such actions that culture is tested, leading either to its confirmation and enforcement, reformation and change, modification and improvement, or even subversion and rejection. The fact that all these are possible show that human agency is not necessarily denied by culture.[145] It is also on account of this that, even within a given culture, there often exist smaller subcultures exhibiting certain distinctive characteristics apart from that of the society in general. When John Paul II describes the human person as not only "an ontic subject of culture, but also its object and term,"[146] he seems to harp on the mutual interaction and influence between culture and the human person, meaning that humans are not mere passive receptacles for culture.

To be sure, the British sociologist, Margaret Archer, has stated that failure to acknowledge the interplay between culture and human agency can either lead to the elision or conflation of the two, or undue exaggeration of the influence of one on the other or of both on each other.[147] For her, acceptance of cultural constraints does not mean endorsement of cultural determinism. There is in human beings, she argues, "the quintessential reflective ability . . . to fight back against conditioning . . . giving them the capacity to respond with originality to their present context."[148] This peculiar ability makes it possible for humans to effect significant changes to their cultural milieu and create a better future for themselves.

---

[144] Luzbetak, *Church and Cultures: New Perspectives*, 168-169.

[145] Ibid., 188, 171; Lars Rodseth, "Another Passage to Pragmatism," *American Anthropologist* 103, no. 2 (2001): 440.

[146] John Paul II, "Address to UNESCO, 2 June 1980," *Origins* 10, no. 4 (1980): no. 7.

[147] Margaret Archer, *Culture and Agency: The Place of Culture in Social Theory*, Revised ed. (New York: Cambridge University Press, 1996), xv.

[148] Ibid., xxvi.

Futhermore, culture is a dynamic reality. Its dynamism enables it to adapt to changing circumstances and times.[149] This, however, does not occur in a haphazard fashion. Just as culture is not made up of arbitrary and unrelated assemblage of beliefs, values, symbols, or customs, so also does it not accept changes arbitrarily. Downs has made the point that "each culture tends to have a logic of its own that makes the various elements of the culture related and interdependent."[150] This view is also echoed by Tanner who nevertheless adds that it is the internal coherence and interrelatedness of cultural elements more than geography that constitute cultural boundaries and distinguish cultures one from the other. According to her, being the principle of social order and cohesion, its elements also need to cohere with one another and be integrally ordered.[151] This also seems to underlie the description of culture by the English historian and sociologist, Christopher Dawson, as "the form of society" without which society becomes mere "crowd or a collection of individuals brought together by the needs of the moment."[152] Cultural change seems to follow the order or internal logic of the cultural system such that any change that is introduced in any aspect or element of a culture, even the most subtle, usually leads

---

[149] It is specifically on account of this dynamism in cultures that Sheila Davaney defines it as "a multitextual network of relations, or total way of life encompassing the myriad relations, and practices that define a historical period or specific geographical location or formative community or subgroup within larger fields." See Sheila Davaney, "Theology and the Turn to Cultural Analysis," in *Converging on Culture: Theologians in Dialogue with Cultural Analysis*, ed. Delwin Brown, Greeve Davaney and Kathryn Tanner (Oxford, NY: Oxford University Press, 2001), 5. Since Luzbetak basically views culture in ideational terms, he makes it clear that cultural change is not so much the change in the external expressions of culture and behaviour as it is the change in the underlying ideas that influence behaviour. See Luzbetak, *Church and Cultures: New Perspectives*, 294.

[150] Downs, *Cultures in Crisis*, 31.

[151] Tanner, *Theories of Culture*, 32-34. Here, Tanner compares the coherence of the various elements of a cultural system to that exisitng between the different parts of a work of art, a text, a narrative, or ideas in a person's mind. This coherence can either be semantic (meanings) or syntactic (structure) or functional.

[152] Christopher Dawson, *Religion and Culture: The Clifford Lectures Delivered at the University of Edinburg in 1947*, 2nd ed. (New York: Meridian Books, 1958), 48. See also Louis Luzbetak, *The Church and Cultures: An Applied Anthropology*, 59-64; ibid., 59ff.

to adjustments in its other aspects in order to accommodate the new situation.[153]

Each element acquires its meaningfulness within the context of the whole. This internal coherence also makes it sometimes difficult for cultures to welcome external practices or changes, even when such are seen by the people as clearly beneficial. It is one thing, Downs contends, for a practice or even a value system to be seen as useful; it is yet another for it to fit into the internal logic of the culture in question.[154] This explains why some cultural elements borrowed by a culture from other cultures or traditions do not usually remain the same in the new culture. If the culture is to adopt it, it usually reshapes it so as to agree with its internal coherence. This also happens when culture loses some elements. In both cases the culture also undergoes some readjustments in order to accommodate the new situation and regain its coherence.[155] This point needs to be taken seriously by Christianity as it relates with cultures.

Furthermore, cultural change can either be externally induced through contact and interchange with other cultures, or through forces internal to the culture or society in question. According to Luzbetak, in anthropology, when the former is the case, it is termed diffusion. The latter is called origination. Change, he notes, can also be fast (as in revolutions) or slow, radical or shallow. It can come about either by incorporation of new cultural elements, or by displacement, removal or disappearance, weakening or strengthening, blending or replacement of older ones.[156] Moreover, not all changes do augur well with the members of the society. While some changes lead to the advancement of the human person and greater freedom, some others impact negatively on him or her.[157] But this is expected since culture is a human creation that needs constant critique, corrections, and improvements. Lonergan has reasoned that, being "man-made" it may not avoid being improved upon since humans always want to improve

---

[153] See Downs, *Cultures in Crisis*, 31; Luzbetak, *Church and Cultures: New Perspectives*, 292; Tanner, *Theories of Culture*, 36.

[154] Downs, *Cultures in Crisis*, 31-32.

[155] See Tanner, *Theories of Culture*, 36.

[156] Luzbetak, *Church and Cultures: New Perspectives*, 292-293, 305-308. See also Shorter, *Toward a Theology of Inculturation*, 45-49.

[157] Arij Crollius, "Presentation," in *Cultural Change and Liberation in a Christian Perspective*, ed. Arij Crollius (Rome: Gregorian University Press, 1987), ix.

on the wisdom inherited from their ancestors in order to build a better future for themselves and their progeny.[158]

Culture is characteristically diverse. Just as societies, peoples and circumstances in which they live differ one from the other, so also do their cultures differ. Tanner has identified diversity as "the primary indicator of culture for the anthropologist."[159] This cannot be less dramatic than obvious in the words of Herder when he writes: "Had Greece been populated with Chinese, our Greece would never have existed: had our Greeks been fixed where Darius led the enslaved Eretrians, they would have formed no Athens, they would have produced no Sparta."[160] No wonder, then, the statement of Dawson that culture is "based on common tradition and conditioned by a common environment."[161]

This does not mean that cultures are closed systems that do not interact with one other. Quite the contrary, they constantly interact with and enrich one another, the rate of which has drastically increased today owing to the rapid advancement and sophistication in communication and transportation. But, in spite of all these contacts, which sometimes tend to threaten the notion of cultural pluralism and uniqueness across societies, no two cultures are exactly the same. There are similarities and commonalities among cultures just as there are dissimilarities and divergences; all are not identical, since each is confronted by problems and challenges that differ from those of others.

Without a doubt, acknowledging the uniqueness and diversity of cultures will help one to be much less enthusiastic to use one's culture as yardstick for another's, or to uncritically impose results of researches in one social group on others. It calls for a deeper and better knowledge of each culture in order to be in a better position to say something meaningful about it or to interpret the behaviour of its people. That explains why anthropologists place more value on understanding the distinctive nature or characteristics of the different cultures than they do on searching for commonalities among them

---

[158]   Lonergan, *A Second Collection*, 93.

[159]   Tanner, *Theories of Culture*, 26.

[160]   Herder, "Ideas towards a Philosophy," 39.

[161]   Dawson, *Religion and Culture*, 47. See also Bernard Meland, *Faith and Culture* (Carbondale, IL: Southern Illionis University Press, 1953), 85; Tanner, *Theories of Culture*, 26.

that can help one to group them together.[162] It is undoubtedly true, for instance, that the knowledge of the culture of a nation in Africa may be of some help in understanding others. At the same time, this can also be a hindrance because one may likely see all the others not just as similar to, but as identical with, the one he or she knows. This can lead to untoward and unwarranted conclusions and deductions.

CONCLUSION

Effort has been made in this chapter to examine how the understanding of culture has influenced theological mediation and the church's missionary activity. We examined the old classicist conception of culture, as well as the modern, more empirical, pluralist view. Part of our discoveries is that the old conception of culture adopted by the church in the fourth century helped to make Christian missionary activity more like an expansion of the western culture than it is the propagation of the kingdom of God. This, of course, had its repercussions as we have shown. The newer modern conception represents a further development and broadening of the old, as a result of which culture assumes a way of life of any given society, and is characteristically a diverse and dynamic category. We also saw the postmodern stress on tensions, ambiguity and power struggles in the process of cultural formation. In the chapter that follows, we will examine how Vatican II represents a significant forward leap in the church's understanding of culture.

---

[162]   Tanner, *Theories of Culture*, 30.

2

SIGNIFICANCE OF CULTURE IN THE SECOND VATICAN COUNCIL

INTRODUCTION

A significant shift in the magisterial teaching on the meaning of culture from more evaluative, elitist perspective to more descriptive and anthropological one only happened in the second half the last century. The first indication of this, though faint, can be spotted in Pius XII's 1944 *Allocution to the Pontifical Mission Aid Societies*, where he clearly acknowledges that each society possesses its own culture that needs not suffer destruction whatsoever. The pontiff precisely cautions against the imposition of foreign cultures on any society being evangelised, and advocates rather that missionaries carry out their work with due respect for the indigenous peoples and cultures.[1] Almost a decade later, he reiterates his belief that no culture should be denied its inalienable right to existence that is natural to it: "The right to existence, the right to the respect from others, the right to one's own good name, the right to one's own culture and national character . . .

---

[1] Pius XII, "Allocution to the Pontifical Mission Aid Societies," *AAS* 36 (1944): 210. Shorter is one of those who argue that this is where the first hint to this shift can be found. See Aylward Shorter, *Towards a Theology of Inculturation* (MaryKnoll, NY: Orbis, 1994), 18.

are exigencies of the law of nations dictated by nature itself."[2] Accordingly, to accord all cultures equal status of existence and legitimacy is never in this sense a matter of concession or privilege, but an affirmation of an irreducible reality of human contingency and existence. This understanding, no doubt, influenced his approval of the instruction from the Propaganda Fide permitting Chinese Christians to participate in ancestor veneration and the civil honour paid to Confucius, thus, ending the centuries-old Chinese rites controversy.[3]

Though the efforts of Pius XII in affirming cultural pluralism, as expressed in these documents, need to be well appreciated, it also needs to be noted that there are pointers to the evaluative, classicist notion of culture in some other writings of his.[4] For instance, in the encyclical, *Evangelii Praecones* of 1951, while trying to justify his call for support for the missionary activities of the church, the pontiff argues that the church, through these missionary activities, aims at elevating "people to a higher culture."[5] This culture is nothing less than that of Christendom. In fact, such a wavering stand might have informed the insistence of some theologians, like Carrier, that the official church still understood culture exclusively in its evaluative sense even during the time of Pius XII. According to Carrier, it was not until the Second Vatican Council that the official church adopted the "language of anthropologists and cultural sociologists"[6] while referring to culture. He argues that not even the dimmest hint in this direction was offered by any official church document before the

---

2   Pius XII, "Allocution to the Italian Jurists, *Ci Riesce*," 6 December 1953, *AAS* 45 (1953): 795. The English translation: available from http://www.ewtn.com/library/PAPALDOC/P12CIRI.HTM; accessed 20 March 2009.

3   See Congregation for the Propagation of the Faith, "Instruction Concerning Certain Ceremonies and the Oath about the Chinese Rites," in *100 Roman Documents Concerning the Chinese Rites Controversy (1645-1941)*, ed. Ray Noll (San Francisco, CA: The Ricci Institute for Chinese-Western Cultural History, 1992), 88-89.

4   Shorter notices this ambiguity, though he does not go further to point out those writings where it is noticed. See Shorter, *Towards a Theology of Inculturation*, 183.

5   Pius XII, "Encyclical Letter, On the Promotion of Catholic Missions, *Evangelii Praecones*," 6 July 1951, *AAS* 43 (1951): 521.

6   Hervé Carrier, "The Contribution of the Council to Culture," in *Vatican II: Assessment and Perspectives Twenty-Five Years after (1962-1987)*, ed. René Latourelle (Mahwah, NJ: Paulist, 1989), 461.

council. But "at Vatican II, the official Church updated its view of culture almost overnight."[7] It is indeed undeniably clear that a decisive and unmistakable break with "classicism" in the magisterial thought occurred at Vatican II, but the significant evolution of thought leading up to this needs not be ignored as Carrier seems to have done.

VATICAN II AND ITS PERSPECTIVE ON CULTURE

It was in a memo written by John XXIII, following a meeting he had with Cardinal Ruffini on 2 November 1958, five days after his election as pope, that we see the first documented expression of his wish to convene Vatican II. It is, therefore, not inappropriate to argue that the idea "was not accidental to the pontificate or a kind of afterthought; it was co-terminous with the pontificate as a whole, and acted as its goal, policy, programme and content."[8] The announcement of the council came two months later on 25 January 1959, the feastday of the conversion of St. Paul. The pope explains that the idea to convene the council was born through direct inspiration of the Holy Spirit. Later, in the *Motu proprio*, *Superno Dei Nutu* of 5 June 1960, he made clearer how the inspiration came to him.[9] He seems to have been justified in his decision on account of the pivotal role that the council eventually turned out to play in the history of the church. It brought about a completely new way of looking at the church and the world among Catholics. Karl Rahner makes the all-important remark that the experience of the faith and its demands in relation to the world as inaugurated at the council can only be comparable to that experienced in early Christianity after the Council of Jerusalem.[10] The American

---

[7] Ibid., 453-454.

[8] Peter Hebblethwaite, *Pope John XXIII: Shepherd of the Modern World* (Garden City, NY: Doubleday, 1985), 307.

[9] See Bernard Pawley, *Looking at the Vatican II* (London: SCM, 1962), 63-64.

[10] Karl Rahner, *Theological Investigations*, trans. Edward Quinn, vol. 20 (London: Darton, Longman and Todd, 1981), 84-86. Here, Rahner compares the experience of the transition from a geographically restricted Judaeo-Christianity into Gentile Christianity, which implied a waver of circumcision for the Gentile Christians, to the experience at Vatican II when the church rose from its mono-cultural expression of the faith to take seriously the issue of making Christianity a living possession of people from other cultures outside the West.

sociologist, Melissa Wilde, describes it as "a watershed event in the history of the Roman Catholicism."[11]

The understanding of the fundamental inspirations behind the convocation of the council and the 'spirit' that prevailed in its deliberations are very vital for the appreciation of its overall contributions to culture.[12] This is especially very significant given the fact that the approval of the document, *Gaudium et Spes*, which has a whole section dealing specifically with culture, came towards the end of the council's deliberations.[13] It is, therefore, normal to expect that one's treatment of the significance of the council to culture should not ignore these realities; otherwise one might run the risk of suggesting that the official teachings of the Fathers and their lived experiences could be completely isolated one from the other;[14] or, worse still, that the teachings embody eternally valid propositions unrelated to their historical situatedness. To avoid such a risk, we have deemed it necessary to examine these realities.

BASIC ORIENTATIONS OF THE COUNCIL

The noticeable difference often commented on by scholars between Vatican II and most of the preceding councils is occasioned by a number of factors. For one, while the majority of earlier councils were convened mainly to redress perceived doctrinal errors or heresies,

---

[11]   Melissa Wilde, "How Culture Mattered at Vatican II: Collegiality Triumphs Authority in the Council's Social Movement Organizations," *American Sociological Review* 69, no. 4 (2004): 576. Sociologists unanimously argue, according to John Coleman, that the "Council represents the most significant institutionalized religious change since the Reformation." John Coleman, "Vatican II as a Social Movement," in *The Belgian Contribution to the Second Vatican Council*, BETL, no. 216, ed. Mathijs Lamberigts and Leo Dedreck (Leuven: Peeters, 2008), 7.

[12]   Angelo Fernandes maintains that the sixteen documents of the council are, in actual fact, incapable of encapsulating the rich dynamism of the council. Without, however, undermining the importance of the documents, he asserts "that it is the spirit of the Vatican II that matters most." See Angelo Fernandes, *Vatican II Revisited* (Anand: Gujara Sahitya Prakash, 1997), 10.

[13]   We recall that the date this document was promulgated, 7 December 1965, was a day before the end of the council.

[14]   See Carrier, "The Contribution of the Council," 452.

Vatican II was not basically convened to combat any heresy. This does not mean that there were no existing theological errors at the time that needed to be corrected, but to call a council just for such would be inappropriate and superfluous. The church had handled such errors through the ordinary magisterium. Moreover, to come forward with repetitions of condemnations would appear pharisaic in the eyes of the people who also expected from the official church admission of guilt and confession of its own sins. In addition, to focus merely on the condemnation of others' errors may scuttle the much-needed reform within the church itself, as has been the case in the past.[15] As a matter of fact, in his opening address to the council, John XXIII acknowledges that errors existed, which the church had always opposed. He, nevertheless, makes the point that the faithful Catholics might not even need such repetitive condemnatory stance from the council in order for them to decipher truth from falsehood, since these errors were so self-evident. He maintains that what the church intended to do was to promote mercy as a solution instead of being out to condemn.[16]

He further argues that the council was not called to start repeating the doctrines of the church, which all the faithful were already familiar with. According to him, if it were for this, it was not necessary to convene a council.[17] His vision of the council is one that would be deeply anthropological and pastoral in character. It should be a council that would pay greater attention to the mode of presentation of the faith to the modern person. It had to go beyond mere repetitions, and positively show the validity of the Christian doctrine using the updated modern methods of research and modes of thought.[18] Four objectives

---

[15] Hans Küng, *The Council in Action: Theological Reflections on the Second Vatican Council*, trans. Cecily Hastings (New York: Sheed and Ward, 1963), 211-212.

[16] John XXIII, "Opening Address to the Second Vatican Council," 11 October 1962, in *Voices from the Council*, ed. Michael Prendergast and M.D. Ridge (Portland, OR: Pastoral, 2004), xv.

[17] Ibid., xiv-xv. One wonders whether the pope may not be presuming too much by this remark. By "all," does he mean the West or are Africans and other regions also included, who, at the time of the council, were yet to decipher what the church was, and what it intended to preach?

[18] Ibid., xv. See also Andrea Riccardi, "The Tumultous Opening Days of the Council," in *History of Vatican II: The Formation of the Council's Identity, First*

have been identified as rudimentary to his vision of the council: "self-awareness, self-renewal, Christian unity and dialogue with the contemporary world."[19] This way he avoids what Hans Küng describes as "doctrinalizing of the Council," which, according to him, has been the utmost challenge such reforming councils as Vatican II is bound to face.[20]

To be sure, the council provided an occasion for the church to update and renew itself given the prevailing achievements and advancements of the time. This is usually couched in the word, *aggiornamento*.[21] This renewal and/or updating has theological and anthropological, as well as *ad intra* and *ad extra* dimensions to it. It involves improvement on the part of the church of its theological positions so as to make possible a meaningful and critical engagement with the culture of modernity. It also extends to the church's redefinition and purification of itself, as well as renewal of its understanding of the world.[22] As regards the church's relationship

---

Period and Intersession, October 1962-September 1963, ed. Guiseppe Alberigo and Joseph Komonchak (Leuven: Peeters, 1997), 17.

19   Fernandes, *Vatican II Revisited*, 11.

20   Küng, *The Council in Action*, 69. According to Mathijs Lamberigts, the nature of Pope's opening speech seriously encouraged those bishops who really wanted a council where their actual participation in the decision making is fully guaranteed. Mathijs Lamberigts, "*Gaudium et Spes*: A Council in Dialogue with the World," in *Scrutinizing the Signs of the Times in the Light of the Gospel*, BETL, no. 208, ed. John Verstraeten (Leuven: Leuven University Press, 2007), 25-26.

21   According to Lieven Boeve, the best reflection of this *aggiornamento* in the Vatican II is perhaps in the Pastoral Constitution, *Gaudium et Spes*. Lieven Boeve, "*Gaudium et Spes* and the Crisis of Modernity: The End of the Dialogue with the World," in *Vatican II and Its Legacy*, BETL, no. 166, ed. Mathijs Lamberigts and Leo Kenis (Leuven: Leuven University Press, 2002), 83.

22   Carrier, "The Contribution of the Council," 444; Tracey Rowland, *Culture and the Thomist Tradition after Vatican II*, ed. John Milbank, Catherine Pickstock and Graham Ward (London: Routledge, 2003), 19. Theologians often refer to *Lumen Gentium* and *Gaudium et Spes* as two major expressions of the *ad intra* an *ad extra* perspectives of the council respectively. It is worthy of note that it was the Belgian Cardinal, Léon Josef Suenens, that helped to call the attention of the council to these two dominant perspectives through which the churches renewal was to be seen. See Francis Murphy, "Vatican Politics: Structure and Function," *World Politics* 26, no. 4 (1974): 542; Boeve, "*Gaudium et Spes*," 83. For an extensive study of the contribution of Suénens to the council, see

with the world, two major dispositions can be identified among the Fathers of the council. There were, on one hand, those who were more open towards the world and, on the other hand, those who were more defensive of the church in opposition to the world. Some commentators choose to refer to the former as the progressives and the latter as the conservatives,[23] a categorisation that Carrier sees as over-simplistic. He rather sees the difference between the two groups as having to do with the difference in methodological approaches:

> It would be oversimplification to say that the Council was divided into conservatives and progressives. It was more a question of different emphasis in connection as to the work of the Council, as based on two different types of intellectual attitude: on the one hand, the reflection on principles, which was more accustomed to deductive methods, and, on the other, the anthropological and pastoral approach.[24]

Indeed, Carrier's reservation concerning the use of "conservatives" and "progressives" to categorise the Fathers seems adrem, because

---

Mathijs Lamberigts and Leo Dedreck, "The Role of Cardinal Léon-Joseph Suenens at Vatican II," in *The Belgian Contribution to the Second Vatican Council*, BETL, no. 216, ed. Doris Donnelly *et al* (Leuven: Peeters, 2008), 61-217. Concerning *Gaudium et Spes* and *Lumen Gentium*, Cardinal Gabriel Garrone, whose contribution to the formulation of *Gaudium et Spes* was very obvious, is reported as saying that "*Lumen Gentium* is the foundation of the Council; *Gaudium et Spes* is its application." Marcos McGrath, "The Impact of *Gaudium et Spes*: Medellin, Puebla, and Pastoral Creativity," in *The Church and Culture since Vatican II: The Experience of North and Latin America*, ed. Joseph Gremillion (Notre Dame, IN: Notre Dame University Press, 1985), 64.

[23] See, for instance, Wilde, "How Culture Mattered," 576-602. While making a sociological analysis of the outcome of the council, Wilde tends to see it as evidence of the organisational success of the progressives over the conservatives. John O'Malley also sees the council as divided into conservatives and progressives, with the progressive camp eventually dominating in a manner that gave the council an unprecedented specific character. John O'Malley, *Tradition and Transition: Historical Perspectives on Vatican II* (Wilmington, DE: Michael Glazier, 1989), 12-13. Cf. Eugene Bianchi, "John XXIII, Vatican II, and American Catholicism," *Annals of the American Academy of Political and Social Science* 387 (1970): 30-40.

[24] Carrier, "The Contribution of the Council," 445-446.

it may obscure the much deeper theological issues involved in the debate. He notes, however, that as the first session was about to end, with the help and interventions of such Cardinals as Montini, Suenens, König, Lercaro, Bishops Garrone and Wojtyla, the council eventually had to turn towards the world and adopted *resolutely* a pastoral and anthropological approach.[25] But should Carrier be correct in his observation concerning the turnaround of events, then, one needs a different ground to explain the compromise nature of most of the documents, which Carrier himself does not seem to deny. Indeed, many theologians believe that this major tension between the two groups remained unresolved throughout the council's sessions and played itself out in the nature of the documents. O'Malley, for one, does not mince words when he says that the conflict continued during the council debates between those Fathers still operating within "the so-called classicist mentality," and those who were more historically oriented. He believes that this tension lies behind many of the council's documents and even continues to be influential in the post-conciliar scholarship regarding the interpretation of the documents.[26]

Of no less importance too is the impact of the great developments in historical and critical studies on the outcome of the council. This guided the council Fathers towards a much greater awareness of the historicity of the church and the development of its teachings. Actually, John XXIII, while addressing the council in his opening speech, recognises the importance of a sense of history, which he refers to as the "teacher of life."[27] With this, the council was well positioned

---

[25]   Ibid., 446. Mention could also be made in this regard of Cardinal Liénart of Lille (France), whose intervention on 13 October 1962, the second *working day* of the council, marked the first decisive turning point from following stereotypically the pre-determined way of running the council already adopted by the secretariat for the council. His intervention, which elicited an extended applause from the council Fathers, helped to postpone the hurried attempt to elect the members of the different commissions even when the Fathers were yet to know one another. Following his suggestions, extra days were given, and the Conferences of Bishops were called upon to assist in drawing up lists for the election. This action, no doubt, helped to shape the subsequent importance placed on these conferences. See Riccardi, "The Tumultous Opening of the Council," 27-32; Coleman, "Vatican II as a Social Movement," 12-13.

[26]   O'Malley, *Tradition and Transition*, 30.

[27]   John XXIII, "Opening Address," xii.

to reappraise the impact of history and culture on the formulation of the Christian doctrine. It is not surprising, then, that they rejected the original drafts of the documents prepared by the Roman curia, which lacked such engagement with history.[28] Comparing Vatican II with the earlier ones in this regard, O'Malley aptly argues that Vatican II is the prime instance of formulation of the church's teachings "with as much concern for historical context and process as for their validity in terms of traditional metaphysics."[29] This provides appropriate context for dialogue with the world, which has been identified as an object of the church's pastoral action.[30]

There are also a number of other factors that had significant impact on the council's decisions. Among them is the presence of bishops from all parts of the globe, especially from the missionary countries of Africa, Asia and Latin America. This helped a lot in creating the much-needed awareness as regards the diversity of cultures.[31] For Rahner, such significant episcopal representation helped to make evident and actuate the fact that the church was "no longer the European church with its American areas of dissemination and its exports to Asia and Africa."[32] Another important factor was the level of publicity that its proceedings enjoyed. According to O'Malley, the aggressiveness of the council's interest in the media and the endeavour to profer satisfactory response to some of the issues raised by the media helped to boost the confidence of those Fathers who were more open to change.[33] The presence and contributions of experts from different fields of learning, as well as the conspicuous presence of non-Catholic Christian observers were also significant. The presence of these observers, Hans Küng remarks, "is more significant than any number of ecumenical proclamations."[34] It helped to stimulate in the

---

[28] See Herman Pottmeyer, "A New Phase in the Reception of Vatican II: Twenty Years of Interpretation of the Council," in *The Reception of Vatican II*, ed. Guiseppe Alberigo, Jean-Pierre Jossua and Joseph Komonchak (Washington, DC: University of America Press, 1987), 31.

[29] O'Malley, *Tradition and Transition*, 14.

[30] Ibid., 15.

[31] Ibid., 13; Carrier, "The Contribution of the Council," 447.

[32] Rahner, *Theological Investigations*, 80.

[33] O'Malley, *Tradition and Transition*, 14.

[34] Carrier, "The Contribution of the Council," 447. The ecumenical disposition found in the council was already visibly manifested by John XIII in his creation

Fathers the need to scrutinise the conciliar documents more incisively than they would have done. Moreover, it also contributed in putting the issue of the challenge posed by the contemporary world and the church's relationship to it on the front burner during the council's debates.[35]

It is very vital that the above-discussed contributive factors to the fundamental configuration of the council be well noted as I now delve into the council's contributions to the church's understanding of, and relationship with, culture.

TREATMENT OF CULTURE BY VATICAN II

The importance placed on culture today by the church can be better appreciated by considering the unprecedented attention it received from the Fathers of Vatican II. In the Pastoral Constitution on the Church in the World of Today, *Gaudium et Spes*, which is the longest of the council's sixteen documents, a whole chapter covering about one-tenth of the entire document was devoted to the meaning and problem of culture in today's society.[36] This can really be very surprising given the fact that, unlike the other chapters with which the chapter on culture forms the second part of the constitution, it never had any previous history during the preliminary stages of the council.[37]

---

of the Secretariat for Christian Unity in 1960. Hans Küng notes that one needs to recall the attitude of the church to other Christian communions before the council in order to duly appreciate the impact of having them observe the council's proceedings. Küng, *The Council in Action:* 71.

[35]   O'Malley, *Tradition and Transition*, 13.

[36]   In fact, the important place occupied by culture is more evident in the works of theologians after the council and, more especially, in the extraordinary concern shown by John Paul II about culture. See Gallagher, *Clashing Symbols*, 48. Gallagher describes *Gaudium et Spes* as "an unexpected child of the Council... a long document that can be viewed as an essay in theological anthropology on contemporary culture." Ibid., 41-42. For Lamberigts, *Gaudium et Spes* "meant a rupture with the ecclesiastical documents that were produced in the past." Lamberigts, "*Gaudium et Spes*: A Council in Dialogue with the World," 26.

[37]   Roberto Tucci, "The Proper Development of Culture," in *Commentary on the Documents of Vatican II: Pastoral Constitution on the Church in the Modern World*, vol. 2, ed. Herbert Vorgrimler (New York: Herder & Herder, 1969), 246. Tucci maintains that none of the schemata from the various commissions had

It is not only the length of the chapter that is significant here, but also the depth of its concern with culture. Gallagher describes it as the *magna charta* of the church's discussion on culture.[38]

In his analysis of the overall significance of the council with regard to culture, Rahner says it is the first official manifestation and realisation of the church as a world-church. He offers some reasons why this is so. For one, it is the first council in which a bishop whose native land was not Europe participated. Others include: the council's approval of the use of vernacular in liturgy; the realisation of the church's responsibility to the Third World, now seen as an integral part of the church. He also points out the council's understanding of revelation, which indicates some shift from much use of neo-scholastic theology and style which are mainly intelligible to the western minds, to that which can be understood by all people. The council, he notes, also laid the foundations for ecumenism and positive assessment of other religions. In fact, Rahner argues that "either the Church sees and recognizes these essential differences of other cultures, into which it has to enter as a world-Church, and accepts with Pauline boldness the necessary consequences of this recognition or it remains a western Church and thus in the last resort betrays the meaning of Vatican II." [39]

DESCRIPTION OF CULTURE

The first pointer to this landmark achievement of the council can be seen in the very first paragraph of the chapter on culture, where the meaning of culture is offered in answer to the question raised in

---

an express treatment of the church's relation with culture, even though the need for one had been adumbrated in the appendix of the schemata drafted by the Commission for the Lay Apostolate. For more on how the chapter on culture eventually emerged, see Tucci, "The Proper Development of Culture," 246-254.

[38] Gallagher, *Clashing Symbols*, 48.

[39] Rahner, *Theological Investigations*, 77-89. See especially p. 86. See also Karl Rahner, "Towards a Fundamental Theological Interpretations of Vatican II," *Theological Studies* 40, no. 4 (1979): 716-727. In a similar vein, Johann-Baptist Metz says of Vatican II that it "is a prime example of moves towards a culture promoted by the Church itself which is based on the acknowledgment of the other in their otherness." Metz, "Unity and Diversity," 83. See also Collet, "From Theological Vandalism," 28.

the first conciliar debate on the topic regarding the confusion often associated with the word. Due to lack of agreement among experts on the precise meaning of culture, the Fathers opted for a description of the concept rather than its definition.[40] The text reads:

> It is a feature of the human person that it can attain to real and full humanity only through culture; that is, by cultivating the goods of nature and values. Wherever human life is concerned, therefore, nature and culture are very intimately connected.
>
> The term "culture" in general refers to everything by which we perfect and develop our many spiritual and physical endowments; applying ourselves through knowledge and effort to bring the earth within our power; developing ways of behaving and institutions, we make life in society more human, whether in the family or in the civil sphere as a whole; in the course of time we express, share and preserve in our works great spiritual experiences and aspirations to contribute to the progress of many people, even of the whole human race.
>
> Human culture necessarily takes on a historical and social aspect, and the term 'culture' often has a sociological and ethnological connotation. In this sense one can talk of a plurality of cultures . . . [41]

In the above description, the text brings out the relationship between nature and culture in an unambiguous fashion, and thereby highlights the importance of culture to human existence. It establishes that it is only through culture can the human existence be authentically and fully realised, meaning that it is impossible to exist as humans without culture. Culture humanises us and brings order into our lives. To survive culturally is to survive humanly.[42] In effect, at the very heart of a person's being is his or her engagement with culture. That being

---

[40] See Tucci, "The Proper Development of Culture," 225.

[41] Vatican Council II, "Pastoral Constitution on the Church in the World of Today, *Gaudium et Spes*," 7 December 1965, in *Decrees of the Ecumenical Councils: Trent to Vatican II*, ed. Norman Tanner (London: Sheed & Ward, 1990), no. 53. Hereafter, *GS*.

[42] Eugene Hillman, "Good News for Every Nation via Inculturation," *Louvain Studies* 25, no. 4 (2000): 344.

the case, the human being is not a creature who is merely nature, or nature with the addition of culture, but a being who is simultaneously nature and culture. Were human being to be exclusively nature or culture, he or she would not be a human being.[43] Through this, the council recovers the intricate, convoluted and dialectical relationship between nature and culture, which the original meaning of culture as husbandry expresses. Thus, culture becomes, as Eagleton describes it, "a matter of self-overcoming as much as self-realization."[44] This is actually what John Paul II underscores when, in his address to UNESCO, he expressly refers to culture as that through which a person surpasses himself, and by so doing, comes to the realisation of who he or she actually is.[45]

Gallagher sees more to this. He understands the council as not only linking culture to the human nature but also to human *autonomy* towards self-realisation. The statement of the council that it is only through culture that the human person can reach an authentic and full realisation of his or her humanity, he says, brings out clearly "two foundation stones of Catholic thinking on culture . . . that culture is intimately linked with the dignity of the person and with *the call of freedom* to become more fully human."[46] This invariably means that the call for the promotion of proper development of culture is also a call for the promotion of freedom within the context of the overall promotion of our humanity, which is always open to fuller realisation. It corresponds to the creator's plan for the human person at creation. Moreover, by linking culture to the human nature, the council succeeds in showing that culture is a universal phenomenon of human societies that should not be seen as an exclusive possession of select few. Tucci argues that it was simply in order to achieve this end that the close connection between nature and culture was introduced during the revision of the document.[47] In fact, the council's concern that plurality

---

[43]   Lambert, "*Gaudium et Spes*," 41-42.

[44]   Terry Eagleton, *The Idea of Culture* (Oxford: Blackwell, 2003), 5-6.

[45]   John Paul II, "Address to UNESCO," 2 June 1980, *Origins* 10, no. 4 (1980): no. 7.

[46]   Gallagher, *Clashing Symbols*, 43. The emphasis is mine.

[47]   Tucci, "The Proper Development of Culture," 255. He says: "This was intended to eliminate from the start any misconception that the term bore a restricted meaning valid only for those who have received an elaborate education, i.e. 'cultivated persons' in the sense of the Latin 'humanus civilisque cultus.'"

of cultures be acknowledged and respected is unmistakeable.[48] Gallagher observes that "even if not stated openly, it is evident [in the council's document] that there can be no 'uncultured' nations and the monopoly exercised by the more aristocratic meaning of culture has been broken for good."[49] Little wonder that the council speaks of socio-cultural regions as it addresses how Christianity can effectively take root outside the West.[50]

In its description of culture, the council carefully combines the traditional, classicist view of culture whereby it emphasises more the development of the personal, intellectual and physical capabilities of the individual, with the modern understanding of culture, which is more anthropological. In effect, culture does not merely involve self-transcendence, but ways of life of different societies and human communities. This way, it tries to update itself in line with the development of the concept in the secular scholarship.[51] Nevertheless, since it does not offer any specific definition of the concept, at certain instances in the document, it uses it in the classicist and elitist sense, while at other points it employs it in a manner that is more anthropological. This is one of the weakneses noticed in its handling of the concept. This will be discussed later in the chapter.

---

[48] *GS* 53. Indeed, the council unequivocally recognises that differences exist across people and cultures, which arise from diversity in the "ways in which objects are utilised, labour is applied, the self is expressed, religion is practiced, customary ways of behaving take shape, laws and juridical institutions are established, sciences and arts develop and beauty is pursued." Ibid.

[49] Gallagher, *Clashing Symbols*, 44. See also Tucci, "The Proper Development of Culture," 256.

[50] Vatican Council II, "Decree on the Missionary Activity of the Church, *Ad Gentes*," 18 November 1965, in *Decrees of the Ecumenical Councils: Trent to Vatican II*, ed. Norman Tanner (London: Sheed & Ward, 1990), no. 22. Hereafter, *AG*.

[51] Hervé Carrier, "The Church Meeting Cultures: Convergences and Perspectives," in *The Church and Culture Since Vatican II: The Experience in North and Latin America* ed. Joseph Gremillion (Notre Dame, IN: University of Notre Dame Press, 1985), 141. See also Carrier, "Understanding Culture," 18.

Gospel, Theology and Culture

Very imperative is the way the relationship that exists between gospel and culture is handled. This relationship, the council makes clear, is theologically founded on the mystery of the incarnation of the Son of God. Through his Incarnate Son, God has revealed himself to different people in accordance with their culture and age. Just as God assumed the human nature in order to offer his salvation to all, the gospel should be allowed to assume the different cultures of the people to whom its message is addressed. The council urges that the cultural achievements of various people and nations be well utilised in spreading the gospel among them.[52] This way, it avoids treating culture as an abstract phenomenon, but as a real "context for theological reflection and pastoral projection."[53] In order to strike a balance between the tendency towards over-exaggeration of the church's cultural patrimony and (following Cardinal Lercaro's speech during the council's debate) the tendency towards uncritical acceptance of cultural poverty of the church, the council states that such engagement with culture will not only bring about enrichment to the cultures concerned but also to the church itself.[54] There is thus a demand for humility from both the church and different cultures so that they can both learn from each other in an atmosphere of mutual respect and dialogue. In order to harmonise the principle of integration of gospel values into particular cultures with the transcendence of these values over all cultures, the council affirms that there is no particular people or culture, whether of the past or of the present, to which the church is "exclusively and indissolubly" tied. Rather, in order to realise its mission, it enters into communion with all.[55]

---

[52] *GS* 58.

[53] Carrier, "The Contribution of the Council," 455.

[54] *GS* 58. See Tucci, "The Proper Development of Culture," 267; Gallagher, *Clashing Symbols*, 46.

[55] *GS* 58; Tucci, "The Proper Development of Culture," 266. See also Georges De Schrijver, "*Gaudium et Spes* on the Church's Dialogue with Contemporary Society and Culture: A Seedbed for the Divergent Options Adopted in Medellin, Puebla, and Santo Domingo," in *Vatican II and Its Legacy*, BETL, no. 166, ed. Mathijs Lamberigts and Leo Kenis (Leuven: Leuven University Press, 2002), 298. For De Schrijver, this position was taken by the council so as to bring a

The council clearly spells out two important tasks of theologians in this regard. On one hand, it stresses the need for them to be deep in their knowledge of the revealed truth, and on the other hand, it recognises the importance of improvement of theological methods, in order to meet the challenges of the time.[56] To achieve this end, theology should incorporate research findings in the secular sciences in order to enrich its mediation and make the faith more intelligible to the people through their specific cultural worlds. It is only thus would the faith be better expressed both in the pastoral and the liturgical lives of the church.[57]

Rather than argue for a kind of too easy interaction between cultural achievements of the age and the gospel, the council acknowledges that some difficulties and tensions do exist. It, nevertheless, admits that they are not necessarily detrimental to the faith, for from them also could be derived some positive gains for the church: "These difficulties do not necessarily harm the life of faith, rather they can stimulate the mind to a deeper and more accurate understanding of the faith."[58] By so doing, it avoids outright condemnations and unnecessary apologetics.

Globalisation and Cultural Development

There is an expression of some reservations by the council towards the enormous scientific achievements and the expansion of

---

balance between the church's openness to cultural expressions of the Christian faith and its critical stance towards the same.

[56] *GS* 62. We note here the importance placed by the council on the need to make formation in theology more open to the laity whose contributions will bring enhancement to the discipline itself. See also Tucci, *"The Proper Development of Culture,"* 283.

[57] *GS* 62.

[58] Ibid. It should be noted that during the preparation of this document, there was a long discussion on the need to mention at this point the case of Galileo. But, according to Tucci, such a suggestion was not allowed based on two reasons: first, there has not been any council that pronounced any condemnation of Galileo; second, it might not be appropriate for the whole issue addressed in the schema to be reduced just to the Galileo case. Tucci, "The Proper Development of Culture," 279. See also Gallagher, *Clashing Symbols*, 48.

contemporary culture, which, it states, has brought with it "a new age in human history."[59] This new age is characterised by the tendency to submerge local cultures by the forces of globalisation, thus, posing some dangers to the cultural specificity of societies:

> Customs and habits are daily becoming more uniform . . . ; the increasing contacts between nations and groups in society are opening to each and everyone the treasures of various forms of cultures, and thus a more widespread form of human culture is gradually developing which is extending and expressing the unity of the human race all the more as it gives better recognition to the peculiarities of different cultures.[60]

One can easily recognise from the foregoing that the council is worried about how to strike a balance between the benefits of an increase in cultural exchange among different people with the accompanying rapid upsurge in homogenisation of cultures, on one hand, and the need to promote the distinctive heritage of each cultural group, on the other hand, having authentic human development as its end.[61] According to the council, this new cultural situation can only be plausible if it serves to preserve the cultural specificities of different people. It also recognises a rapid growth in specialisation and divergences in different fields of contemporary culture, making it difficult for people to have an integral vision of reality. It, therefore, affirms that everyone should make it a point of duty to ensure that the integral vision of man is not hampered by this cultural development. In short, it appeals for greater attention to be paid to integral development and understanding of the whole human person, with the "values of understanding, will, conscience and fellowship" given more prominence.[62]

---

[59] *GS* 54.

[60] *GS* 54. See also De Schrijver, "*Gaudium et Spes*," 297.

[61] Leo Nauwens argues that such fear of submerging local cultures is often over-exaggerated by scholars. According to him, there are certain unavoidable factors that work against it within cultures. For his discussion on some of these factors, see Leo Nauwens, "Clash between Globalization and Local Cultures," in *Liberation Theologies on Shifting Grounds: A Clash of Socio-Economic and Cultural Paradigms*, BETL, no. 135, ed. Georges De Schrijver (Leuven: Leuven University Press, 1998), 280-283.

[62] *GS* 61.

Taking the above issues into consideration, the need for the promotion of favourable conditions for the proper development of culture is highlighted. Culture, it states, needs autonomy and independence in order to develop in accordance with principles proper to it.[63] But this autonomy and independence remains unchallengeable in as much as cultural development is directed towards its proper end—the development of the individual and the common good of all: "It rightly calls for respect and enjoys a certain inviolability, without prejudice to the rights of the person and of the particular and general community within the bounds of the common good."[64] According to the council, if this end is kept in view, it will encourage the promotion of new humanism of co-responsibility, decrease the likelihood of agnosticism, the feeling of absolute self-sufficiency, with the ensuing disregard for the desire for higher order of things.[65] When this proper end is not taken into consideration, as Mathew Levering argues, what we have is a "false autonomy," by which "human culture becomes destructive."[66] The council also stresses the need for independence of culture from economic and political forces, which always divert culture to serve their own interests.[67] Here one senses an implicit caution against totalitarianism's claim to dictate principles and norms for culture and to create a culture of its own.[68]

There is also the affirmation of the need to pay proper attention to everyone's rights and duties with regard to culture. All human beings have this inalienable right to culture and its benefits. It is a

---

63   *GS* 59, 36.

64   *GS* 59. In fact, by expressing this idea, the council is simply echoing a thought already contained in *Quadragesimo Anno* of Pius XI, in which he states that, though both the economic and moral orders should each depend on their own separate principles in their own right, they should not be so dichotomised as to affirm absolute independence of the former from the latter. Pius XI, "Encyclical Letter, On Reconstruction of the Social Order, *Quodragesimo Anno*, 15 May 1931," *AAS* 23 (1931): 190.

65   See *GS* 55, 57.

66   Mathew Levering, "Pastoral Perspectives on the Church in the Modern World," in *Vatican II: Renewal within Tradition*, ed. Mathew Lamb and Mathew Levering (Oxford: Oxford University Press, 2008), 170. Levering tries to understand this end christologically. He makes the point that the end to which culture should be directed finds its ultimate fulfilment in Christ.

67   *GS* 59.

68   Tucci, "The Proper Development of Culture," 271.

right, the council argues, that abhors every form of "discrimination on the ground of race, sex, nationality, religion or social condition."[69] It, therefore, urges that everything possible be done to make people become aware of this, as well as their duty towards the development of culture.[70] In this connection, it advocates for making it possible for people to acquire higher studies to achieve proper cultural enhancement.[71] This way, the council emphasises once more that culture is not restricted to some special individuals, but is rather an essential constituent of the life of every society.

EVALUATING THE COUNCIL'S CONTRIBUTION

There is no doubt that Vatican II's approach to culture is much more comprehensive and up to date compared to that adopted by the official church before it. That notwithstanding, there are some elements of weakness in its treatment of culture. One thing that has often bothered many scholars is why and how such a modern approach to culture omits a clear inclusion of religion as an aspect of culture.[72] The style and language of the document has also been a source of worry to some critical minds. Just like the language of Vatican II documents generally, it lacks some technicality and precision that one may ordinarily expect from a document of such theological importance. From his general assessment of the documents of the council, O'Malley considers them unequalled in history as regards their technical looseness and verbosity. The language of earlier

---

[69] *GS* 59. This thought has been hinted on by Paul VI in *Octogesima Adveniens*. See Paul VI, "Apostolic Letter, *Octogesima Adveniens*, 14 May 1971," *AAS* 63 (1971): no. 2.

[70] *GS* 59, 60. As regards the relationship between one's right to culture and his duty to it, Tucci affirms that "Culture is not primarily a right but a duty." Therefore, person's right to culture flows from his or her duty to it and not vice versa. According to him, culture "is only a right because it is a fundamental duty. Precisely because man has the duty of cultivating himself, of developing all his powers and capacities, he has also the right to what he needs to fulfil that duty." Tucci, "The Proper Development of Culture," 274. Gallagher also shares the same idea. See Gallagher, *Clashing Symbols*, 47.

[71] *GS* 60.

[72] De Schrijver, "*Gaudium et Spes*," 296.

councils, he says, tends to be more concise, precise and juridical. This is not the case with Vatican II where the language is generally fluid, exhortatory, non-judgemental, reconciliatory and more or less homiletical.[73] Though such a style can be said to be fitting for a council the major aim of which is pastoral, and which wants to show some openness to the future and never intends to sound canonical or dogmatic, there are some inevitable problems with it. One readily-observed problem is that it easily lends the documents to a myriad of interpretations.[74] Their verbosity has been judged as making the documents often "boring to read, almost impossible to teach, and further complicates their interpretation."[75]

This is particularly true of *Gaudium et Spes* in which culture is very extensively treated. Tracey Rowland is in no way comfortable with the document's terminological inexactitude. She accuses it of claiming to be in principle what it is not in practice. Rowland considers as inappropriate its designation as a "constitution" because, according to her, its form is not in any way constitutional or juridical. The situation is even worsened by the official English translation of the title, whereby the Latin "*mundo huius temporis*" [beter translated, 'in the world of today/in the contemporary world'] is translated "in the modern world." According to Rowland, the council seems to consider the word "modern" as simply synonymous with contemporary, even though it "is a theologically and philosophically loaded term."[76] The expressions, like "modern man" and "modern world," are constantly referred to without examining them theologically. This leaves them open to very many interpretations.[77] Furthermore, there is neither a clearly defined theological framework nor a standard with which the culture of modernity is analysed nor do the conciliar Fathers

---

[73]　O'Malley, *Tradition and Transition*, 25, 26.

[74]　Ibid., 27-28; Turbanti argues that such looseness could be said to have contributed to the emergence of, for example, the Lefebvre group and the South American Liberation Theologians holding two diametrically opposed positions with regard to the interpretation of the council. Giovanni Turbanti, "The Attitude of the Church to the Modern World at and after Vatican II," *Concilium*, no. 6 (1992): 92.

[75]　O'Malley, *Tradition and Transition*, 28.

[76]　Rowland, *Culture and the Thomist Tradition after Vatican II*, 18.

[77]　Ibid., 18, 20.

see modernity as "*a specific cultural formation*," the pre-conciliar scholarship in this direction notwithstanding.[78]

Considering too the concept of culture as contained in *Gaudium et Spes*, one also notices some imprecision. The council rightly acknowledges the multifacetedness of the concept, and is able to examine the different dimensions or senses of it. But at a long run, since it wants to avoid giving perhaps any questionable definition of the concept, it fails to pull these dimensions together into a coherent whole. Having left the reader with such incoherency, one would have expected it to, at least, specify in the various contexts it uses the term, the particular sense in which it is being employed. Unfortunately, this is not done. Thus, even if one acknowledges the comprehensive nature of the council's treatment of culture, he or she sees also that its analysis of the concept remains shallow. In fact, Rowland is of the opinion that the document lacks proper hermeneutics of culture.[79]

Little wonder that, in its Constitution on the Sacred Liturgy, *Sacrosanctum Concilium*, while acknowledging the need to take into consideration the peculiar situations of the different cultures of the world during the reform of the liturgy, it seems to have simultaneously advocated for imposition of the western (Roman) perception of the liturgy on others. This is seen in its call that the liturgical rites be outstanding in their "noble simplicity," brevity and clarity, and should shun unnecessary repetitions. It also demands that they be easily understood by the people without much details.[80] Surely, such "noble simplicity" being canvassed here may not tally with the African perception of how liturgical celebrations should be. This may also be true of other regions. For Africans, liturgy should be elaborate, colourful and deeply involving. It is good to the extent that it is able to appeal not only to the intellect but also to the emotions and the deepest yearnings of the people. These needs may not be adequately addressed by the Roman "noble simplicity." But it is quite unfortunate that the

---

[78] Ibid., 21. Emphasis in the original.

[79] Ibid., 20-23. Rowland points out that the council should have been more critical in its analysis by making clear areas where it uses culture (following, for example, T.S. Eliot's insight) either as self-formation (*Bildung*), as culture of a specific group or civilisation (*Geist or ethos*), or that of the society as a whole (*Kultur*).

[80] Vatican Council II, "Constitution on the Sacred Liturgy, *Sacrosanctum Concilium*," 4 December, 1963, *AAS* 56 (1964): no. 34.

document appears not to have been sufficiently appreciative of the significance of these variations and the need to put them into serious consideration.[81]

Another issue is the council's fundamental concept, *aggiornamento*, which some have argued lacks any theoretical framework. Its vagueness has led to different camps among post-conciliar theologians regarding the attitude of the church towards the world and the nature of its dialogue with it, as adopted during the council. It was not until the Extraordinary Synod of 1985 that its understanding as updating theological knowledge to meet the challenges of modernity came in force.[82] While some theologians appear to have too optimistic vision of the world and the church's dialogue with it, others at the other end of the spectrum react against such optimism and their opinions seem to suggest closing the chapter of the church's dialogue with the contemporary culture. These two different attitudes represent two major camps as regards the reception of *Gaudium et Spes* generally. Boeve describes the former as progressives and the latter as neo-conservative theologians. Theologians, like Joseph Ratzinger (later, Pope Benedict XVI), Boeve argues, would, time and again, caution against over-optimistic and often-exaggerated openness to the modern world, insisting that dialogue with it does not simply mean a mere adjustment of the Christian faith to the modern world, but a critical engagement, involving a re-evaluation of the ambiguity of the modern world with all that entails.[83] Boeve reasons that, at a long run, however, these neo-conservative thinkers suggest going back to the pre-modern Christian master narrative as a solution to the problem. A third group to the discussion, representing the post-modern thinkers, like Boeve, insists on the utilisation of the postmodern critical consciousness in the dialogue between the Christian faith and the present culture. A return to Christian master narrativity is nothing but

---

[81] See Gerald Arbuckle, *Culture, Inculturation, Theologians: A Postmodern Critique* (Collegeville, MN: Liturgical, 2010), 141-142.

[82] This is the argument of Rowland Tracey. According to her, it was the polyvalency of the word, as used by the council, that made theologians understand it variously in such senses as to "accommodate," "follow," "mimic," "ape," "meeting some external standard." Such a situation made the word unable to offer any "guidance for a philosophical or theological interpretation of the 'spirits' of the 'modern world.'" Rowland, *Culture and the Thomist Tradition after Vatican II*, 19-20. See also See O'Malley, *Tradition and Transition*, 45.

[83] Boeve, "Gaudium et Spes," 87.

a return to the hegemonic, authoritarian closeness to otherness, which does not reflect the present detraditionalised context, and is to that extent counter-productive.[84] Indeed, Boeve suggests that it is only by becoming an open narrative that Christianity can achieve the needed fruitful dialogue with the post-modern situation.[85] This demands greater determination and frankness on the part of the church.

Indeed, to be fair to the council, and to ensure its better reception, two extremes must be avoided. One is being too restrictive as to the limits of the possibilities that the council offers. The other is being too forward as to the openness offered by it to the world. A more appropriate interpretation and reception should try to strike a balance between the letters of the texts and the general 'spirit' of the council. Failure to harmonise these two effectively can lead to more hermeneutical confusions.[86] It is also crucial to understand the council as a transitional one in which the tension between continuity and change is inevitable. Understood this way, it would, therefore, be a surprise were one to see more precision in the documents, especially in its treatment of culture, as is the case. Herman Pottmeyer sees the disagreement among the council Fathers over the way of presenting the church's teaching, the course of the council's renewal and the eventual compromise nature of the documents as expected, given the transitional nature of the council. According to him, for the council to have challenged the one-sided nature of the church's earlier stand on issues and juxtaposed them with yet other sides of the story is an

---

[84] Ibid., 86-87, 90-93.

[85] For more on this, see Lieven Boeve, *Interrupting Tradition: An Essay on Christian Faith in a Postmodern Context*, trans. Brian Doyle (Leuven: Peeters, 2003), 86-111. See also Lieven Boeve, *God Interrupts History: Theology in a Time of Upheaval*, trans. Brian Doyle (New York: Continuum, 2007), 38-43. For Boeve, to stress discontinuity with the modern culture is not a solution, just as the correlationists' easy continuity with it is not plausible. That is why he proposes that a process of recontextualisation be adopted in which interruption becomes the "exponent of the contemporary critical consciousness." With it, the current postmodern context could be critically engaged, yet avoiding the two extremes of bridge and rupture that the two other solutions embody. Cf. Terrence Meriggan, "What's in a Word? Revelation and Tradition in Vatican II and in Contemporary Theology," in *Vatican II and Its Legacy*, BETL, no. 166, ed. Mathijs Lamberigts and Leo Kenis (Leuven: Leuven University Press, 2002), 59-61.

[86] Pottmeyer, "A New Phase," 42-43.

achievement in itself. It is left for the church, he states, and its latter theologians to labour harder in bringing about greater precisions and synthesis.[87]

The truth remains that the council made a significant contribution towards stimulating a more ardent awareness in the church of cultural diversity and church's historicity. A remarkable shift from the age-long classicist mentality of traditional theology towards a more pluralist and anthropological understanding of culture, and stimulation of the much-needed dialogue between the church and culture, which bore its fruits in the post-conciliar magisterial thought and theological reflections are gains that may not be reasonably waved aside.[88] It is the gains of such documents as *Gaudium et Spes* that influenced the Synod of Bishops on Evangelisation in 1974; Paul VI's insistence in *Evangelii Nuntiandi* that culture should become the focal point for any evangelisation; and the Synod on Catechesis (1977). The extraordinary interest on culture by John Paul II can also be understood in this light.[89] We shall see in the third chapter of the work how the new understanding of culture has led, since after the council, to greater emphasis on evangelisation of cultures and the development of inculturation theology. In the mean time, it is important to examine how such landmark achievement of the council imparted generally on the understanding of theology's relationship with culture.

---

[87]   Ibid., 38. See also Walter Kasper, "The Theological Anthropology of *Gaudium et Spes*," *Communio* 23 (1996): 138. Kasper recognises some imprecision in *Gaudium et Spes* regarding the reference to man as God's image as used in Gn 1: 26 and the reference too to Christ as the image of God (Col 1:15). But he argues that no one should expect a council to have undertaken such a systematic definition of how these terms are related to each other. This, he maintains, is a task left for subsequent theological developments.

[88]   See Albert Outler, "After-Thought of a Protestant Observer of Vatican II," in *The Church and Culture since Vatican II: The Experience of North and Latin America*, ed. Joseph Gremillion (Notre Dame, IN: University of Notre Dame Press, 1985), 153; O'Malley, *Tradition and Transition*, 30.

[89]   We recall John Paul II's great encyclicals in this direction: *Catechesi Tradendae* (1979), *Slavorum Apostoli* (1985), *Redemptoris Missio* (1991), *Ecclesia in Africa* (1995), among others. John Paul II has also addressed this issue in a great number of his speeches to different groups of people and in his travels round the globe. Very significant too is his setting up of the 'Pontifical Council for Culture' in 1982.

IMPLICATIONS FOR THEOLOGY OF THE RECONCEPTUALISATION OF CULTURE

The influence of the development in the concept of culture is very glaring and the transformation brought by it is so broad that it would be surprising were theology not affected by it.[90] Today, more than ever, theologians have made a significant shift from the view of human knowledge and experience whereby they seem to be understood as ahistorical, universally valid and permanent phenomena. On account of better appreciation of the historical nature of human existence in the world, greater attention is paid to the study of how context influences acquisition and development of knowledge, theological or otherwise.[91]

One significant effect that this has had in theology is an increasing appreciation of religion as an aspect of culture, thus, calling into question the claim to the possession of abstract universal essences by religious formulations and doctrines. As a religion, Christianity cannot exist independently of culture. Though it embodies transcendent truth, in a very significant sense, it is conditioned and heavily influenced by culture in its beliefs, practices, symbolic forms and texts.[92] That is why mere study, in theology, of ideas and general principles dislocated from, or without reference to, their different contexts and situations of origin and development is no longer fashionable. Instead, historical context of ideas, practices and formation of texts are interestingly enough studied today in order to ascertain the extent they are influenced by forces at play within their respective contexts.[93] This calls for the church's re-appraisal of its role and mission as the universal sacrament of salvation. It is in this light that one can understand Paul VI speaking in 1971 of the difficulty the church

---

[90] See Linell Cady, "Loosening the Category that Binds: Modern 'Religion' and the Promise of Cultural Studies," in *Converging on Culture: Theologians in Dialogue with Cultural Analysis and Criticism*, ed. Delwin Brown, Sheila Davaney and Kathryn Tanner (Oxford, NY: Oxford University Press, 2001), 18.

[91] Sheila Davaney, "Theology and the Turn to Cultural Analysis," in *Converging on Culture: Theologians in Dialogue with Cultural Analysis*, ed. Delwin Brown, Greeve Davaney and Kathryn Tanner (Oxford, NY: Oxford University Press, 2001), 5. See also Thomas Groome, "Inculturation: How to Proceed in a Pastoral Context," *Concilium*, no. 2 (1994): 122-123.

[92] See Shorter, *Towards a Theology of Inculturation*, 27.

[93] Cady, "Loosening the Category that Binds," 20.

encounters in its social teachings, especially in terms of their universal validity, not only for the entire church, but also for the humankind as a whole.[94]

It has become evident today, more than ever, that theology is a cultural practice, in so far as it is part of the activities of man or woman as a member of a given society, sharing a common way of life and influenced by contacts and mutual exchange of ideas among people. In Tanner's estimation, this is the most fundamental contribution that the anthropological understanding of culture has made to theology.[95] Theologians now appreciate more the fact that to theologise is to do so from somewhere, from a particular cultural specificity, which imprints its unmistakable character and limitations on the activity. As such, the assumptions, for instance, of a single neoscholasticism formerly understood to be a universally applicable theological method no longer appears plausible.[96] Edward Schillebeeckx puts it very succinctly that every theology, western or otherwise, is nothing other than a theology that is local. Each carries with it every form of social prejudice and cultural bias as any other.[97] According to Schreiter, to act as if one is not aware of the influence of "context, interests, relationships of power, special concerns" in every act of theologising "is to be blind."[98] It is not surprising today that theologians have begun to employ cultural analysis and criticism. This, Cady observes, is a welcome development because it "holds out promise of theology's escape from its intellectual and institutional confinement that has contributed to its increasing marginalization and irrelevance."[99]

Besides, the local churches are now seen as very important factors to reckon with in the church's understanding of itself and for an effective fulfilment of its divine mission. There is greater awareness of the need to embrace cultural diversity as a welcome

---

[94]   Paul VI, "*Octogesima Adveniens*," no. 3, 4.

[95]   See Kathryn Tanner, *Theories of Culture: A New Agenda for Theology* (Minneapolis, MN: Ausburg Fortress, 1997), 63, 67.

[96]   Rahner, *Theological Investigations*, 96. See also Tissa Balasuriya, "Towards the Liberation of Theology in Asia," in *Asia's Struggle for Full Humanity*, ed. Virginia Fabella (Maryknoll, NY: Orbis, 1980), 21.

[97]   See Robert Schreiter, *Constructing Local Theologies*, ix.

[98]   Ibid., 3.

[99]   Cady, "Loosening the Category that Binds," 33.

richness to the church, or as Lonergan would say, as testimonies to its esteemed vitality.[100] Nowadays, theologians devote a considerable amount of time studying particular communities in their concrete life situations and experiences, with the belief that the common person has significant contributions to make in the theological practice. In this way, the populace are believed to be involved in active determination of their own destiny and are not just passive receptacles of highly intellectualistic theological definitions of the elite and highly placed authorities.[101] In a sense, then, Christian theology becomes primarily concerned, though not exclusively, with practical Christian ways of living, to the extent that there is theological aspect to every form of Christian activity.[102]

The fact that cultures are understood to be characteristically diverse challenges the theologian to search for ways of recasting the symbols employed in communicating the message of Christianity in such a way that this diversity is taken seriously yet in harmony with the demands of the faith. This is important because symbols or images used in a particular situation may not fit into another, and may even communicate messages contrary to the demands of the faith. Those used, for instance, in a predominantly Christian society may be inappropriate in a non-Christian or post-Christian environment.[103] The seriousness with which theologians take this is reflected in many theological works of today. In various ways one sees languages that stress otherness, difference and specificity.[104] They no longer merely highlight those "commonalities that once were thought to hold a society or a tradition or even an intellectual discipline together, but to the fragmentation, inherent plurality, and unrelenting dynamics of dominion and resistance that constitute all cultural processes."[105]

---

[100] Bernard Lonergan, *Method in Theology* (New York: Seabury, 1979), 300.

[101] See Davaney, "Theology and the Turn to Cultural Analysis," 6. See also Balasuriya, *Towards the Liberation*," 20.

[102] Tanner, *Theories of Culture*, 70.

[103] Aidan Nichols, *Christendom Awake: On Reenergizing the Church in Culture* (Edinburgh: T. & T. Clark, 1999), 10-11.

[104] See Stephen Bevans, *Models of Contextual Theology*, Revised and Expanded Edition (Maryknoll, NY: Orbis, 2002); Boeve, *Interrupting Tradition*; Boeve, *God Interrupts History*.

[105] Davaney, "Theology and the Turn to Cultural Analysis," 6.

The dynamic nature of cultures should also be a matter of concern for the theologian. As we have seen in the previous chapter, culture is in a continuous change and mutation within itself as the society progresses, encounters new problems and challenges. It is never fossilised or crystallised. As it undergoes these changes, the meanings conveyed by cultural elements also change. This might render the previous image used within the cultural ambient to express the Christian faith no longer relevant, unless it is reaffirmed in the new cultural situation necessitated by the change. For the western cultures, this metamorphosis is very fast. In others, like those of Africa and Asia, it could really be slow. Besides, some cultural systems do not easily admit changes due to the strength of their cohesiveness. An instance of this, which has been extensively studied by scholars, is the pastoral Maasai of the East African Rift Valley in Kenya.[106] The swiftness or otherwise of the change has a corresponding demand on, and challenge for, the theologians. He or she sees to it that the faith remains alive and relevant to a given people at any particular point in time.[107]

It is crucial to realise that culture exerts much influence on religion just as religion does on culture. The theologian or missionary should know that he or she is an agent of change and that any significant change he or she introduces in the religion of a people may also exert considerable influence on the people's culture as a whole. Luzbetak developed this thought very well and succinctly puts it this way: "It is, therefore, impossible to bring about changes in religion

---

[106] See Shorter, *Towards a Theology of Inculturation*, 25. For studies on the conservativeness of the Maasai people and their resistance to change, see Willis Hotchkiss, *Then and Now in Kenya Colony* (New York: 1937); Elspeth Huxley, *The Sorcerer's Apprentice* (London: Chatto & Windus, 1949); Valeer Neckebrouck, *Resistant Peoples: The Case of the Pastoral Maasai of East Africa*, Inculturation: Working Papers on Living Faith and Cultures, ed. Ary Crollius (Rome: Pontifical Gregorian University Press, 1993). Such people may fear to admit any changes to avoid the disturbance of the equilibrium enjoyed in their cherished pattern. In fact, at certain instances of the change process, as Crollius notes, conflicts are sure to ensue, which, however, could be a price to be paid for eventual enrichment. See Ary Crollius, "The Meaning of Culture in Theological Anthropology," in *Inculturation: Its Meaning and Urgency*, ed. John Walligo *et al.* (Nairobi: St. Paul, 1986), 61.

[107] Nichols, *Christendom Awake*, 11.

and morality without, in some way, affecting the entire organism, the entire culture."[108] This important realisation is also corroborated by Standaert, who argues that such mutual influence is undeniable, so long as we admit that religion itself is a phenomenon that is basically human. According to him, this can be better understood by considering the influence exerted by Christianity on the European culture, especially during the medieval times, or that on the culture of the Middle East by Islam.[109]

Technological advancement has indeed made it easier for people from different cultural backgrounds to meet and exchange their cultural traits often on unexpected scales. One easily realises that one's culture is just one possible way of life among many, which are in constant contact and inter-communication. It is in the process of this acculturation that one appreciates the beauty of the other. Edward Said makes it clear that "all cultures are involved in one another; none is single, all are hybrid, heterogeneous, extraordinarily differentiated, and unmonolithic."[110] Thus, the theologian, in the service of evangelisation, should, as a matter of necessity, recognise the implications of the constant interaction among different cultures. He or she should be able to manage the tension often created by the acculturation process in such a way that the otherness of each people's culture with respect to being, values, yearnings, orientations and interests is respected. As the Christian faith interacts with cultures, it should also be borne in

---

[108] Louis Luzbetak, *The Church and Culture: An Applied Anthropology for the Religious Worker* (Techny, IL: Divine Word, 1970), 343. Their reciprocal influence on each other, argues Mariasusai Dhavamony, "is too evident to be demonstrated." See Mariasusai Dhavamony, *Christian Theology of Inculturation* (Roma: Editrice Pontificia Universita Gregoriana, 1997), 44.

[109] See Nicholas Standaert. *Inculturation: The Gospel and Cultures*, trans. Anton Bruggeman and Robert Murray (Philippines: St. Paul, 1990), 53. See also Joseph Omeregbe, *A Philosophical Look at Religions* (Lagos: Joja, 1996), 300. Omeregbe observes that religions are largely defined by the cultures from which they grow. Such could be said of Christianity and the Jewish-Greco-Roman culture; the Arabic culture and Islam; Indian culture and Buddhism; Hinduism and Jansenism. See also Nicholas Lobkowicz, "Christianity and Culture," *The Review of Politics* 53, no. 2 (1991): 373-389; Ernst Troeltsch, "The Place of Christianity among the World Religions," in *Attitudes toward Other Religions*, ed. Owen Thomas (New York: Harper & Row, 1969), 73-91.

[110] Edward Said, *Culture and Imperialism* (London: Chatto and Windus, 1993), xxix.

mind that the latter can only welcome changes from the Christian faith when it is clear to them that their security is not endangered by the new alternative.[111] These, among many others, are some of the issues that the anthropological understanding of culture brings to the fore. Every theologian devoted to the cause of deepening of the faith should take these seriously.

CONCLUSION

We discussed in the chapter how Vatican II tried to update the official church's understanding of culture in line with the developments in the secular sciences. Its understanding of culture marks a shift in the magisterial teaching from classicist view to anthropological, empirical one. This later conception acknowledges the plurality of cultures. The challenges that this new understanding poses to the theologians of today, as have been examined, are enormous. Theologians have come to take the historicity of human experience seriously. The role played by culture in making the faith more intelligible to the people has also been given much attention. The church and its theologians have come to realise the need to re-examine some theological axioms hitherto assumed to enjoy universal applicability. John Paul II, in his address to the Pontifical Council for Culture in 1983, voices out a two-fold dimension by which the church responds to this new awareness: "that of the *evangelization of cultures* and that of the *defence of man and of his cultural development*."[112] In the next chapter, I will explore more how the demands of this dimensions can better be met by the church and its theologians.

---

[111] Luzbetak, *The Church and Culture: An Applied Anthropology*, 64-65.
[112] John Paul II, *Discourse to the Plenary Assembly of the Pontifical Council for Culture*, 18 January 1983, no. 4; available from http://www.vatican.va/ holy_father/john_paul_ii/speeches/1996/documents/hf_jp-ii_spe_18011983_ address-to-pc-culture_en.html; accessed 13 April 2009. The emphasis is mine.

3

CHRISTIAN FAITH AND CULTURES: INCULTURATION MODEL

INTRODUCTION

In the preceding chapter, it was made clear how the development in the understanding of culture helped Vatican II in its concern for, and affirmation of, the promotion of cultural pluralism within the framework of the nature of the church and realisation of its universal mission. One of its merits, as noted, is that it enabled the council to discuss the need for a better relationship between Christian faith and culture. Though the council talks about this relationship and the importance of utilising the resources of culture in the presentation of the good news for men and women of today, it does not articulate in greater detail how this relationship is to be practically realised. This was a task to be undertaken within the post-conciliar scholarship. The present chapter goes beyond mere acknowledgement of the need for better relationship between the faith and culture or the challenges it poses, and discusses the basic pattern to be followed as they relate with each other. This will be embarked on in the light of the dire need today to make Christianity a living reality for different people and cultures;

a need born out of the church's realisation that it is only when it really becomes local that its mission can be made visible and actualised.[1]

I argue in the chapter that inculturation offers the best model for the realisation of the goal of making the faith 'incarnate' in each locality. It is only through inculturation that the church can properly affirm and adequately address the challenges posed by the plurality of cultures in its theology and evangelising mission. Through it the different cultures are taken seriously as dialogue partners with Christian faith and tradition; a dialogue that is doubtless "of vital importance for the future of the Church and of the world."[2] Just as the different communities, cultures and traditions of the New Testament writers made them render different accounts of the common narrative of Jesus Christ, so also can different local churches in their cultural embeddedness bear authentic witness to Christ even amidst the differences necessitated by their circumstances. The importance and the urgency of the situation has been articulated by David Tracy when he says: "Catholic Christianity can no longer afford to be Eurocentric anymore than early Christianity could afford to be purely Judaic if it would reach the Gentiles in ways that they could understand and appropriate the common faith in their own cultural forms."[3]

---

[1]   While not intending to go into the ecclesiological discussions as contained in the council's documents, it might be pertinent to remark that the council's understanding of the church helped a lot in the inculturation endeavour. Its recognition of the particular churches as the primary reality of the church is very encouraging in this regard, for "it is in and from these particular churches there exists the one unique catholic church." See Vatican Council II, "Dogmatic Constitution on the Church, *Lumen Gentium,* 21 November 1964," in *Decrees of the Ecumenical Councils: Trent to Vatican II*, ed. Norman Tanner (London: Sheed & Ward, 1990), no. 23. Hereafter, *LG.*

[2]   John Paul II, "Address to the First Meeting of the Pontifical Council for Culture, 18 June 1983," in *The Church and Cultures since Vatican II: The Experience of North and Latin America*, ed. Joseph Gremillion (Notre Dame, IN: University of Notre Dame Press, 1985), no. 4.

[3]   David Tracy, "World Church or World Catechism: The Problem of Eurocentrism," *Concilium* 204, no. 4 (1989): 29. He debunks those assertions which identify Europe with Christianity. Tracy argues that this cannot stand, especially in the present day circumstances, when the fact of Christianity being a world-church stares everyone in the face. Owing to this, he clearly states, "any refusal to acknowledge that reality theologically... should be resisted theologically." Ibid., 31. Equally important in this regard is the concern of

I shall first investigate the meaning of inculturation and its various implications. Secondly, in order to achieve more terminological clarity, which "is an essential tool in research,"[4] inculturation shall be differentiated from other terms sometimes confused with it, though related to it in one way or another. Thirdly, I will argue why and how inculturation, despite its emphasis on giving proper attention to local cultures and local churches, would neither pose a divisive force in the church, nor threaten its catholicity. This leads to the examination of Christological foundation for inculturation. The last section of the chapter deals with some hurdles in the way of authentic inculturation and how they can be more effectively overcome.

UNDERSTANDING INCULTURATION

Inculturation could be said to be a relatively recent term in theology, and was first employed by theologians about the middle of the last century.[5] Though fairly new, it has been adjudged by many theologians as a term that is capable of articulating most adequately

---

Hermann Häring about the need to respect the multicultural situation of the world of today in matters relating to the formulation of the Christian doctrine. He clearly understands any attempt to apply a single theological system to all as a mono-cultural imposition which, according to him, is nonsensical. Hermann Häring, "Experiences with the 'Short-Formula' of the Faith," *Concilium* 204, no. 4 (1989): 72.

[4] Melville Herskovits, *Man and His Works: The Science of Cultural Anthropology* (New York: Knopf, 1970), 525.

[5] The first appearance of this word in theological discourse, according to Efoé-Julian Pénoukou, could be traced to the 19th Week of Missiology in Louvain in 1959. Then, it was used to describe the feature of the universal church by which it was open to the diversity of human cultures. Efoé-Julien Pénoukou, "Inculturation," *Encyclopedia of Christian Theology* 2 (2005): 767. The popularity of the word owes much to the Jesuits. Its appearance has been described by Richard Cote as sudden and "unannounced yet charged with potent meaning, and... has kept theologians busy ever since." Richard Cote, *Re-Visioning Mission: The Catholic Church and Culture in Postmodern America* (New York: Paulist, 1996), 37. It was only in 1979 that it found its way, for the first time, into the papal vocabulary. In that context, Pope John Paul II employed it as a synonym for acculturation. See John Paul II, "Apostolic Exhortation on Catechesis, *Catechesi Tradendae*, 16 October 1979," *AAS* 71 (1979): no. 53. Hereafter, *CT*.

the needed respect and promotion of healthy cultural pluralism in the process of expression of Christian faith.[6] A Filipino theologian, Virginia Fabella, describes it as a theological process that "not only allows for pluralism but actually encourages it."[7] It re-enforces the conviction that the peculiarity of the historical and cultural experiences of different people calls for a distinctive approach to evangelisation, in order to address their unique and legitimate hopes and aspirations.[8] By so doing, it not only respects the variety that exists in Christian tradition but also the integrity of other religious traditions. It allows for a more meaningful dialogue with those traditions that could be considered secular or non-Christian.[9] With inculturation, it is easier for Christian faith to dialogue with cultures without denigrating them, or treating them with any form of impertinence.

With regard to the formulation of Christian doctrine, inculturation emphasises the particular and the concrete situations in which people live and where the witness to the faith is borne, and does not merely presume a universally permanent doctrine valid at all times and in all circumstances, without the need for reformulation of any sort.[10] Owing to the plurality of cultures, it allows for corresponding plurality of responses and approaches to Christian doctrine, and this, according to Paul Poupard, will definitely be "translated into plurality of theologies."[11] It is able to do this because it does not

---

[6] Hervé Carrier describes the attitude of pluralism thus: "that we accept the desirability of a human order respecting the complexity of ideologies, the diversity of life projects. We acknowledge the fact that there are realities simply not reducible to unity by force... a new type of social unity [which] respects cultural disparities." Hervé Carrier, "The Church Meeting Cultures: Convergences and Perspectives," in *The Church and Culture since Vatican II: The Experience in North and Latin America*, ed. Joseph Gremillion (Notre Dame, IN: University of Notre Dame Press, 1985), 146-147. See also Donald Gelpi, *Inculturating North American Theology: An Experiment in Foundational Method* (Atlanta, GA: Scholars, 1988), 1.

[7] Virginia Fabella, "Inculturation," *in Dictionary of Third World Theologies*, ed. Virginia Fabella and Rasiah Sugirtharajah (Maryknoll: Orbis, 2000), 105.

[8] See Gelpi, *Inculturating North American Theology*, 1.

[9] Ibid., 1-2.

[10] Cf. John Thiel, "Pluralism in Theological Truth," *Concilium*, no. 6 (1994): 59-63.

[11] Paul Poupard, *Church and Culture: Challenge and Confrontation, Inculturation and Evangelization*, trans. John Miller (St. Louis, MO: Centra Bureau, CCVA, 1994), 127.

adhere to the aristocratic notion of culture, which is more deductive, but relies on the more descriptive understanding of culture, which has to do with the concrete lives of people in their respective societal settings.[12] With inculturation, the local community plays an essential role and is understood as the maker of its own theology, though in dialogue with the universal church.[13] This means that any genuine inculturation begins from below, not from above, thus, ensuring the much valued ingenuity and originality needed in the process. This entails (using insights from Vatican II) sincere respect and utilisation of people's philosophy and wisdom, their cultural endowments and general worldview.[14] John Walligo sees in this effort a serious concern to take the thought-pattern or conceptual apparatus of a given people into serious consideration in the presentation of the message. He maintains that this effort stems from the fact that the more these resources are utilised, the more the people come to better understanding of Christ and the gospel, and all the more its dynamism and challenges to their situations are manifested.[15] In African society, for instance, it would mean utilising African concepts, wisdom, philosophy and worldview, which serve as prism through which the people perceive and express who God is, the nature of the human person, the meaning of the world around them and their relationship with it. This presupposes a thorough knowledge of the culture of the people; otherwise, no proper dialogue with it will be possible.[16] It

---

[12] Peter Schineller, *A Handbook on Inculturation* (Mahwah, NJ: Paulist, 1990), 23.

[13] Peter Schineller, "Inculturation as the Pilgrimage to Catholicity," *Concilium* 204, no. 4 (1989): 99. Cf. Vatican Council II, "Decree on the Missionary Activity of the Church, *Ad Gentes*, 18 November 1965," in *Decrees of the Ecumenical Councils: Trent to Vatican II*, ed. Norman Tanner, vol. 2 (London: Sheed & Ward, 1990), no. 21. Hereafter, *AG*.

[14] *AG* 22.

[15] John Walligo, "Making a Church That Is Truly African," in *Inculturation: Its Meaning and Urgency*, ed. John Walligo et al. (Nairobi: St. Paul, 1986), 12. Luke Mbefo believes that, if the conceptual apparatus of a people is adequately utilised in the effort, then, a cultural integration is achieved and this will make "Christianity not alien and alienating from the culture that receives it." Luke Mbefo, *The True African: Impulses for Self Affirmation* (Onitsha: Spiritan, 2001), 43. Cf. Jürgen Werbick, "Can the Universal Catechism Help Overcome the Crisis in Handing on the Faith?," *Concilium* 204, no. 4 (1989): 56-57.

[16] Gerald Arbuckle has made it clear that once the evangeliser or a theologian lacks an adequate knowledge of the culture of the people among whom he or

also calls for greater creativity on the part of theologians. Only thus can the message be properly and meaningfully expressed. The doctrine formulated therefrom, thus, bears the imprint of the culture concerned. Lack of such imprint, Lonergan maintains, "would point to a merely perfunctory assimilation."[17] That is why, in one of his addresses to the Pontifical Council for Culture, John Paul II tasks them to find ways of making the message of the church accessible and understandable to the contemporary frames of mind and sensibility.[18] Without the concreteness and the particularity of people's situations being seriously addressed this way, the process of evangelisation runs the risk of losing, as Paul VI puts it, "much of its force and effectiveness."[19]

Accordingly, the process of inculturation surely corresponds to the proper theological understanding of the nature of Christian experience of salvation, which, as David Tracy has argued, is always contextual. For him, the experience of salvation, just like every other human experience, necessarily goes with some understanding and interpretation, both of which cannot be effectively realised outside one's historical and cultural embeddedness.[20] In other words, every experience of salvation involves the individual taken in his or her humanity not merely as an architect of culture but also as one under its influence. Christian experience of salvation, Tracy argues, involves experience of faith in God revealed in the person of Jesus Christ. This faith is realised, not in a notional assent to some propositions, but in a radical trust in God who is made known in the person of Jesus Christ. This radical trust, this faith, he maintains, "is praxis and praxis

---

she is working, he cannot function effectively. It is very fundamental to the dialogue with the culture. To neglect this, he argues, is both "[t]heologically and humanly... unjust." See Gerald Arbuckle, *Culture, Inculturation, Theologians: A Postmodern Critique* (Collegeville, MN: Liturgical, 2010), xxiii.

[17] Bernard Lonergan, *Method in Theology* (New York: Seabury, 1979), 301.

[18] John Paul II, "Address to the First Meeting," no. 3.

[19] Paul VI, "Apostolic Exhortation on Evangelization, *Evangelii Nuntiandi*, 8 December 1975," *AAS* 68 (1976): no. 63. Hereafter, *EN*.

[20] David Tracy, "World Church or World Catechism: The Problem of Eurocentrism," *Concilium* 204, no. 4 (1989): 31-32. For Tracy, in any particular cultural context, salvation involves an experience of relief from some sort of bondage, as well as an experience of a demand to live for a new kind of life in Jesus Christ.

is always embedded in a particular culture."[21] Inculturation works on this principle and tries to respond to the felt need to make this understanding effective in the church's life and outlook by insisting on the formulation of Christian faith taking the need of each cultural situation into serious consideration.

I assert, therefore, that inculturation refers to a renewed approach in the mission of the church to evangelise cultures. Its end coincides with the overall purpose of evangelisation, which, according to Paul VI, consists in "transforming humanity from within and making it new."[22] That is why it is described as representing "an ideal of sound evangelization."[23] It expresses an increased awareness in the church of the need to evangelise cultures from within, so that the locus of the praxis of the faith is properly permeated and addressed.[24] It is a model that works with, and stresses much, the use of 'incarnation' and 'redemption' approaches in the process of evangelisation.[25] This ensures an authentic and adequate expression of the faith "within the shifting sands of the cultural variables,"[26] as Luke Mbefo would have it, yet effecting the needed fundamental challenge to the cultural situation. According to Oliver Onwubiko, it represents "a new vision of an old problem in the church or a new approach to a solution of an old problem, or still a new interpretation of an old solution of the church

---

[21]   Ibid., 33.

[22]   Paul VI, *EN* 18. Addressing the Pontifical Council for Culture, John Paul II also recognises, as a presupposition for evangelisation, that the gospel penetrates the specific cultural identity of each people opening it up for mutual exchange with other cultures and the "universal values," which, according to him, are "the values of Catholicity." John Paul II, "Address to the First Meeting," no.5.

[23]   Gelpi, *Inculturating North American Theology*, 1.

[24]   See Häring, "Experiences with the 'Short-Formula' of the Faith," 72. Michael Gallagher points out that it is this fact of evangelising from within the culture itself that is the most outstanding feature that distinguishes inculturation from other approaches. Michael Gallagher, "Inculturation: Some Theological Perspectives," *International Review of Mission* 85, no. 337 (1996): 175.

[25]   Cf. Eugene Hillman, "Inculturation," in *The New Dictionary of Theology*, ed. Joseph Komonchak, Mary Collins and Dermot Lane (Dublin: Gill & Macmillan, 1987), 513. See also Francis Sullivan, *The Church We Believe in: One, Holy, Catholic and Apostolic* (New York: Paulist, 1988), 93.

[26]   Mbefo, *The True African*, 43.

and culture encounter."[27] Whatever be the case, the issue remains that it has made the church ever more responsive to its responsibility to make serious effort in creatively confronting from within each people's culture the fissure existing between the culture and the gospel, which Paul VI recognises as "the drama of our time."[28] In effect, with inculturation, Christian faith gets proper integration into the culture of a particular people. By this integration, the faith becomes, more or less, received by them, because it has been made their way of life—their culture.

TOWARDS A DEFINITION

The encounter between faith and culture that happens in the process of inculturation is very dynamic and too deep to be visualised as mere mixture, intermingling, much less adaptation or assimilation. Hence, Pedro Arrupe defines inculturation thus:

[T]he incarnation of Christian life and of the Christian message in a particular cultural context, in such a way that this experience not only finds expression through elements proper to the culture in question (this alone would be no more than a superficial adaptation), but becomes a principle that animates, directs and unifies the culture, transforming and remaking it so as to bring about 'a new creation.'[29]

Experts often refer to and laud the above definition in the context of discussions on inculturation.[30] The definition, no doubt, has some

---

[27]   Oliver Onwubiko, *Theory and Practice of Inculturation: African Perspective* (Enugu: SNAAP, 1992), 1.

[28]   Paul VI, *EN* 20. See also Vatican Council II, "Pastoral Constitution on the Church in the World of Today, *Gaudium et Spes*," 7 December 1965. In *Decrees of the Ecumenical Councils: Trent to Vatican II*, ed. Norman Tanner, vol. 2 (London: Sheed & Ward, 1990), no. 43. Hereafter, *GS*.

[29]   Pedro Arrupe, "On Inculturation," *Acta Romana Societastis Iesu* 17, no. 1 (1979): 257.

[30]   See, for example, Aylward Shorter, *Towards a Theology of Inculturation* (MaryKnoll, NY: Orbis, 19940, 11; Inoibong Udoidem, *Pope John Paul II on Inculturation* (Lanham, MD: University Press of America, 1996), 2. The definition offered by Ary Crollius is almost the same as that of Arrupe. He only

merits. First, it sees inculturation as having to do with some form of interaction between the Christian message, faith experience, and respective cultural contexts. Second, it is able to differentiate inculturation from mere adaptation. Third, it recognises the fact that when inculturation is properly carried out, the culture encountered by Christian faith is transformed. Having said that, I must, however, note that there seems to be a cryptic suggestion in the definition that it is only the culture that is transformed in the process, and not Christian faith too. When Christian faith is integrated into a culture simply to animate, orient, unify and transform the culture without the faith having to involve a change in itself, then it might seem that one understands Christian faith as a pure entity that remains changeless as it encounters cultures in the process of inculturation. It is precisely for this reason that Thomas Grenham argues that the above definition by Arrupe does not adequately reflect the recognition that "Christianity is a religious cultural system."[31] If it does, then, it should have shown that it is also subject to change. Christianity only exists in terms of culture. Thus, inculturation always involves contact between two or more cultures.[32] In fact, for Grenham, Arrupe's definition may have

---

introduces some slight modifications: *"the inculturation of the Church is the integration of the Christian experience of a local Church into the culture of its people, in such a way that this experience not only expresses itself in elements of this culture, but becomes a force that animates, orients and innovates this culture so as to create a new unity and communion, not only within the culture in question but also as an enrichment of the Church universal."* Ary Crollius, "Inculturation: Newness and Ongoing Process," in *Inculturation: Its Meaning and Urgency*, ed. John Mary Walligo *et al.* (Nairobi: St. Paul, 1986), 43. Emphasis in the original.

[31] Thomas Grenham, "Interculturation: Exploring Changing Religious, Cultural, and Faith Identities in an African Context," *Pacifica* 14, no. 2 (2001): 192. Indeed, Christianity cannot exist outside of culture. Poupard describes it as a "cultural phenomenon." See Poupard, *Church and Culture*, 134.

[32] See Michael Amaladoss, *Making All Things New: Dialogue, Pluralism and Evangelization in Asia* (Maryknoll, NY: Orbis, 1990), 121-122. That is why Joseph Blomjous prefers to use the term, "interculturation" instead of "inculturation." For him, the former brings out more the mutuality and reciprocity of cultural exchange involved in the relationship between Christian faith and human cultures. Joseph Blomjous, "Development in Mission Thinking and Practice 1950-1980: Inculturation and Interculturation," *AFER* 22, no. 6 (1980): 393. Grenham also opts for "interculturation." He justifies his choice thus: "It enables us to see that Christian evangelisation is not one-sided but

been influenced by his lack of consideration of the fact that in the process of inculturation, Christian faith also encounters a diversity of cultures with different religious worldviews apart from the Christian. According to him, if he was aware of this, he should have known that, during the process, "'a new transformation' would take place simultaneously for Christianity and a diverse religious worldview."[33] Added to this is the fact that Arrupe seems to view culture as a passive receiver of the transforming actions of Christian faith in the process of inculturation, and as a system without life, direction, or unity before the encounter, such that the faith now animates, directs, and unifies it. But this is far from what we have learned so far concerning the nature and characteristics of culture.

In view of the above observations and the discussions so far, I propose that inculturation be rather defined as *an encounter between Christian faith and a particular culture by which the faith is integrated or "incarnated" into the culture in accordance with the demands of effective evangelisation and dialogue, involving a mutual exchange and change between the two without destruction of their respective identities*. But there is no presumption that this integration is seamless. It involves conflicts, negotiations, tensions and strains between and within the Christian faith and the culture in question. In addition, it principally occurs at the deeper cognitive level of culture beyond the phenomenological, which is "the level of underlying meaning and values,"[34] where religious beliefs operate in any culture. Thus, John Paul II, while discussing inculturation, talks of the gospel penetrating

---

is a mutual partnership of witness and dialogue or conversation regarding the gospel. This means that the process of evangelising must always be cognizant of the fundamental 'good news' already contained within specific cultures." Grenham, "Interculturation," 193. Though we understand the point these authors are making, may we remark that one needs not call the process "interculturation" in order to be aware of these realities. They are already contained in the concept of inculturation. In fact, instead of opting for "interculturation," as Blomjous and Grenham suggest, Michael Amaladoss and Shorter rather insist that 'interculturation' is a normal process that characterises every genuine 'inculturation.' See Michael Amaladoss, *Beyond Inculturation: Can Many Be One* (Delhi: Society for Promotion of Christian Knowledge, 1998), 20-23; Shorter, *Towards a Theology of Inculturation*, 13-16.

[33]   Grenham, "Interculturation," 193.

[34]   Shorter, *Towards a Theology of Inculturation*, 35. See also John Paul II, "Address to the First Meeting," no. 4.

"the soul of living cultures."[35] The pattern that this integration process takes needs to be better clarified. This will also shed more light on the definition I offered above.

Pattern of the Encounter between Christian Faith and Culture

To achieve the kind of integration needed in an effective inculturation, there should be a sincerely mutual dialogue between Christian faith and culture resulting in what Vatican II describes as "marvelous exchange."[36] None should stand above and speak to the other. It is not merely "speaking to," but "speaking with," for real dialogue is not vertical but horizontal. Both must establish deep-rooted mutual interaction. Without this, no meaningful progress can be made.[37] This accounts for John Paul II's understanding of inculturation as "the incarnation of the Gospel in native cultures—and also the introduction of these cultures into the life of the Church."[38] Paul Poupard describes this as a symbiosis.[39] Both partners need each other for a truthful and fruitful encounter. Owing to this, Richard Cote sees it as a process whereby "the core mobilizing symbols of a culture"[40] and the gospel engage each other in a mutual encounter and authentic dialogue in which none is considered to be higher than the other. He believes inculturation could be anything but genuine unless this is taken very seriously.[41]

This encounter should not be visualised as bringing God into a culture where he is absent or unknown. Rather, it involves an encounter between the faith and a particular culture where, in one

---

[35]   Ibid.

[36]   *AG* 22.

[37]   See Robert Schreiter, "Inculturation or Identification with Culture," *Concilium*, no. 2 (1994): 22.

[38]   John Paul II, Encyclical Letter, "The Apostles of the Slavs, *Slavorum Apostoli*," 2 June 1985, *AAS* 77 (1985): no. 21. Hereafter, *SA*.

[39]   Poupard, *Church and Culture*, 25.

[40]   Cote, *Re-Visioning Mission*, 41

[41]   Ibid.

way or the other, God has been present.[42] The current theological understanding of divine revelation and grace is that God is present and has been revealing himself to all men and women throughout history in diverse hidden ways, which reached its fulfilment in the person of Jesus Christ.[43] That is why Vatican II, taking up the *logos spermatikos*[44] of the Fathers of the church, speaks of the seed of the word already present in all cultures, even before the gospel is proclaimed.[45] This entails that one respects and listens to this presence and not ignore it. Hence, Laurenti Magesa reminds us that in inculturation, "the Word of God in the gospel encounters the Word of God in a culture. The revelation of God in the Christian scriptures meets the God who is already present in the values of a culture and in the history of a people."[46] Accordingly, he sees inculturation as an effort to reach out

---

[42]   Groome argues that, if one were to maintain that God is not already present in the culture of any people, it implies God is selective in his treatment of people, which is contrary to the Christian convictions: Thomas Groome, "Inculturation: How to Proceed in a Pastoral Context," *Concilium*, no. 2 (1994): 123. See also *LG*, 16.

[43]   See Gerald O'Collins, *Theology and Revelation* (Cork: Mercier, 1968), 37.

[44]   This term has its origin in the Greek philosophy. Its use by Philo of Alexandria, in his attempt to harmonise Greek philosophy and the theology of the scriptures, influenced its introduction into Christian theology. *Logos* has been used to denote power, reason, word, discourse, etc. Among the Fathers, Justin Martyr is reputed as being the first to employ the term very outstandingly in his theology. The Fathers use it to refer to the Son, the divine Word, through whom the universe came into being. For these, see: Richard Norris, ed. *The Christological Controversy* (Philadelphia, PA: Fortress, 1980), 5-6.

[45]   *AG* 11. See also *LG* 16. Maurice Otunga describes this image of the 'seed of the word' as a more dynamic one with regard to integrating the faith into cultures when compared to '*praeparatio Evangelii*' image applied to African cultures before Vatican II. Maurice Otunga, "African Cultures and Life-Centered Catechesis," *Teaching All Nations* 15, no. 1 (1978): 25-26. This concept was developed by the Fathers of the Church. See Justin Martyr, *Apology* II, 8, 10. For this document, see Barnard Leslie, trans., *St. Justin Martyr: The First and Second Apologies*, Ancient Christian Writers, vol. 56, ed. Walter Burghardt, John Dillon and Dennis McManus (New York/Mahwah, NJ: Paulist, 1997), 79-81.

[46]   Laurenti Magesa, *Anatomy of Inculturation: Transforming the Church in Africa* (MaryKnoll, NY: 2004), 143. See also Schineller, "Inculturation as the Pilgrimage to Catholicity," 99; Marcello Azevedo, *Inculturation and the Challenges of Modernity* (Rome: Pontifical Gregorian University, 1982), 27; Donal Dorr, *Mission in Today's World* (Maryknoll, NY: Orbis, 2000), 91. Dorr

for what belongs to God in a given cultural context. It enables the culture to assess itself and know areas where it really manifests God's word and areas where it distorts it.[47] This understood, it becomes easier to comprehend what John Paul II was driving at, in his address to the Kenyan bishops, when he identifies Christ as "an African."[48]

Since culture is a human creation, it remains an ambiguous reality. It cannot be perfect. It needs constant criticisms and purification. Thus, in this mutual encounter, the gospel never ceases to challenge and critically purify those unwholesome elements of the culture that are at variance with the true values promoted by it (the gospel).[49] Hence, there is no way, as Carrier argues, any true inculturation could coincide with condoning, much less encouraging, unjust structures, immoral practices and ungodly ideologies. It rather goes against such elements that do not conduce to the upliftment of the human person, or cultural advancement of the people.[50] "This means that the gospel exercises a critical function with regard to the elements threatening, or at least posing an obstacle to, real humanization"[51] in a particular culture. However, those cultural endowments of the people that are good are fostered and made nobler in order to serve as avenues for

---

talks of the "Spirit of God" already present and embodied in people's cultures before ever the good news of Jesus Christ is preached to them.

[47]   Magesa, *Anatomy of Inculturtion*, 144.

[48]   John Paul II, "The African Bishop's Challenge," 7 May 1980, *Origins* 10, no. 2 (1980): no. 6. See also Paul Beauchamp, "The Role of the Old Testament in the Process of Building Local Churches," in *Bible and Inculturation*, ed. Ary Crollius, Working Papers on Living Faith and Cultures (Rome: Pontifical Gregorian University, 1983), 2.

[49]   John Paul II, "Encyclical Letter, On the Permanent Validity of the Church's Missionary Mandate, *Redemptoris Missio*, 7 December 1990," *AAS* 83 (1991): no. 54. Hereafter, *RM*; Peter Schineller, "Inculturation: Why So Slow?," *Journal of Inculturation Theology* 4, no. 2 (1997): 135.

[50]   Carrier, "The Church Meeting Cultures," 150.

[51]   Claude Geffré, "Double Belonging and the Originality of Christianity as a Religion," in *Many Mansions?: Multiple Religious Belonging and Christian Identity*, ed. Catherine Cornille (Maryknoll, NY: Orbis, 2002), 98. See also Walter Principe, *Faith, History and Cultures: Stability and Change in Church Teachings*, The Pere Marquette Theology Lectures, no. 22 (Milwaukee, WI: Marquette University Press, 1991), 43.

the propagation of the gospel.[52] This exercise brings growth and enrichment not only to the culture itself, but also to the church.[53]

Furthermore, the experience of the mutual exchange also brings about transformation to Christian faith. As Uzochukwu Nwala maintains, it is not just a unidirectional exercise whereby Christianity merely transforms the culture in question "to its own image."[54] On the contrary, Christianity's symbiotic relationship and experience with the culture also entails a re-shaping, re-interpretation and re-expression of the content of the faith and its actual practice. It is in view of this that Claude Geffré maintains:

> In its attempt at inculturation the church is thus challenged to question itself about its spontaneous forms of expression and to practice discernment with regard to the fundamental elements of the Christian message and more contingent structures derived from the dominant culture with which it has been historically associated.[55]

This being the case, it becomes evident that, in any genuine inculturation, both the faith and the culture are enriched and transformed.[56] Thus, just as their encounter is governed by the principle of mutual exchange, so also their influences on each other. Just as culture needs faith for it to grow and blossom all the more, so does faith need culture for it to be of benefit to the people and be lived out. In acknowledgment of this fact, John Paul II states that "the synthesis between culture and faith is not just a demand of culture, but also of faith. A faith which does not become culture is a faith which has not been fully received, not thoroughly thought through, not fully lived out."[57]

It is also pertinent to note that, for this mutual transformation to be enriching, it should not rob any of the two of its essential

---

[52]   *LG* 13.

[53]   Paul VI, *EN* 63.

[54]   Uzodinma Nwala, *Igbo Philosophy* (Lagos: Lantern, 1985), 236.

[55]   Geffré, "Double Belonging," 98.

[56]   Ibid., 97. See also Emilio Alberich, "Is the Universal Catechism an Obstacle or a Catalyst in the Process of Inculturation?," *Concilium* 204, no. 4 (1989): 92.

[57]   L'Osservatore Romano, 28 June, 1982, cited in Shorter, *Towards a Theology of Inculturation*, 231.

character.[58] Thus, inculturation vouches for and safeguards both the cultural as well as the Christian identity and authenticity. None should be compromised in the process. No inculturation takes place if the people's cultural identity is destroyed.[59] If it happens, the faith cannot be adequately received.[60] On the other hand, variations in its cultural expression are not expected to bring about betrayal of Christian faith or the gospel. If in the process the culture becomes absolutised such that the faith is so radically transformed as to lose its essential identity, there is also no inculturation in the real sense of the word. This, John Paul II points out, "amounts to what St. Paul very forcefully calls 'emptying the cross of Christ of its power.'"[61] It is against this background that one can understand the instruction issued by the Congregation for the Doctrine of the Faith in which words of caution were addressed to liberation theologians concerning subjecting the gospel to Marxist ideology.[62]

---

[58] Gelpi, *Inculturating North American Theology*, 32. See also Michael Angrosino, "The Culture Concept and the Mission of the Roman Catholic Church," *American Anthropologist* 96, no. 4 (1994): 825; Magesa, *Anatomy of Inculturation*, 142.

[59] Groome, "Inculturation," 124.

[60] See John Paul II, "Address to the Bishops of Nigeria, 15 February 1982," *Origins* 11, no. 37 (1982): no. 3.

[61] John Paul II, *CT* 53. Cf. I Cor 1, 17.

[62] Congregation for the Doctrine of the Faith, *Instruction on Certain Aspects of the "Theology of Liberation," Libertatis Nuntius*, 6 August 1984; available from http://www.vatican.va/roman_curia/congregations/cfaith/documents/rc_con_cfaith_doc_19840806_theology-liberation_en.html; accessed 11 April 2012. In the document, concerns are raised about certain kinds of theology of liberation. There is some warning against an uncritical employment of Marxist social analysis and the concept of class struggle in theology. The document also raises concern about the understanding of personal sin as employed in these struggles. This, it stresses, leads to the reduction of the gospel of Christ to a mere earthly gospel. This is done at the expense of a holistic evangelisation and human dignity. It also expresses worry over the atheistic and totalitarian tendencies inherent in Marxism. Added to this is the fact that justice and political freedom cannot be achieved if personal perfection is not promoted. For some critical comments on this document, see Joseph Bernardin, "Comment on 'Theology of Liberation' Document," *AFER* 26, no. 6 (1984): 373-374; Laurenti Magesa, "Instruction on the 'Theology of Liberation:' A Comment" *AFER* 27, no. 1 (1984): 3-8; Simon Smith, "The Vatican Document on Liberation Theology," *AFER* 26, no. 6 (1984): 372-373.

From the discussion so far, one can agree with Groome who sees inculturation as a dialectical encounter between the gospel and culture; a dialectics that involves "a *threefold* dynamic of affirming and cherishing, of refusing or questioning, and of moving on to new and transformed possibilities for both."[63] Hence, it often encompasses a complex and unrelenting convolution of processes and involves a certain measure of uneasiness, tension and conflict; even more so, given the fact that culture is not simply a seamless phenomenon, but one in which so many interest and competing objectives are manifest. It is not a question of easy accommodation or adaptation of the faith to a given culture or a facile continuity between the two.[64]

---

[63]   Groome, "Inculturation," 121. Emphasis in the original.

[64]   Modern correlation method has been criticised on this. As a theological term, it was coined by Paul Tillich. One of the chief advocates of this method, the American Catholic theologian, David Tracy, in his proposal for a 'revisionist' theology, sees the principal function of theology as that of setting human experience and language into critical correlation with the Christian tradition. This task, he argues, involves "the dramatic confrontation, the mutual illuminations and corrections, the possible basic reconciliation between the principal values, cognitive claims, and existential faiths of both a reinterpreted post-modern consciousness and a reinterpreted Christianity." See, David Tracy, *Blessed Rage for Order: The New Pluralism in Theology* (New York: Seabury, 1975), 32. Lieven Boeve has provided a detailed critique of this approach, especially given today's postmodern situation of the West. The following are some of his criticisms of the method: it presumes there is a fundamental continuity between Christian tradition and modern culture; it assumes that Christianity can provide answers to all the questions raised by modernity; it sees the modern culture as simply secular without taking into consideration other religious alternatives, forms, fundamental life options and plurality in the society; it concedes to the secular context the right to provide the yardstick for gauging the authenticity of the Christian tradition and its critical re-visioning, even when that entails watering down the contents of the latter. Boeve proposes recontextualisation, which entails a theological method of interruption. This, according to him, is able to account for the reality of continuity and discontinuity between the Christian tradition and the contemporary postmodern context. It also involves the acceptance that Christian narrative simply represents a definite, unique particularity amidst other possible particularities with which it engages in dialogue. Implied here too is the acknowledgment of the radical otherness and plurality characteristic of today's society, as well as the diversity internally characteristic of Christianity itself. As against the correlationist's stance of easy continuity between Christian tradition and context and anti-correlationist's argument for discontinuity with the context,

Such assumptions may point to lack of appreciation, on one hand, of the diversity of Christian faith, and on the other, of the complexity of culture, the politics and ideological underpinnings of cultural formation, cultural dynamics and change. Inculturation always involves questions related to how one is to achieve real integration of the faith into the culture without imposition and consequent "destruction" of the culture, on one hand. On the other hand, one is also confronted with questions related to how the faith can actually relate with a particular culture without being, in a certain sense, "de-Christianised." This tension will always be there in any genuine inculturation process. It is only in such a situation will the relationship between the two lead unto growth and newness.

INCULTURATION AND OTHER RELATED CONCEPTS AND APPROACHES

I have noted earlier that inculturation is a relatively new term in theology. Before its emergence, a plethora of terms had been employed over the years in an attempt to fashion out the best model or approach to be adopted in relating Christian faith and culture. Part of the setbacks experienced today in inculturation is because of the way people confuse it with some of the terms, which in themselves represent approaches quite different from that adopted by inculturation in dealing with faith and culture. That is why it is necessary to make some clarifications concerning their applications and usages.

TRANSLATION

Translation basically argues for integrating the faith into any given culture by first purifying it of all the foreign cultural accumulations resulting from its previous contacts with other cultures. They are seen as coatings that obscure the real and original message. Having

---

interruption, he argues, holds continuity and discontinuity in continuous tension. Interruption forces each narrative to open itself to the other yet without losing its particularity. For these, see Lieven Boeve, *God Interrupts History: Theology in a Time of Upheaval*, trans. Brian Doyle (New York: Continuum, 2007), 30-49.

removed these coatings, the faith is assumed to be pure. Then comes the second stage, which is its translation into the new situation. Scholars usually employ the image of 'husk and kernel' to describe the relationship between faith and culture that is manifest in translation. While the husk comprises the different cultural contexts into which the faith has previously been successfully integrated, the kernel represents the fundamental Christian revelation or the presumed 'pure' faith.[65]

Translation, therefore, presumes that there is an essentially supracultural or supracontextual core or essence of Christian faith that can be understood independently of culture or context. According to Stephen Bevans, there is generally no agreement among the advocates of this approach as to what constitutes this core. For some, it is Christ Incarnate. For others, it could be the Trinity, the Bible, or some injunctions and doctrines contained in the Bible.[66] The primary concern of this model is the preservation of this presumed pure and changeless core. The culture of the people into which the faith is to be translated is accorded a secondary status. It merely functions as the vehicle for the transmission of the message. Translation seems to construe revelation in terms of God's direct communication of certain

---

[65]   Robert Schreiter, *Constructing Local Theologies* (Maryknoll, NY: Orbis, 1985), 7. Other images used to explain it are those of 'clothing' and 'vegetation.' In the 'clothing' image, the cloth or garb represents the culture, while the gospel or the faith is represented by that which the cloth covers. So, just as the garb used in covering or wrapping an object can be removed in order to reveal what lies under it, so also is it assumed that culture can be isolated from the faith in order for the latter to be properly comprehended and integrated into a given culture. When the image of 'vegetation' is employed, the soil is understood as the culture in which the faith is planted, nurtured and grown, while the faith is seen as the seed sown in the soil (culture). See Volker Küster, *The Many Faces of Jesus Christ: Intercultural Christology*, trans. John Bowden (London: SCM, 2001), 21. Some scholars use translation synonymously with accommodation. Though the two operate with the same basic idea of separation of the content of the message from its cultural form, Volker Küster argues that translation is the modern variant of accommodation. According to him, the model has been with Christianity right from the time the spread of the gospel meant crossing cultural borders. He further argues that this was the model adopted in China and India by two Jesuit missionaries, Matteo Ricci (1552-1610) and Roberto de Nobili (1577-1656) respectively. See Ibid., 20-22.

[66]   Stephen Bevans, *Models of Contextual Theology*, Revised and Expanded Edition (Maryknoll, NY: Orbis, 2002), 40.

truths, doctrines, or teachings to human beings, thus, isolating it completely from human experience, history, and culture.[67]

The strength of translation lies in the fact that it makes effort to remain faithful to the church's tradition without any betrayal. It makes sure all the achievements in the church's tradition are kept intact and made present to a given people using appropriate equivalents within their culture.[68] It believes in the relevance of the Christian message in the world, and thus reinforces the need, on the part of the church, to treasure it accordingly. In addition, its recognition of the ambiguity of culture is also commendable. This ambiguity is part of the reason why it advocates for the shedding, in the first place, of the previous cultural expressions of the gospel or the faith in order to get at the core of the message. This way cultural romanticism of a sort is avoided. Furthermore, it is neither time-consuming nor too demanding. Much involvement of the theologian or the people is not needed, and can thus be employed without much familiarity with the culture where Christianity is about to be rooted. As such, it can be useful when immediate pastoral need is felt, especially at the initial stage when Christian faith is introduced into a particular cultural milieu.[69]

The danger with this approach comes to the fore when it is no longer used as a temporary measure intended to address an urgent situation, especially at the initial stage of evangelisation, but taken as the only method to be adopted. This danger arises because the Christian tradition that is being safeguarded is not made very meaningful to the people living here and now in a particular context. The secondary place it assigns to the culture of the people cannot help matters in making Christianity a living reality for them. When culture is considered merely as a medium for communicating the Christian message, its importance in the life of the people is seriously undermined. What often happens is to search for elements in the culture that seem to be equivalent to those already contained in Christian tradition, and which can be used to replace the latter. Underlying this is the presumption that such parallels always exist even when it is not clearly so. Moreover, because cultural analysis is

---

[67]   Ibid., 41.

[68]   Schreiter, *Constructing Local Theologies*, 9.

[69]   Stephen Bevans, *Models of Contextual Theology*, 42-43; Schineller, *A Handbook on Inculturation*, 15; Schreiter, *Constructing Local Theologies*, 7.

not done very deeply, it often results in peripheral association of one cultural pattern with another, which might easily lead to crisis. It also betrays the authentic meaning of texts and symbols.[70]

In addition, Christ is not seen as already present and at work in the culture into which the faith is to be translated. He is rather understood to be introduced into the culture during the process. This partly explains why the people's culture is accorded an ancillary position, and no genuine dialogue encouraged between it and the faith. It is against this background that Schineller describes translation as an imposition.[71]

Another problem with this approach is the implications of the basic image of 'kernel and husk' with which it operates. It works with the assumption that Christian faith and culture are static realities that lack dynamic interaction with each other. Culture is there merely to provide the wrap for the content—the faith. This does not provide the real picture of what actually takes place when there is genuine encounter between the two. It ignores the implications of cultural metamorphosis, the mutual influence that each has on the other, and what this implies with regard to the people concerned.[72]

This feeds on the presumption that the faith can be made to stand free of previous cultural accretions in order to be translated into another culture. This is, to say the least, very unrealistic, abstractionist and fictitious. There exists nothing like pure, naked, or ahistorical Christianity, which could be recovered and which exists independently of, or prior to its contact with, culture. In no way can Christianity or even the gospel reach us in an unmediated or culturally neutral form.[73] Therefore, to think of or search for an abstract essence

---

[70]   Bevans, *Models of Contextual Theology*, 41; Schreiter, *Constructing Local Theologies*, 8.

[71]   Schineller, *A Handbook on Inculturation*, 16; Schreiter, *Constructing Local Theologies*, 8.

[72]   See Küster, *The Many Faces of Jesus Christ*, 22-23.

[73]   Johann-Baptist Metz, "Unity and Diversity: Problems and Prospects for Inculturation," *Concilium* 204, no. 4 (1989): 81. See also Aylward Shorter, "Inculturation: The Premise of Universality," in *A Universal Faith?: Peoples, Cultures, Religions, and the Christ*, ed. Catherine Cornille and Valeer Neckebrouck (Louvain: Peeters, 1992), 12-13. William Biernatzki makes the point that there is no way any religion could be conceived apart from a particular culture. It is culture that gives it empirical existence and guarantees

of Christianity is like pursuing shadows. Geffré asserts that there is no way Christianity can be considered today without reference to its encounter with the Mediterranean culture: "It would nonetheless be wrong to conceive of the problem of inculturation in terms of a Christianity that would have to cease to be Western in order to become African or Asian."[74] A better approach for making Christianity 'incarnate' in cultures outside the West would be a situation where the western Christianity with all its cultural richness engages fruitfully and creatively with the riches and values of other cultures.[75] Okure has made the point that Africans, for instance, cannot reasonably deny the fact that Christian faith reached them in unavoidably, culturally conditioned form. So, making the faith 'incarnate' in Africa involves contact between this culturally conditioned expression of the faith and African culture. This, she asserts, needs to be recognised and accepted in all sincerity or else the process remains anything but genuine.[76]

---

its accessibility to the people. William Biernatzki, "Symbol and Root Paradigm: The Locus of Effective Inculturation," in *Effective Inculturation and Ethnic Identity*, Inculturation: Working Papers on Living Faith and Cultures, ed. Ary Roest Crollius (Rome: Pontifical Gregorian University Press, 1987), 63. See also Peter Phan, *Being Religious Interreligiously: Asian Perspectives on Interfaith Dialogue* (Maryknoll, NY: Orbis, 2004), 242; Peter Rottländer, "One World: Opportunity or Threat for the Global Church?," *Concilium* 204, no. 4 (1989): 113; Subhash Anand, "The Inculturation of the Eucharistic Liturgy," *VJTR* 57, no. 5 (1993): 273.

74   Geffré, "Double Belonging and the Originality," 96. For Nkéramihigo, such an idea about Christianity with regard to inculturation is a sort of "'docetism" of the universal which risks deadening the edge of its blade, namely the power to be incarnated." Christianity, he further contends, cannot be conceived in terms of an abstract universal, which hangs in the air seeking for concrete expression. Instead, it should be seen as a concrete expression of faith in Jesus Christ, which has the power to be universalised and proclaimed to the whole world. Théoneste Nkéramihigo, "Inculturation and the Specificity of Christian Message," in *Inculturation: Its Meaning and Urgency*, ed. John Walligo et al. (Nairobi: St. Paul, 1986), 70. See also Michael Gallagher, *Clashing Symbols: An Introduction to Faith and Culture*, 2nd ed. (London: Darton, Longman and Todd, 2003), 118.

75   Geffré, "Double Belonging and the Originality," 96. Cf. Nkéramihigo, "Inculturation and the Specificity of Christian Message," 67.

76   Teresa Okure, "Inculturation: Biblical/Theological Basis," in *32 Articles Evaluating Inculturation of Christianity in Africa*, ed. Teresa Okure and Paul van Thiel (Eldoret: AMECEA Gaba, 1990), 58.

From the foregoing, it is clear that translation is clearly different from inculturation. It falls short of the much-needed creative and deep engagement between the faith and culture.

ADAPTATION

This term had been in popular usage before Vatican II. That explains the council's extensive use of it in its effort to emphasise the need to take the cultures of different people seriously in the church's mission and life. To be sure, adaptation does take the culture of the local people more seriously than does translation. It advocates for deeper contact between Christian faith and culture than does translation. Schriter has identified three forms that adaptation can take. One needs to know how these forms operate in order to learn what is involved in adaptation. The first form involves the practice whereby a foreigner or a local theologian tries to develop a theology for the local situation after the manner of theology developed in another culture and understood as the norm. The so-called normative theological tradition is usually that of the West. So, if the culture into which the faith is to be integrated is outside the West, the theologian uses concepts, names and worldview of the people and tries to force them into the pre-fabricated mould of western theological tradition and method.[77] Thus, there is always a particular pattern posited, according to which the local theology must be modelled.

The strength of this form of adaptation lies in the fact that it takes the local culture into consideration in the theological practice. Again, the local theology thus developed can easily enjoy acceptability within the theological tradition taken as the norm. Theologians trained in the tradition can easily understand it because that is what they are more familiar with.[78]

---

[77]   Schreiter, *Constructing Local Theologies*, 8. According to Schreiter, Placide Tempels represents one of those who had tried to undertake such a theology. In one of his works, Tempels tries to use the scholastic philosophical framework to work out a philosophy and a theology for the Bantu people. He sees their whole worldview as directed and permeated by the idea of "vital force or energy." See Placide Tempels, *Bantu Philosophy*, trans. Colin King (Paris: Présence Africaine, 1959).

[78]   Schreiter, *Constructing Local Theologies*, 10.

Since the western theological tradition is rigorously intellectualistic, this form of translation seems to see any genuine theology as such. Thus, any theology that is not founded on a solid intellectual framework does not worth its salt. In case of systematic theology, it must have a sound philosophical footing to be acceptable. But granted such a method may yield sure and certain knowledge, it is not the most suitable approach in addressing adequately the issues that could be raised by all cultures. No genuine theology can emerge by literally forcing cultural elements of a given culture into imported framework.[79] To base, say African theology, merely on the procedure and strict intellectual methodology worked out in the West may not at a long run produce a theology that can adequately address African problems.[80] This might end up attending merely to issues peripheral to the people's faith. This is because the contact it advocates between Christian faith and a particular culture is extrinsic.[81] An approach of this sort is what Paul VI describes as decorative style of evangelisation, which does not reach the very root of cultures.[82]

The second form of adaptation is where a particular concept of the New Testament Church is posited as a philosophical framework for a theology. Schreiter says this is more prevalent among Protestants. But this approach is not realistic because, according to him, no such unified New Testament Church exists.[83]

The third form of adaptation is that which advocates for planting of Christian faith in a particular culture like a seed and allowing both of them to freely grow together. According to Schreiter, this model is a good one, in that it preserves the integrity of both the Christian faith and the culture. Thus, a genuine theology can develop from it. However, he accuses this approach of being too idealistic. It is rarely possible that such ideal circumstances could be found.[84]

---

[79] Ibid., 9-10.

[80] Justin Ukpong, "African Inculturation Theology," *Voices from the Third World* 9, no. 4 (1986): 28.

[81] Ary Crollius, "What Is So New about Inculturation? A Concept and Its Implications," *Gregorianum* 59 (1979): 723.

[82] Paul VI, *EN* 20.

[83] Schreiter, *Constructing Local Theologies*, 10. See also Stephen Sykes, *The Identity of Christianity* (London: SPCK, 1984), 11.

[84] Schreiter, *Constructing Local Theologies*, 11-12.

In short, adaptation approach cannot live up to the demand of real integration of Christian faith into cultures on account of its superficiality. It cannot be substituted for inculturation.[85] Schineller has even accused it of being an imposition of a sort.[86] According to Cote, the major distinguishing mark between it and inculturation is that, while the latter begins from within the culture and works itself outwards, it works the opposite direction—from outside the culture to its inner dimension. Failure to identify this difference, he maintains, has led to many inappropriate initiatives in the church's liturgy and its overall pastoral life.[87]

INDIGENISATION

Indigenisation refers mainly to the making of local churches that are native to the people in outlook, led and managed by the natives and not by foreigners. It was first used by Protestant scholars in the 1950s, when expatriate missionaries managed many of the local churches, to emphasise the need for their replacement by the natives. According to Volker Küster, the need for independence of churches fostered by indigenisation was based on the three principles of *"self-governing, self-supporting, self-propagating"* advanced by two protestant theologians, Rufus Anderson (1796-1873) and Henry Venn (1796-1880) in response to the paternalistic excesses of western missionaries, especially in Asia.[88] In effect, adaptation reinforces the primary role of the local clergy and the faithful in charting their own course, especially as regards making the faith at home in their culture.[89] This is based on the conviction that an insider, who is a product of a particular culture, typically has more knowledge of the

---

[85] Aylward Shorter, *African Christian Theology: Adaptation or Incarnation* (London: Chapman, 1975), 150. See also Cote, *Re-Visioning Mission*, 41; Eugene Hillman, *Toward an African Christianity* (Mahwah, NJ: Paulist, 1993), 84.

[86] Schineller, *A Handbook on Inculturation*, 17.

[87] Cote, *Re-Visioning Mission*, 41. See also Schreiter, *Constructing Local Theologies*, 13.

[88] Küster, *The Many Faces of Jesus Christ*, 22. Emphasis in the original.

[89] Cf. David Hesselgrave, *Communicating Christ Cross-Culturally* (Grand Rapids, MI: Academie, 1978), 83.

cultural patterns at work in his or her locality than any foreigner might claim to have. Any help from an outsider is, therefore, considered supportive and secondary.[90]

Granted this term expresses the indispensable and irreducible role of the local community in the process of making the faith answer the questions raised by their peculiar cultural situation, if care is not taken, it can easily lead to exclusivism of a sort. If a given culture and its people become too self-centred, the danger is that they cut themselves off from the riches of intercultural communication and exchange with others.[91] Just having indigenous men and women does not suffice in making the faith well received in a culture. In many instances, as experience has shown, some of such indigenous leaders turn out to be at the forefront of the move to clamp down on some reasonable initiatives for genuine inculturation. Many were even trained outside their cultural milieu and promoted to their various leadership positions by forces external to the people.[92] The continued influence of these forces on them should not be neglected.

Schreiter sees the problem with the word as rather historical. Its connection with the fight against colonialism in some areas, he affirms, makes it unfit for use in theology. Mere mentioning of it reminds the people of their colonial past and whatever that entails. According to him, this is true especially among the Indians and East Africans, for whom the term implies the old policy whereby the local leadership replaced the British personnel serving the colonial government.[93]

---

[90] Schineller, *A Handbook on Inculturation*, 18. Cf. Hesselgrave, *Communicating Christ Cross-Culturally*, 83.

[91] Schineller, *A Handbook on Inculturation*, 18. See also Joseph Osei-Bonsu, *The Inculturation of Christianity in Africa: Antecedents and Guidelines from the New Testament and the Early Church* (Frankfurt: Peter Lang, 2005), 15; Shorter, *Towards a Theology of Inculturation*, 150. According to Angrosino, when this term appeared initially, the Vatican theologians approved it. However, because the word has a tone that is somehow patronising, it was later abandoned. Angrosino, "The Culture Concept," 825.

[92] Cf. Kraft, *Christianity in Culture*, 319-320.

[93] Schreiter, *Constructing Local Theologies*, 5.

CONTEXTUALISATION

This term is used by many theologians in almost the same way inculturation is used to express the phenomenon of the integration of Christian faith into cultures. It literally means "to weave together." So, in the context of our discussion, its literal meaning is weaving together Christian faith and culture.[94] Many a time it is used in such a way that it is a comprehensive term covering the various attempts to genuinely engage the context in the work of evangelisation, which has inculturation as one of them.[95] For some, the two are simply synonymous. Except for few sceptical voices during the first few years of its emergence, it generally enjoys great favour among theologians, and has been a preferred term for the World Council of Churches.[96]

The difference between inculturation and contextualisation stems from the fact that, while the former emphasises culture, the latter lays emphasis on the context.[97] It is based on this that one can argue for either of the two.

Contextualisation has some advantages. For one, 'context' has such a generic meaning that makes it possible for the process of contextualisation to be applied to a greater variety of situations. Even among people of the same culture, there could still be some differences in situations, which may warrant a different approach in relating the faith to them. It is not only this. It also makes clearer the continuous

---

[94]   Schineller, *A Handbook on Inculturation*, 19.

[95]   See Justin Ukpong, "Contextualization: A Historical Survey," *AFER* 29, no. 5 (1987): 278-286.

[96]   The term was actually popularised in 1957, when Rockefeller Foundation offered some grants for the reform of theological education in view of training leaders who were to help contextualise the gospel in the mission countries. Since then, the World Council of Churches has always used it in any discussion on cross-cultural communication of the Christian message. Schineller, *A Handbook on Inculturation*, 19. See also Anscar Chupungco, "Inculturation," in *The New SCM Dictionary of Liturgy and Worship*, ed. Paul Bradshow (London: SCM, 2002), 224; Shorter, *Towards a Theology of Inculturation*, 11; Angrosino, "The Culture Concept," 825.

[97]   Aylward Shorter, *Evangelization and Culture* (New York: Geoffrey Chapman, 1994), 30.

changing nature of human situations and, therefore, the need to make the faith relevant to them even as they change.[98]

One of its possible disadvantages is that its emphasis on the present context might make it lack "continuity with the past."[99] Culture, on the other hand, denotes not only the present circumstance but also inherited characteristics that are transmitted from generation to generation. As such, its usage does more justice to history than context. Moreover, the wobbling nature of context has its problems. Contexts are diverse, erratic and hardly stable. Thus, theology constructed from it will most certainly be "a chameleon-like theology that lacks constancy and solidity."[100]

The arguments proffered by some theologians for preferring contextualisation to inculturation are sometimes based on a false understanding of culture. Seeing culture as having only to do with myths, legends or arts, they argue that it is not fit for use in discussions concerning the complexities of modern society. For them, the use of context offers more grounds for theology's engagement with these realities.[101] But, if the concept of culture is properly understood, one realises that it is so comprehensive as to cover issues pertaining to modernity and other intricacies of contemporary society. Hence, in its employment of 'culture,' inculturation not only does more justice to history than does contextualisation, but is also capable of being used to analyse today's realities.[102]

Before concluding this section, there are two other concepts from cultural anthropology with which inculturation bears some proximity, which we need to give some attention to: **enculturation** and **acculturation**. I deem it important to do so because some have

---

[98] Peter Schineller, "Ten summary Statements on the Meaning, Challenge and Significance of Inculturation as Applied to the Church and Society of Jesus in the United States, in Light of the Global Process of Modernization," in *On Being the Church in a Modern Society*, Inculturation: Working Papers on Living Faith and Cultures, ed. Ary Crollius (Rome: Pontifical Gregorian University Press, 1983), 55; Schineller, *A Handbook on Inculturation*, 19. See also Fabella, "Inculturation," 105.

[99] Schineller, *A Handbook on Inculturation*, 19.

[100] Ibid., 19-20. See also Shorter, *Evangelization and Culture*, 30.

[101] Bevans is one of those theologians. See Bevans, *Models of Contextual Theology*, 26-27.

[102] Shorter, *Evangelization and Culture*, 30.

conjectured that inculturation is a fusion of these two anthropological concepts, on one hand, and the theological concept of incarnation, on the other.[103] Acculturation simply means the process of transmission of cultural traits between two or more cultures by first-hand contact with each other.[104] According to John Berry, for acculturation to take place, two things are required. First, there is a contact between the cultures involved. Second, there should be a change in at least one of the contacting cultures, with the cultural traits most often flowing more from the dominant culture into the weaker one. In fact, he maintains that the process generally involves three stages: of contact, of conflict and of adaptation. Conflict, in some cases, may not be so evident, he notes, but it is usually the case before any change could be effected. It occurs due to lack of readiness for cultures to easily compromise their long-standing cultural heritage. It is in the resolution of this conflict that the third stage of acculturation takes place—adaptation. Anthropologists believe that these processes of acculturation occur not only on the societal or macro-level but also on the individual or micro-level.[105] Enculturation denotes the process by which an individual learns to live as a member of a particular society. Marcello Azevedo defines it as "a process by which the human individual becomes inserted into his/her own culture."[106] According to

---

[103]   See Küster, *The Many Faces of Jesus Christ*, 23-24.

[104]   Marvin Mayers, *Christianity Confronts Culture: A Strategy for Cross-Cultural Evangelism* (Grand Rapids, MI: Zondervan, 1974), 10.

[105]   John Berry, "Acculturation as Varieties of Adaptation," in *Acculturation: Theory, Models and Some Findings*, ed. Amado Padilla (Boulder, CO: Westview, 1980), 11-12. See Raymond Teske and Bardin Nelson, "Acculturation and Assimilation: A Clarification," *American Ethnologist* 1, no. 2 (1974): 351-352. Some anthropologists distinguish three types of acculturation: blind acculturation, imposed acculturation and democratic acculturation. Blind acculturation occurs when people of different cultural groups meet and intermingle with one another, so much so that they exchange their cultural traits without any intention of doing so. Imposed acculturation, on the other hand, is witnessed when one culture arrogantly and forcefully imparts its traits on another. The democratic type does not involve any form of coercion at all, but works with the principle of mutual respect and is witnessed where there is recognition of cultural pluralism and tolerance. There are other ways according to which acculturation could be classified. For these and the ones described above, see Teske and Nelson, "Acculturation and Assimilation," 355-357.

[106]   Azevedo, *Inculturation and the Challenges of Modernity*, 7.

the American Anthropologist, Melville Herskovits, one undergoes the enculturation process from cradle to the grave. In the earliest stages of life, one has to go through a continuous conditioning in order to conform to the societal demands. By way of imitation or by the use of punishment and reward, a child comes to adapt to the way of life of the society. It is only as the child grows up, and the level of his or her conscious acceptance of values increases, that he or she can consciously be exposed to alternative choices from which he or she can make some selections.[107]

The proximity of acculturation to inculturation lies in the fact that the faith cannot be communicated without the medium of culture. Hence, every inculturation process involves contact between two cultures: that with which the faith encounters/reaches a particular society and the culture of the society itself. In other words, every inculturation necessarily involves acculturation.[108] Furthermore, since the local church is understood as the subject of the church's mission, mission could also be seen as a process whereby the local church becomes inserted into the culture of its people. This is nothing but enculturation. But, despite the closeness of inculturation to these two terms, none of them can be identified with it.[109]

---

[107] Herskovits, *Man and His Works*, 40.

[108] Küster, *The Many Faces of Jesus Christ*, 24. Indeed, acculturation can at best be regarded as a stage in the inculturation process, whereby the previous cultural expression of the Christian message meets with the culture of the local people. Shorter is of the view that inculturation always involves acculturation phase, which, however does not preclude the needed deep insertion of the Christian faith into culture that follows afterwards. Shorter, *Evangelization and Culture*, 84. See also Ndubuisi Udeafor, *Inculturation* (Enugu: SNAAP, 1994), 39. For more on the relatedness and differences between these two, see Schineller, *A Handbook on Inculturation*, 22; Crollius, "Inculturation: Newness and Ongoing Process," 33; Poupard, *Church and Culture*, 34. All these authors basically believe that the two are related but also differ significantly, since the Christian faith cannot merely be regarded as one culture among others. Its evangelical character, they argue, should also be taken into serious consideration.

[109] Küster, *The Many Faces of Jesus Christ*, 24. We also note the difference between inculturation and enculturation. Crollius argues that the difference between the two lies in the fact that in enculturation, the individual does not have a culture until he or she becomes inserted or enculturated into one. But the church could not be said to undergo the same experience. He observes that, instead, the church, in the process of inculturation, already has some culture consequent upon

INCULTURATION, CATHOLICITY AND UNITY OF THE CHURCH

What it means to say that the church is catholic has been variously perceived at different times in the history of the church. It is also observed that discussions on catholicity have often been accompanied by that on the church's unity, since the two concepts are apparently correlative, such that any upset in either of them immediately affects the other.[110] It is observed too that contemporary debates on inculturation have often, either directly or indirectly, referred to these. Inculturation is now and again viewed as a threat to these two marks of the church, especially by those Diego Irarrazaval describes as having "a uniform and centralizing logic."[111] This is because inculturation encourages expression of Christian faith in ways with which the church may not have been identified with since about two thousand years of its existence. Added to this is the fact that it advocates for much greater consideration of the concrete and the particular, unlike what obtains in the traditional theology.[112] Moreover, it is quite easier to assume that, for there to be unity, more uniformity should be encouraged than variations or changes, which inculturation advances. In effect, any form of variation or diversity is, many a time, seen as divisive and, therefore, to be resisted. That is why resistance to the efforts made to inculturate the faith is sometimes perceived by some as proof of one's loyalty to the one, universal church.[113]

What needs to be noted is that unity, though not necessarily opposed to external uniformity, goes much further and deeper.[114]

---

its previous insertions into other cultures. It is with this that it encounters the new culture. Crollius, "Inculturation: Newness and Ongoing Process," 36.

[110] Hans Küng, *The Church*, trans. Ray and Rosaleen Ockenden (London: Search, 1968), 296.

[111] Diego Irarràzaval, *Inculturation: New Dawn of the Church in Latin America*, trans. Phillip Berryman (Maryknoll, NY: Orbis, 2000), 18.

[112] Peter Schineller, "Inculturation as the Pilgrimage to Catholicity," 99.

[113] See Teresa Okure, "Inculturation: Biblical/Theological Basis," 57.

[114] Any undue emphasis on uniformity in today's society does not do justice to the prevailing diversity and promotion of cultural autonomy. Such, as Schineller argues, "will lead to schism unless sufficient breathing space is allowed for local expression." See Schineller, "Inculturation as the Pilgrimage to Catholicity," 100. See also Mort Kane, "African Liturgy and the Papal Visit to Zaire," *AFER* 26, no. 4 (1984): 247.

Besides, unity itself presupposes diversity and pluriformity, just as universality or catholicity does in relation to particularity; otherwise one may ask as Shorter does: "Unity of what?"[115] In essence, I argue that unless inculturation is truly undertaken by the church, its claim to catholicity and unity is anything but real. In what follows, the concept of catholicity will first be explored. This is followed by demonstration of how the two marks of the church are functions of genuine inculturation.

THE CONCEPT OF CATHOLICITY

Catholicity, in its classical Greek usage has a wide range of meanings. Its adjectival form, *katholikos* (derived from *kath' holou*, meaning literally "according to the whole" or "through the whole"), was employed when referring basically to something that is general, complete, full, total, or perfect, as opposed to something that is partial, incomplete and particular.[116] The New Testament records only one occurrence of the word in Ac 4: 18. Here, its Greek adverbial form, *kath'holou*, is 'untheologically' used in combination with the negative particle *me* to denote a negation that is thorough, complete and total—"not at all."[117] It is significant to note that in this single biblical usage, it never refers to the church; a fact, Hans Küng argues, has been a contributory factor to the proliferation of myriads of interpretations

---

[115] Aylward Shorter, *African Christian Theology*, 152.

[116] Thomas Raush, *Towards a Truly Catholic Church: An Ecclesiology for the Third Millennium* (Collegeville, MN: Liturgical Press, 2005), 138. See also J. N. D. Kelly, "'Catholic and Apostolic' in the Early Centuries," *One in Christ* 7, no. 3 (1970): 275. It is in this sense that Greek philosophers used it while referring to such universal concepts, like goodness and beauty, in contrast to particular things that are beautiful or good, which merely embody such universals. See Sullivan, *The Church We Believe In*, 84. The usage of this word in this sense is also seen in the works of such early Christian writers, like Justin Martyr, who speaks of "catholic resurrection;" Tertullian—"the catholic goodness of God;" Irenaeus—"the four catholic winds." It is this sense of the word that has survived in the caption—Catholic Epistles—given to the epistles of Peter, Jude, etc, which were seen as addressed not to any particular community, but to the whole church. See Herbert Thurston, "Catholic," *The Catholic Encyclopedia* 3 (1980): 449.

[117] Avery Dulles, *The Catholicity of the Church* (Oxford: Clarendon, 1985), 13-14.

associated with the word among theologians down the centuries. Just like the classical Greek usage, Latin too employs the term *catholicus* or *universalis* when referring to 'the whole' or general.[118] Even though each age down the centuries has added its own touch to the understanding of the term, this original meaning of the word has not been lost in theological circles when applied to the church.

Historical Development

The church was first referred to as catholic (*ecclesia catholica*) during the patristic era. St Ignatius of Antioch was the first to employ it in his letter to the Smyrnaeans about the year 110 CE, where he writes, "Wherever the bishop is, there let the multitude [of the people] also be; even as, wherever Jesus Christ is, there is the Catholic Church."[119] These words of Ignatius have had a long history of interpretations. For some, like Francis Sullivan and Hans Küng, Ignatius most probably contrasts the bishop as the head of the local congregation to Christ who is the head of the whole, entire, universal (catholic) church.[120] For others, 'catholic,' as used in the saying, simply expresses the authenticity of the church where the bishop presides, since he represents Christ.[121]

Its second oldest appearance was in the *Martyrdom of Polycarp* (160 CE), where it was employed at four different places to qualify the church.[122] J. N. D. Kelly observes that in this text, catholicity bears the primary meaning of 'universal,' thus, referring to the universal church in contrast to local congregations. But he observes too that the use of the word to designate intensity of doctrine is also present.[123] Moreover,

---

[118]   Küng, *The Church*, 296. See also Walter Ong, "T. S. Eliot and Today's Ecumenism," *Religion and Literature* 21, no. 2 (1989): 5-6.

[119]   Ignatius of Antioch, *Smyrn.* 8:2. See Joseph Lightfoot, *The Apostolic Fathers* (Grand Rapids, MI: Baker, 1987), 84.

[120]   Francis Sullivan, *From Apostles to Bishops: The Development of Episcopacy in the Early Church* (New York: Paulist, 2001), 120; Sullivan, *The Church We Believe In*, 85.

[121]   See John O'Grady, *The Roman Catholic Church: Its Origin and Nature* (Mahwah, NJ: Paulist, 1997), 122.

[122]   *Martyrdom of Polycarp*, 41.

[123]   Kelly, "'Catholic and Apostolic,'" 277.

the fact that in this letter (17, 2), Polycarp was specifically saluted as "an apostolic and prophetic teacher, bishop of the catholic Church at Smyrna" shows the use of this word to denote some kind of oneness, uniqueness, thus, distinguishing their *true* church from any other heretical group or sect that might surge up within the community.[124] In fact, by the second half of the second century, in both East and West, catholicity had come to denote both "the one, true Church of Christ as opposed to all heretical and schismatic groups, and points to the universality of the former as the guarantee of its authenticity."[125] Clement of Alexandria and Tertullian both used the term to denote "the true Church."[126]

This sense of the word became more pronounced beginning from the third century, when the term unmistakably assumed a polemical dimension. Catholicity became more or less synonymous with orthodoxy. It became a term frequently used when referring to the 'orthodox' Church in contrast to those deemed dissidents.[127] This polemical usage became more obvious in the fourth century, owing to Christianity's acquisition of official status within the Roman Empire. Every Roman citizen was more or less compelled "to be a Christian, more particularly a 'Catholic' Christian. Paganism and heresy became political crimes, 'Catholicity' became orthodoxy, defended by law."[128] Consequently, "instead of the reality of catholicity, there develops the claim to catholicity."[129] It is this claim that subsequently crystallized into the insertion of the term "catholic" in the Nicaean creed (325).[130]

With Cyril of Jerusalem (in his *Catechetical Lectures*), one finds a much more detailed examination of the concept of catholicity. The catholicity of the church, Cyril argues, rests on five major reasons:

> It is called Catholic then because it is spread throughout the world, from end to end of the earth; also because it teaches universally

---

[124] Ibid., 278. See also Sullivan, *The Church We Believe In*, 85.
[125] Kelly, "'Catholic and Apostolic,'" 278.
[126] O'Grady, *The Roman Catholic Church*, 122.
[127] Küng, *The Church*, 298; Thurston, "Catholic," 449.
[128] Küng, *The Church*, 298.
[129] Ibid.
[130] Kelly, "'Catholic and Apostolic'," 278-279. In fact, in the baptismal creed of Egypt, the creed of Epiphanius, and that of Cyril of Jerusalem, the term "catholic" is also used. See O'Grady, *The Roman Catholic Church*, 123.

and completely all the doctrines . . . and because it subjects to right worship all [hu]mankind . . . further because it treats and heals universally every sort of sin . . . and it possesses in itself every conceivable virtue . . . [131]

St. Augustine and Optatus of Mileve also helped to develop the understanding of catholicity in terms of universal extension of the church, especially in their arguments against the Donatists, who claimed to be the only genuine church of Christ. The Donatists' claims, the two insisted, could not be sustained since they only enjoyed a very limited spread in Africa. For any church to be true, it must be the one church present everywhere (*ubique diffusa*).[132] Vincent of Lérins is another prominent figure within the period. His criteria for catholicity was: "that which is believed everywhere, always, and by all."[133]

Theologians of the middle Ages, like Aquinas, Bonaventure, and Albert the Great also made significant contributions in this regard. Generally, they tried to articulate and synthesize what the Fathers of the Church had already said. Catholicity of the church, they reasoned, meant not only its universal expansion in time and place but also its numerical superiority. [134]

The use of catholicity as a polemical tool once more witnessed a boost after the definitive severance of Eastern and Western churches in the fifteenth century following the Council of Florence, and the fissure of the Western church into different factions in the succeeding century. Each of the contending factions used it to prove its authenticity against

---

[131]   Cyril of Jerusalem, *Catecheses*, 18: 23. See Leo McCauley and Anthony Stephenson trans., *The Fathers of the Church: A New Translation*, vol. 64 (Washington, DC: The Catholic University of America, 1970), 132.

[132]   M. E. Williams, "Catholic," *New Catholic Encyclopedia* 3 (2003): 275; Kelly, "'Catholic and Apostolic'," 279.

[133]   Vincent of Lérins, *Commonitories*, I, 2. See Rudolph Morris trans., *The Fathers of the Church: A New Translation*, vol. 7 (Washington, DC: The Catholic University of America, 1949), 270.

[134]   See Dulles, *The Catholicity of the Church*, 14-15; Küng, *The Church*, 298; Paul Meagher, "Catholicity," in *Encyclopedic Dictionary of Religion*, ed. Paul Meagher and Thomas O'Brien (Philadelphia, PA: Sisters of St Joseph, 1979), 677. John of Ragusa also noted in one of his unpublished works the different aspects of the church which serve to prove its catholicity. See Gustav Thils and R. Kress, "Catholicity," *New Catholic Encyclopedia* 3 (2003): 293.

others. Generally, for Roman Catholicism of the period (especially as evident in Counter-Reformation and neo-Scholasticism),which was battling against the splitting of the western Christendom, a church that is truly catholic is the one that enjoys wider geographical coverage and is at the same time visibly united under a single supreme authority.[135] This claim was accompanied by visible expansion of the church and sending of missionaries to non-European territories.[136] Greek Orthodox theologians saw catholicity as complete adherence to the plenitude of faith transmitted by the apostolic Fathers and the great councils of fourth and fifth centuries.[137] Though Martin Luther, on his own part, replaced the word 'catholic' in the creed with 'Christian' (in German, *christlich*), early Lutheran theologians, like Philipp Melanchton and John Gerard, claimed the catholicity of their church based on their "adherence to the Scripture and to the common teaching of the Fathers of the ancient, undivided Church."[138] Anglicans too claimed to be catholic based on their ability to accommodate all shades of opinions and conflicting doctrines.[139] Practically, almost all Christian denominations defended their being catholic.[140] This exclusive, apologetic claims and counter-claims to catholicity continued among theologians until Vatican II came into the scene with its reforms.[141]

---

[135]   Dulles, *The Catholicity of the Church*, 15-16.

[136]   O'Grady, *The Roman Catholic Church*, 124.

[137]   Dulles, *The Catholicity of the Church*, 15.

[138]   Ibid., 16; Küng, *The Church*, 299.

[139]   Meagher, "Catholicity," 678.

[140]   It is important to remark that many authors today, while referring to the "Catholic Church" as a denomination within Christianity, often use the capital "C" and when using it in its adjectival form, they employ the small "c." This is also the case with the usage of "Catholicism" while referring to the Catholic Church and "catholicity" when reference is made to this special attribute which all Christians ascribe to the church of Christ. Thus, Sullivan argues, "The church that subsists in the Catholic Church is catholic, but catholicity is not found exclusively in Catholicism." See Sullivan, *The Church We Believe In*, 84.

[141]   See T. Liddy, "Catholic," in *Encyclopedic Dictionary of Religion*, ed. Paul Meagher and Thomas O'Brien (Philadelphia, PA: Sisters of St Joseph, 1979), 670.

Vatican II and Recent Theological Thinking on Catholicity

A remarkable shift in the way the official church understands its catholicity came with Vatican II. In the Dogmatic Constitution on the Church, *Lumen Gentium*, the council speaks of catholicity as a mark of the church of Christ, and not just of the (Roman) Catholic Church. Though it argues that this church of Christ subsists in the Catholic Church[142] (meaning, of course, that the fullness of catholicity can only be realised in communion with it[143]), it also admits that elements of sanctification and truth which belong to this church of Christ are not restricted to the visible frontiers of the Catholic Church.[144] This enabled it to avoid the mere age-long claim to catholicity and went further into a deeper theological thinking on it. This catholicity, it recognises, is inseparably linked with unity, and everyone, without exception is "called to be part of this catholic unity of the People of God."[145] It is actually by expanding this unity, the council notes, that it becomes perfected.[146] That is why it decries the divisions among Christians which it acknowledges is a major setback to the church's move towards reaching the "fullness of catholicity proper to her."[147]

The council recognises that this catholicity proper to the church is a gift from the Lord himself. The church is, therefore, called upon to work tirelessly to bring all together under the headship of Christ "in the unity of the Spirit."[148] This means that, though the church received it as a gift, catholicity cannot yet be said to be a finished or finally accomplished actuality for the church. It "is never lacking to the Church. But it is dynamic and expansive; it continually presses forward to a fullness and inclusiveness not yet attained."[149] That is why the church cannot be tired of working hard to ensure that it evangelises

---

[142] *LG* 8.
[143] Vatican Council II, Decree on Ecumenism, *Unitatis Redintegratio*, 21 November 1965, *AAS* 57 (1965): no. 4. Hereafter, *UR*.
[144] *LG* 8; *UR* 13.
[145] *LG* 13.
[146] *AG* 6.
[147] *UR* 4.
[148] *LG* 13.
[149] Dulles, *The Catholicity of the Church*, 24.

all cultures,[150] in as much as it also makes frantic effort in the field of ecumenism. No wonder, then, the council further acknowledges that the richness of variety experienced in the Eastern churches is also part of "the full catholic and apostolic character of the Church."[151] It is in the light of the above that Dulles remarks that the understanding of catholicity as put forward by the council "may therefore be called cautiously ecumenical rather than narrowly confessional;"[152] a catholicity that does not restrict itself to "a monotonous repetition of identical elements but rather as reconciled diversity."[153] It, therefore, becomes very evident that, once diversity or multiplicity is denied in any understanding of catholicity, it degenerates into mere uniformity and "false totality."[154]

As a matter of fact, theologians have tried to explain the catholicity of the church by reason of its relationship to Christ, to whom, Dulles argues, catholicity belongs in three senses: "by his very constitution as the Incarnate Word . . . [B]y reason of his primacy over all creatures, and . . . in so far as he is head of the Church."[155] The catholicity of the church is, therefore, made possible because Christ subsists in it in the fullness of its body "united with its head," by reason of which it contains in its fullness the necessary means of salvation.[156] In this sense, then, the church's catholicity becomes "a participation in Christ's own fullness."[157] This, Miroslav Volf refers to as the intensive understanding of catholicity, which, according to him, is its primary meaning.[158] But the church is also catholic by reason of its universal mission, by which it is commanded by Christ to spread

---

[150] In fact, *Ad Gentes* says of the church's missionary activity that "[i]t perfects her Catholic unity by expanding it." See *AG* 6.

[151] *UR* 17.

[152] Dulles, *The Catholicity of the Church*, 21.

[153] Avery Dulles, "The Church is Catholic," in *The Many Marks of the Church*, ed. Williams Madges and Michael Daley (New London, Conn: Twenty Third, 2006), 46.

[154] Miroslav Volf, *After Our Own Likeness: The Church as the Image of the Trinity* (Grand Rapids, MI: Eerdmans, 1998), 262.

[155] Dulles, *The Catholicity of the Church*, 33. Cf. Jn 1: 14, 16; Col 1: 15-17, 19; 2: 9-10; Eph 1: 10, 23; Rm 8: 19-23.

[156] *Catechism of the Catholic Church*, Revised ed. (London: Chapman, 1999), no. 830, 831. Hereafter, *CCC*.

[157] Dulles, *The Catholicity of the Church*, 41.

[158] Volf, *After Our Own Likeness*, 267.

the gospel to all nations (Mtt 20: 19-20).[159] Volf refers to this as the extensive understanding of catholicity, which is, however, inseparably bound up with the first:

> For there cannot be fullness of salvation for some without the fullness of salvation for all; nor can there be fullness of salvation for human beings without the fullness of salvation for the entirety of created reality. Because of its own dynamic, intensive catholicity pushes towards extensive catholicity.[160]

Actually, recent theological thinking on the church's catholicity have often revolved around these two senses.

INCULTURATION AT THE SERVICE OF THE CHURCH'S CATHOLICITY AND UNITY

I argue here that the more inculturation is encouraged and practiced, the more the church grows in its catholicity and more *realistically* united it becomes.[161] Indeed, without mincing words Schineller clearly states: "the process of inculturation is the only possible way to full catholicity."[162] Therefore, people "must see the changes brought about by authentic inculturation not as a loss or diminishment, but as growth in the true catholic nature of Christianity."[163] That understood, any attempt to scuttle genuine inculturation in the church, in some sense, jeopardises the church's catholicity.[164] Doubtless, John Paul II is well aware of this when he

---

[159] *CCC* 830, 831.

[160] Volf, *After Our Own Likeness*, 267.

[161] This does not, however, rule out the fact that the more diversity is fostered, the more there is also the likelihood of disunity in the church. But this refers to diversity without authentic inculturation and not "inculturated diversity." Cf. Peter Schineller, "Inculturation as the Pilgrimage to Catholicity," 105. See also Kjell Blükert, "The Church as Mosaic: Catholicity in a Pluralistic Context," *International Journal for the Study of the Christian Church* 6, no. 2 (2006): 175.

[162] Schineller, "Inculturation as the Pilgrimage to Catholicity," 100.

[163] Schineller, "Inculturation: Why So Slow?," 134.

[164] Aylward Shorter, "Inculturation: The Premise of Universality," in *A Universal Faith?: Peoples, Cultures, Religions, and the Christ*, ed. Catherine Cornille and

states: "The Church is also catholic because she is able to present in every human context the revealed truth . . . in such a way as to bring it into contact with the thoughts and just expectations of every individual and every people."[165] It is only when the church is truly inculturated in every place that it can be said to be 'present' to all nations and thus becomes a universally tangible sign and instrument of redemption.[166]

There is no way we can talk about the universality of the church when the concrete and particular manifestations of God's grace in specific cultural contexts are not appreciated by the church or are simply neglected. Karl Rahner argues about the ubiquitous presence of divine grace, conceived as divine free, undeserved and forgiving self-communication. He writes, "the very commonest of everyday things harbours the eternal marvel and silent mystery of God and his grace."[167] Indeed, Rahner, Thomas O'Meara writes, conceives the world history as "a history of grace."[168] Having acknowledged the reality of this presence, Tracy argues that it is only when this presence in the concrete particular places are focused upon and appreciated that the universality of the church can be rightly affirmed. This is true, he continues, because it serves as a clue that leads to the concrete whole, and there is no way the universal can be grasped if the particular is not. "For if God is love, if all is graced, then the surest route to that love and to that universality is here, now, in the really concrete, the 'each', the local and the particular joined to the universal."[169] He, thus, believes that realisation of true catholicity of the church can only be achieved when the faith is adequately expressed in many other

---

Valeer Neckebrouck (Louvain: Peeters, 1992), 1.

[165]   John Paul II, *SA* 18.

[166]   Cf. *LG* 1. See also Principe, *Faith, History and Cultures*, 43.

[167]   Karl Rahner, *Belief Today*, trans. Ray and Rosaleen Ockendon (New York: Sheed and Ward, 1967), 14. For more on Rahner's understanding of grace, see John Galvin, "The Invitation of Grace," in *A World of Grace: An Introduction to the Themes and Foundations of Karl Rahner's Theology*, ed. Leo O'Donovan (New York: Crossroad, 1981), 67. See also Quentin Quesnell, "Grace," in *The New Dictionary of Theology*, ed. Mary Collins Joseph Komonchak, Dermot Lane (Dublin: Gill & Macmillan, 1987), 446.

[168]   Thomas O'Meara, "A History of Grace," in *A World of Grace: An Introduction to the Themes and Foundations of Karl Rahner's Theology*, ed. Leo O'Donovan (New York: Crossroad, 1981), 77.

[169]   Tracy, "World Church," 30.

cultural forms apart from the European.[170] The above description is what Amalorpavadass calls "universality through particularity," in the process of inculturation.[171]

For the church's claim to catholicity to be real, it must ensure it is able to provide meaning to people of every locality in the uniqueness of their existence.[172] This is true particularly in the world of today where Christianity no longer enjoys unquestioned authority, nor are its truth and validity still accepted based on the ground that it belongs to an authentic ancient tradition. Instead, due to the present detraditionalisation and its effect on Christianity, its relevance and truthfulness has to be proved based on another ground. This ground, Jürgen Werbick maintains, is that it must be able to convince people "by showing that it belongs to the fundamental conditions of true humanity."[173] It must show that it is able to meet people at their deepest level and in their variety of circumstances to give answers to the fundamental questions of human existence amidst the confusions of life. This cannot be accomplished apart from proper encouragement, appreciation and permeation of people's culture, which "being the social group's set of solutions to life's problems, is perforce highly valued and protected . . . [and] lies at the very root of a society's identity, group consciousness, esprit de corps, and survival."[174] Unless Christian faith, in each cultural milieu of its expression, is able to offer meaning at this level, which moulds or patterns the lives of members of the society, it cannot hope for much relevance. That is why

---

[170]   Ibid., 31, 36. See also Geffré, "Double Belonging and the Originality," 28-29.

[171]   Duraisamy Amalorpavadass, "Church and Culture," in *The New Dictionary of Theology*, ed. Joseph Komonchak, Mary Collins and Dermot Lane (Dublin: Gill and Macmillan, 1990), 203.

[172]   In this connection, Leonardo Boff argues: "To be catholic is not to simply expand the ecclesiastical system but to live and witness to the same faith in Jesus Christ, saviour and liberator, within a particular culture." In other words, true catholicity is a function of authentic inculturation. See Leonardo Boff, *Church, Charism and Power: Liberation Theology and the Institutional Church*, trans. John Diercksmeier (London: SCM, 1985), 98.

[173]   Werbick, "Can the Universal Catechism Help," 51. He asserts that the truth can no longer be established by an appeal to the collective unconscious.

[174]   Louis Luzbetak, *The Church and Cultures: New Perspectives in Missiological Anthropology* (Maryknoll, NY: Orbis, 1988), 176-177.

inculturation is a necessary option.[175] By its insistence upon bringing *every* culture into integration with Christian faith, inculturation offers hope for proper legitimisation of the church's claim to catholicity. By its proper integration into the culture, Christian faith enters, as it were, in the words of John Walligo, the people's "blood and veins."[176] It is only when the church is able to achieve this that every people can meaningfully experience Christianity as its own and not as an intruder, because the meaning it offers is fundamental to its existence as a people. In other words, it engenders a welcome ground for authentic existence.

By offering meaning to people in their own distinctive circumstance, inculturation also recognises that each culture, tradition or nation has its own part to play in the universal mission of the church.[177] They are viewed as valuable partners in forging a global communion of the church. Thus, it is never a call for nationalism, cultural chauvinism or ethnocentrism.[178] Instead, it involves a process of exchange of special talents and gifts, in which, to attain "full catholicity," as John Paul II puts it, each part plays its own role, not in isolation, but "must remain open and alert to the other churches and traditions, and, at the same time, to universal and catholic communion."[179] According to Vatican II, in this exchange, each of the particular churches, at the service of the church's catholicity and unity, brings an increment to all the other parts and to the church as a whole.[180] Each has something not only to contribute, but also to learn from others in the match to fullness. In doing so, the universal church gets enriched. Thus, the richness experienced by the church in

---

[175] Cf. Pedro Arrupe, "Catechesis and Inculturation," *Teaching All Nations* 15, no. 1 (1978): 23.

[176] Walligo, "Making a Church That Is Truly African," 22.

[177] Cf. John Paul II, *SA* 19.

[178] Luzbetak defines ethnocentrism as "the universal tendency to regard the ways and values of one's own social group as the norm for everyone… [it] can vary in intensity, ranging from an understandable and forgivable minor excesses in group enthusiasm, loyalty, and pride to uncontrolled xenophobia, unpardonable cultural imperialism, and such utterly outrageous madness as Nazism." Luzbetak, *The Church and Cultures: New Perspectives*, 193. See Gelpi, *Inculturating North American Theology*, 2.

[179] John Paul II, *SA* 27.

[180] *LG* 13.

such diversity does not stand in opposition to its unity.[181] That is why Paul VI clearly states: "Legitimate attention to the individual Churches cannot fail to enrich the Church. Such attention is indispensable and urgent."[182]

This could be better articulated by what Schineller describes as "unity through complementarity," which he considers the best expression of what guides the relationship among the local churches and between them and the universal church, in the process of inculturation. He argues that it alone can actually "point to the full catholicity that is the result of the process of inculturation."[183] This forges a kind of unity where differences do not bring about discrimination. It corresponds with the vision of Vatican II as regards the relationship between the churches of the East and West even amidst the existing variety and differences.[184]

Furthermore, there is a paradox to the whole process. The more the local church, with its peculiarity, remains one with the universal church, the more it is able to properly make the faith 'incarnate' in its particular cultural milieu. Conversely, the farther the local church is from the universal church, the less its ability to effect a genuine inculturation of the faith in its own cultural context.[185] This is because, if it detaches from the universal, then it is deprived of the richness of the universal communion of the churches, which is very important for genuine inculturation. In such a situation, the church gradually dries up after suffering from what Paul VI describes as "withering isolationism." The second danger is that, being alone, it would be more difficult for it to withstand the manipulative forces of the world.[186]

---

[181] *CCC* 814.

[182] Paul VI, *EN* 63.

[183] Schineller, "Inculturation as the Pilgrimage to Catholicity," 100-101.

[184] Vatican Council II. "Decree on the Eastern Catholic Churches, *Orientalium Ecclesiarum*," 21 November 1964, in *Decrees of the Ecumenical Councils: Trent to Vatican II*, ed. Norman Tanner, vol. 2 (London: Sheed & Ward, 1990), no. 2. See also *CCC* 814.

[185] Paul VI, *EN* 64. See also Schreiter, *Constructing Local Theologies*, 21. Cf. Günther Gassmann, "The Church Is a Communion of Churches," in *The Catholicity of the Reformation*, ed. Carl Braaten and Robert Jenson (Grand Rapids, MI: Eerdmans, 1996), 93.

[186] Paul VI, *EN* 64.

Catholicity and unity of the church are functions of true inculturation. It is only through inculturation that the fullness of the means of salvation possessed by the church by reason of the presence of Christ in it can reach all people in the distinctiveness of their historical situations. This way, oneness of the church is forged which is not a result of monolithic uniformity, but rather of unity and communion in diversity.[187] Unless the church is prepared to allow the level of pluralism needed for genuine inculturation, its supposed unity is anything but real, for "real pluralism," Arrupe argues, "is the most profound unity."[188] Only then can we confidently echo the words of Adrian Hastings: "She is not the Church of the Latins or of the white man; not the Church of the West or the Church of the Middle Ages— she is the world Church of every age, the bride of the new Adam, the restorer of the *orbis terrarium*."[189]

HINDERANCES TO AUTHENTIC INCULTURATION

The process of inculturation experiences some hitches, which hinder its full implementation and progress. Some of these arise out of misconceptions regarding what inculturation entails. This has led to some questionable assumptions and illegitimate fears regarding the outcome of the process. These, no doubt, pose real challenges to the inculturation process. It is important that we examine some of these and put them in perspective.

First among these concerns the scope of inculturation within the culture. Some understand inculturation as involving the integration of Christian faith into culture, yet neglecting the issue of its encounter with other religious traditions, which may form part of the people's cultural heritage. One can hardly imagine, for instance, how African or Asian culture can be spoken of without taking into consideration

---

[187] The point we have actually been trying to put across in this regard has been summarised by Sullivan thus: "The more fully inculturated its particular churches are, the more catholic the universal church will be, provided that in the process the essential bonds of communion are not weakened." See Sullivan, *The Church We Believe In*, 93.

[188] Arrupe, "Catechesis and Inculturation," 23.

[189] Adrian Hastings, *One and Apostolic* (London: Darton, Longman & Todd, 1963), 191.

their religious heritage. Religion, no doubt, is an aspect of culture, and the two cannot be separated one from the other. In effect, for one to presume that there can be proper inculturation in the above-named cultures without at the same time taking into consideration the much-needed interaction with the religions forming part of the people's culture would be to miss the point.[190] There is no way inculturation can address the people's hopes and aspirations effectively when it is limited to the non-religious aspects of the culture. To do this, Amalorpavadass contends, amounts to unnecessary limitation and compartmentalisation of the scope of inculturation within the culture. This, he says, is not in line with the creative and redemptive plan of God, the incarnation of the Son of God and the universal mission of the church.[191]

There is yet this assumption that the practice of inculturation is a matter reserved for the younger churches outside the western world, especially for the so-called Third World countries. This assumption can be detected in the instruction, *Varietate Legitimae*, issued in 1994 by the Sacred Congregation for Divine Worship and the Discipline of the Sacraments. As regards liturgical reforms and the need to make the faith rooted in the different parts of the world, it states that, in those countries with long-standing Christian tradition, that is the West, "it is not so much a matter of inculturation, which assumes that there are pre-existent religious values and evangelizes them, but rather a matter of insisting on liturgical formation and finding the most suitable

---

[190] Geffré, "Double Belonging and the Originality," 96. Geffré considers as an illusion any attempt to imagine that there could be a possibility of complete and clear extrication of what is cultural from what is specifically religious, especially in Asian cultures where the Christian faith "is confronted with a complex whole in which the cultural and the religious elements are inextricably intertwined." Geffré, "Double Belonging and the Originality," 98. See also Phan, *Being Religious Interreligiously*, 116, 241-242. Michael Amaladoss, in line with the above observation, wonders (though his reasoning is open to question), why someone who accepts "Indianization" as a way of making Christianity incarnate in India could at the same time be opposed to "Hinduization." He sees such an attitude as a result of a "view of culture as merely secular," which "is not only inadequate, but unreal and untrue." Amaladoss, *Making All Things New*, 123.

[191] Amalorpavadass, "Church and Culture," 205. Cf. Paul VI, *EN* 67. Here, the pope urges that dialogue be fostered with the adherents of African Traditional Religion in order to promote assimilation of their good values that are in line with the demands of Christian faith.

means to reach spirits and hearts."[192] One wonders how such liturgical formation can touch the hearts and minds of people if it is not inculturated. The document seems to ignore the fact that inculturation represents that "most suitable means" of reaching "spirits and hearts."

This presumption that inculturation is an issue mainly for countries outside the West seems to have arisen because most of the initiatives and moves for proper inculturation are initiated from these places, chiefly as a result of their historical past: a history of evangelisation that never took their cultural riches into consideration. No doubt, one may be correct to say that the urgency of inculturation is more noticeably felt in these areas, but one is not being true to reality if he or she expects it to be an exclusive concern of theirs.[193] According to Cote, that the church is already present for a long time in the West and, therefore, seems already assimilated into the societal institutions does not mean that inculturation is already a *fait accompli* in the society:

> [T]he criteria for judging the degree of inculturation that is necessary in a given country cannot be predicated on the basis of how long the Christian faith has been present to that people or how well-ensconced the institutional church may be in the public life and social fabric of a given culture.[194]

Inculturation is, rather, an ongoing process, whereby the church always tries to make the faith meaningful, alive and relevant in any historical circumstance and period in its march toward the *eschaton*. John Paul II

---

[192] See Sacred Congregation for the Divine Worship and the Discipline of the Sacraments, *Varietates Legitimae*, 29 March 1994; available from http://www.adoremus.org/doc_inculturation.html; accessed 23 November, 2013.

[193] Cote, *Re-Visioning Mission*, 38-39. Such 'exclusive' view of inculturation may be seen in an article published by Hillman in 1987, by which he understands inculturation not as a universal phenomenon but rather as "the central and dynamic principle governing the Christian missionary outreach to peoples not yet evangelized, or among whom the church is not yet rooted firmly and indigenously." Hillman, "Inculturation," 510. Cf. Musini Kanyoro, "Called to One Hope: The Gospel in Diverse Cultures," in *Called to One Hope: The Gospel in Diverse Cultures*, ed. Christopher Duraisihngh (Geneva: WCC, 1998), 102.

[194] Cote, *Re-Visioning Mission*, 39.

sees it as "a must for Christians in all countries."[195] The present pontiff, Francis, sees it much the same way.[196] In any society, the way of expression of the faith cannot be static since culture itself is a dynamic phenomenon. It changes along with new challenges that confront the society. Words or modes of expression used today to express the faith may no longer serve the same purpose tomorrow, and, therefore need reformulation and reinterpretation. Since no society is stagnant, none should be reasonably excluded from the process of inculturation. New challenges to the faith are bound to arise from time to time, and they need to be adequately addressed through genuine inculturation.[197]

So, the issue is not whether or not a society needs inculturation but how it is to be carried out. Because of differences in culture and challenges confronting different societies, there is bound to be differences in the approach adopted by each society to inculturation. The methods employed in the pre-Christian societies may not be the same with those adopted for the often-referred-to-as post-Christian societies. Poupard identifies three different groups of societies, each calling for a different approach to inculturation. First are the traditional societies, as in Africa and Asia. Then, there are the communist and Islamic societies, which are examples of those whose cultural development and behaviour are respectively regulated by principles of wide-ranging sociopolitical ideology and Koranic law. The third group comprises those whose cultural development is directed by the sciento-technical rationality, which, due to its materialistic bent, runs counter to the Christian culture. According to him, there is no way these societies will require the same approach to inculturation.[198] The West needs inculturation just as the rural villages in Africa,

---

[195]   John Paul II, "Address to the First Meeting," no. 4. The European bishops have even pointed out that in the field of their pastoral activity, integrating the gospel with the culture remains the greatest challenge. See Poupard, *Church and Culture*, 31. See also Pedro Arrupe, "On Inculturation," 257.

[196]   See Francis, Apostolic Exhortation, *The Joy of the Gospel, Evangelii Gaudium*, 24 November 2013, nos. 68-75; available from http://www.vatican. va/holy_father/francesco/apost_exhortations/documents/papa-francesco_ esortazione-ap_20131124_evangelii-gaudium_en.html#Star_of_the_new_ evangelization; accessed 25 December 2013.

[197]   Werbick, "Can the Universal Catechism Help," 55. See also Fabella, "Inculturation," 105.

[198]   Poupard, *Church and Culture*, 30. See also John Paul II, *RM* 37.

Asia or South America do. The church has as its responsibility to creatively, reflectively, and critically engage the present day society in all regions of the world. Some theologians have even argued that Christianity's dialogue with the process of modernisation, which is more prominently at work in a very fast rate in western societies, is the most challenging aspect of inculturation today.[199]

Furthermore, the move towards authentic inculturation is often hindered by fears that it entails falsification of Christianity. According to Amarlorpavadass, what prompts such fears cannot be unconnected with the fact that some have identified Christianity with its western form. Therefore, any other expression apart from this form cannot but be a false one. Such people, thus, resist any attempt towards genuine inculturation. For them, it involves too much engagement with the cultural context, thereby risking Christianity's identity.[200] This is usually the case with fundamentalist theologians. Such people, more often than not, are over-preoccupied with maintaining the *status quo* and are uncomfortable with anything new or different.[201] Inculturation, indeed, needs some sort of courage on the part of theologians and Christians generally. Everyone must be ready to let go the monolithic

---

[199]   Schineller, "Ten Summary Statements," 55-56. In the article, Schineller demonstrates why and how modernisation could be considered as a culture, which strives not only to dominate and subdue all cultures, but also to sweep them up. With the ambiguities inherent in the modernisation process, he argues strongly that its dialogue with Christianity is much needed, and this can effectively be achieved through inculturation. For further reading, see Ibid. 57-83; Azevedo, *Inculturation and the Challenges of Modernity*, 30-56; Irarràzaval, *Inculturation*, 22-24; Joseph Tetlow, "The Inculturation of Catholicism in the United States," in *On Being Church in a Modern Society*, Inculturation: Working Papers on Living Faith and Cultures, ed. Ary Crollius (Rome: Pontifical Gregorian University Press, 1983), 42-45. See also John Paul II, "Apostolic Exhortation, On the Church in Africa, *Ecclesia in Africa*, 14 September 1995," *AAS* 88 (1996): no. 71.

[200]   Amalorpavadass, "Church and Culture," 204.

[201]   Arrupe, "Catechesis and Inculturation," 23. See also Walligo, "Making a Church That Is Truly African," 17; Schineller, "Inculturation: Why So Slow?," 133. Archbishop Marcel Lefebvre easily comes to mind as a strong opposition to inculturation from the hierarchy. He rejected the whole document of Vaticn II, especially those on liturgical reforms, and described the council, in the words of Yves Congar, as a manifestation "of neo-modernist and neo-Protestant tendencies." Yves Congar, *Challenge to the Church: The Case of Archbishop Lefebvre*, trans. Paul Inwood (London: Collins, 1977), 14.

expression of the faith. Everybody should have the courage to risk even making mistakes and learning from them in the process;[202] otherwise, no meaningful progress can be achieved.

Certainly, any genuine effort at inculturation of the local churches must have to contend with the issue of power. There is always this tension between the local churches and the Roman curia, which always cling to the Roman 'typical' nature of the church's structure and function. It is against this kind of attitude that Gregory Baum accuses the church of living out in reality some form of authoritarianism contrary to its own official teachings.[203] In the area of liturgical inculturation, Peter Phan asks whether a genuine inculturation can result when the centralised church hierarchy claims to dictate both the pace and the course of inculturation, even when it knows little about the cultures concerned. He wonders whether such is not a case of an imposition of Latin/Roman culture on others.[204] The situation is sometimes worsened by those local ecclesiastical authorities who are obsessed with the "*Roman locuta est*" mentality.[205] Decrying how such attitudes hinder genuine celebration of Christian faith in India, Subhash Anand notes:

---

[202] Okure, "Inculturation: Biblical/Theological Basis," 74-75. In the same vein, Amaladoss argues that inculturation is such a dynamic process that "experimentation becomes necessary, normal and accepted, with all the uncertainty and possibility of failure that go with experimentation. Not to risk is to condemn oneself to safe immobility and to become quickly irrelevant." Amaladoss, *Making All Things New*, 124.

[203] Gregory Baum, "The Church against Itself," *Concilium* 204 (1989): xiv-xv. See also Shorter, "Inculturation: The Premise," 10-11.

[204] Phan, *Being Religious Interreligiously*, 223. See also Shorter, "Inculturation: The Premise," 13, 17-18.

[205] This is the short form of "*Roman locuta est, causa finita est,*" meaning "Rome has spoken, the case is closed." This saying originated from amplification of Augustine's words during the period of the church's struggle with Pelagian heresy in the 5th century. Referring to Pope Innocent I's reply to the letter written to him by African bishops on this issue, in which Pelagius and Coelestius were excommunicated, Augustine writes: "You see, there have already been two councils about this matter, and their decisions sent to the Apostolic See; from there receipts have been sent back here. *The case is finished.*" Augustine, Serm. 131, par. 10, in Edmund Hill, trans., *The Works of Saint Augustine: A Translation for the 21st Century*, vol. 4 (New York: New City, 1992), 322. Emphasis is mine. See also S. J. McKenna, "Pelagius and Pelagianism," *New Catholic Encyclopedia* 11 (1967): 62.

Those outsiders who wish to preserve rites of foreign origin in India are guilty of ecclesiastical colonialism. Those in India who are comfortable with and cherish these rites, the remnants of an [sic] earlier processes of inculturation, seem to be suffering from some kind of theological fixation.[206]

The question of power can also present an obstacle or a challenge to authentic inculturation in a society where minority cultures are subdued by the dominant culture. One of the questions that often arise is how to manage the tension between them to be sure the minority are taken into consideration. In such situations, there are often questions related to the sharing of economic resources and political representation. How can one address these issues without doing disservice to authentic inculturation? Taking the Indian situation as a case in point, Phan questions whether inculturation has to do with dialogue with "the Hindu culture or that of the *Dalits*, who make up the larger membership of the church?"[207] In fact, the discussion could be continued to point out other potential areas of tension. But these, at least, have shown that inculturation is not after all an easy project, and as such cannot justifiably ignore these realities.

Also worthy of consideration as a hindrance to inculturation is the often-noticed obsession with preservation of one's culture. This is more prevalent among the so-called Third World countries. The desire to recover the integrity of their cultures, which they believe have been destroyed in the past through evangelisation and colonialism, easily leads to a certain kind cultural romanticism. As such, only the good side of the culture is emphasised without much attention to those areas that need some form of transformation.[208] In certain cases, the culture might be viewed as not having any negative element within it. This also goes with the assumption that a particular culture contains all that is needed to reach its perfection without any external influence.

---

[206]   Anand, "The Inculturation of the Eucharistic Liturgy," 273.

[207]   Phan, *Being Religious Interreligiously*, 223.

[208]   Schreiter, *Constructing Local Theologies*, 29. Beauchamp is of the view that it is not only the evil aspects of a culture that needs scrutiny. Even the good aspects do. According to him, this is the case because "the good part of a culture can resist God all the more powerfully since it is good." Beauchamp, "The Role of the Old Testament," 14.

To critique the culture may thus be viewed as lack of adequate appreciation of its merits. Thus, it becomes difficult to surrender the culture to the scrutinising effects of the gospel message. Inherent in such a romantic claim is the denial both of human sinfulness and the gains of cultural contact.[209] If such a trend is not checked, no meaningful progress can be achieved in the process of inculturation in those contexts.

Lastly, inculturation is often understood as restricted to some aspects of the life of the people or the church. In Nigeria, for instance, once one mentions inculturation, the minds of the people immediately go to the liturgy. This is not surprising because, in most of the dioceses, this is the only aspect of the church's life where inculturation seems to be taken seriously. Such restrictions undermine the immense possibilities open for inculturation. Inculturation should embrace the entire life of the church in a given society. It should also address the implications of the social, the political and the economic structures of a given society and how they affect the masses. In a word, inculturation aims at the total wellbeing of the people and how the faith can facilitate this. Unless it ultimately aims at concrete realisation in the lives of the people of the salvation wrought by Christ on the corss, it is not worth its salt.

The church must rise above these hindrances discussed above in order to achieve a meaningful impact on the people. What this entails can only be more effectively comprehended in the light of the mystery of the Incarnate Word.

CHRISTOCENTRICISM OF INCULTURATION PROBLEMATICS

Unless one really appreciates the mystery of God-made-man and all it entails, he may not adequately understand or come to grips with the demands of effective inculturation. To put it differently, the difficulties associated with inculturation and the skewed understanding of its implications can only give way for better clarity if one embraces the full implications of the mystery of incarnation, which is "the very centre of the reality from which we Christians live, of the reality which

---

[209]   Schreiter, *Constructing Local Theologies*, 29.

we believe."[210] Failure to acknowledge this and value it for what it is makes the whole inculturation endeavour empty and fruitless. That accounts for Vatican II's insistence on the need for the church to follow the path of incarnation in its relationship with different cultures. It is only through it, the council argues, can the church effectively appropriate "in a marvellous exchange, all the riches of the nations which have been given to Christ as an inheritance."[211] Incarnation, therefore, remains the theological foundation for inculturation.

It is precisely by being incarnate that Christ's actions acquire redemptive significance. Therefore, inculturation, which seeks to make the redemptive value of the faith felt in every cultural milieu, cannot pretend to ignore the significance of making the faith concretely embodied in these places. It is specifically in this divine action in history, which serves as the paradigm for the mission of the church, that is rooted the principle of inculturation.[212] Poupard makes it clear that all inculturation should be modelled after the incarnation. Inculturation, according to him, is primarily an "imitation of the incarnation of the Word."[213] The Bishops of Africa and Madagascar, at their 1974 Synod in Rome, unanimously rejected the theology of adaptation based on the fact that it was out of date and not based on the principle of incarnation. For them, the theology of incarnation remains the sole guiding principle for inculturating Christianity in the continent.[214]

Incarnation reveals to us, as depicted in John's Gospel, the mystery of the Word becoming flesh and living among us (cf. Jn 1: 14). By employing the Semitic sounding term 'flesh' as a synonym for 'man,' John implicitly highlights the radicality of Christ's humanity which this mystery inaugurates.[215] By incarnation, God takes flesh

---

[210]   Karl Rahner, *Theological Investigations*, vol. 4, trans. Kevin Smyth (London: Darton, Longman and Todd, 1966), 105.

[211]   *AG* 22.

[212]   Hillman, "Inculturation," 512.

[213]   Paul Poupard, *Church and Culture*, 21. See also John Paul II, *RM* 52. For Mariasusai Dhavamony, it is "the archetype of the inculturation of the Gospel." Mariasusai Dhavamony, *Christian Theology of Inculturation* (Roma: Editrice Pontificia Universita Gregoriana, 1997), 95.

[214]   "Statement of the Bishops of Africa," *AFER* 17, no. 1 (1975): 58.

[215]   Pénoukou, "Inculturation," 770. According to the World Council of Churches, the taking of flesh by the Word has very important implications for inculturation

in the womb of a woman of Nazareth. In this way, Christ, the second person of the Blessed Trinity, is revealed as one who "is the same perfect in divinity and perfect in humanity, the same *truly* God and *truly* man."[216] His humanity is thereby shown to be real and not just a disguise or external clothing covering his divinity. In him, humanity and divinity, though distinct, are hypostatically united. This intimate union entails that in the Incarnate Word, the human nature is neither absorbed nor compromised; the divine nature is neither lost nor demeaned.[217]

When this Christological principle is applied analogically to the relationship between faith and culture, it yields much challenging results. By the very fact of becoming flesh, the Incarnate Word could be said to be, in a sense, "the first to inculturate himself."[218] His incarnation starkly demonstrates that revelation cannot be said to take place apart from human culture. It constitutes the avenue for the expression and communication of divine revelation. Just as Christ assumes our human nature to offer us redemption, so should the faith 'assume' the different cultures in order to make God's message of salvation present to them.[219]

Moreover, just as by his incarnation Christ becomes *truly* man while remaining *fully* God, the church is seriously challenged to make the faith intimately united with different cultures of the world in such a way that the identity of neither the faith nor the culture in question is jeopardised or compromised by their union. It follows, therefore, that if in any way the identity of the faith is upheld to the

---

and its relationship to the Christian mission: "If proclamation sees mission in the perspective of the *Word* to be proclaimed, inculturation sees mission in the perspective of the *flesh*, or the concrete embodiment, which the Word assumes in a particular individual, community, institution or culture." See "Results of the SEDOS Seminar on the Future of Mission, Rome, March 1981," *SEDOS*, no. 7 (1981): 123.

[216] Council of Chalcedon (451), in *Decrees of the Ecumenical Councils: Nicaea I to Lateran V*, ed. Norman Tanner (London: Sheed & Ward, 1990), 86. Emphasis is mine. See also Gerald O'Collins, *Incarnation: New Century Theology* (London/New York: Continuum, 2002), 2.

[217] Council of Chalcedon (451), in *Decrees of the Ecumenical Councils*, 86. See also Council of Constantinople II (553), in *Decrees of the Ecumenical Councils: Nicaea I to Lateran V*, ed. Norman Tanner (London: Sheed & Ward, 1990), 117.

[218] Pénoukou, "Inculturation," 770.

[219] Dhavamony, *Christian Theology of Inculturation*, 93, 95.

detriment or diminution of the cultural identity of the people, authentic inculturation does not happen. Shreiter is clear on this when he says: "Without a culture having its own integrity and dignity, as well as the participation of its people, there can be no inculturation of the faith."[220] What has happened instead is, to say the least, an act of injustice or violence. The same is also true when the culture is absolutised to the detriment of the identity of the faith. What this entails is that, in the light of incarnation, there should be no pretence on the part of the church to be either "more divine" or "less human," or vice versa, than the Incarnate Word himself.[221]

Furthermore, by becoming incarnate, God, in the person of Jesus Christ, was subjected to human weaknesses, though without sin. Jesus was a Jew, a Nazarene. In him, "God became *this man in this people.*"[222] Just like every other Jew, he lived his life within the limitations offered by the Jewish cultural milieu. He walked the streets of Palestine and got enculturated into the society beginning from his family and moving to the wider Jewish community. Just like any other devout Jew, he was groomed in the understanding of the Torah, frequented the synagogue (Lk 4:16) and prayed in the Temple (Lk 2:41-51). In fact, as one would expect, the Jewish culture shaped his understanding of reality and his ability to cope with the challenges it offers. In a word, the first-century Palestianian culture helped to mould his identity. It may not have been otherwise. He became vulnerable and subject to human dependency and limitations. He even went to the extreme of that humanity by his suffering and 'shameful' death (cf. Phil 2:6-8).[223] In the light of this, the church is summoned to humbly acknowledge and accept, through inculturation, the limitations

---

[220] Robert Schreiter, "Inculturation or Identification," 21.

[221] Hillman, "Inculturation," 512.

[222] Beauchamp, "The Role of the Old Testament," 3.

[223] Cf. O'Collins, *Incarnation: New Century Theology*, 60; Gerald O'Collins, "The Incarnation: The Critical Issues," in *The Incarnation: An Interdisciplinary Symposium on the Incarnation of the Son of God*, ed. Stephen Davis, Daniel Kendall and Gerald O'Collins (Oxford, NY: Oxford University Press, 2002), 6; Rahner, *Theological Investigations*, 110. Rahner sees in incarnation an instance where the human reality is perfectly and fully actualised. According to him, this entails that one realises oneself to the extent one is prepared to offer oneself up. This paradox has strong implication for the church in the process of actualising its mission in the world. As such, the more it spends itself for others in the

imposed on it by its historicity as far as its truth claims are concerned.
Hillman puts it well:

> Against a recurring monophysite tendency to "divinize" the
> church by regarding it in an overly spiritualized and ahistorical
> manner that minimizes or even denies the ephemeral nature of the
> historically conditioned nature of the limited elements in its life,
> the incarnation approach takes seriously the implications of the
> human finitude, flesh, history, creativity, temporality, vulnerability
> and fallibility.[224]

It is only through this can the faith permeate each cultural milieu and
be very effectively expressed and lived even within the limitations
offered by these cultures. It is by the church's humble identification
with each situation, together with its problems and weaknesses, can
Christian faith offer healing to the culture, just like Christ who, by
being fully one with us, is able to effect our healing from within.[225]
Since God, by manifesting himself through the incarnation, no longer
seems distantly separated from humanity, the church is challenged
to come nearer to the people, thereby bringing the faith very close to
them through the process of inculturation. Unless the faith is allowed
to follow this path in its encounter with culture, all efforts will always
end up with superficial adaptation, or imposition.

What is more, by assuming an ordinary and particular existence
in the world, Christ charges us not to neglect the particular and the
concrete and all it entails in the work of evangelisation. Instead, we
should be concerned with "each natural, human, or spiritual reality
where we happen to be."[226] Gerald O'Collins brings out very clearly
the implications of incarnation with regard to the particular when he
writes:

> By assuming a particular, and in many ways a very ordinary, human
> existence, the eternal Word sheds light on the significance and

---

process of making the gospel a living reality for the people, the more its own
reality is actualised.

[224] Hillman, "Inculturation," 512.
[225] Cf. O'Collins, *"The Incarnation: The Critical Issues,"* 26.
[226] Irarràzaval, *Inculturation*, 30.

lasting importance of the particular and often unspectacular life we all live. We receive our eternal salvation not by escaping from the specifics of our embodied and everyday existence but by working through them.[227]

Jesus shows us the need to appraise the particularities of our existences and never ignore using them as avenues for gaining the salvation to which the work of the church is directed. From this, one should then be theologically confident in utilising the opportunities offered by the particularity of cultures, no matter how challenging or 'degrading' one may think they are, in spreading the good news. It is in this sense that Paul speaks of becoming all things to all people so that they might be saved (I Cor 9: 22). The Fathers of Vatican II succinctly articulates it this way:

> The Church, so that it may be able to offer to all the mystery of salvation and the life brought by God, ought to insert itself into all these groups with the same thrust with which Christ himself, by his incarnation, bound himself to the particular social and cultural conditions of the people among whom he lived.[228]

According to Gallagher, this important realisation shows that it is not only cultures that need Christ. In certain sense too, Christ needs cultures so as to carry on and bring to completion the process of making himself 'incarnate' in the different historical contexts.[229] It is clear then that inculturation ensures that the theological implications of incarnation with respect to the particular is concretely realised.

It is important to observe that Jesus, though he was nurtured by the Jewish culture, nevertheless critiqued the culture of his day. He was never a mere conformist. He criticised the legalistic tendencies in Jewish piety and condemned the showy attitude of the Pharisees (Mt 23: 1-36). He also criticised the disregard shown to the poor and the less-privileged in the society, and found in them comfortable companions. When the Temple was turned into a market place, he zealously fought for its sanctity by driving the traders away and

---

[227] O'Collins, "The Incarnation: The Critical Issues," 26.

[228] *AG* 10.

[229] Gallagher, *Clashing Symbols*, 122.

upturning the money changers' tables (Mk 11: 15-17). So many other biblical passages show such critical disposition of his to the Jewish culture. This is the kind of critique expected in any society where a genuine inculturation takes place.[230] Its importance has been highlighted by Paul VI when he remarks that, in its evangelisation, the church should not only be concerned with the spreading of good news to wider areas "but also of affecting and as it were upsetting, through the power of the Gospel, [hu]mankind's criteria of judgment, determining values, points of interest, lines of thought, sources of inspiration and models of life that contrasts with the word of God and the salvific design."[231]

This process remains a continuous one. Incarnation is never an event that just happened and ended at annunciation or an event which is, as it were, a prelude to Christ's redeeming acts. On the contrary, incarnation is a reality that persists even after Christ's birth, and spans through his life, passion, death and resurrection. Christ continues to assume the human nature even in his risen glorified state. In other words, after his transformation in glory, he still remains the second person of the Blessed Trinity in whom, by virtue of the hypostatic union, the human and the divine natures exist without any diminution.[232] Christian faith cannot bring hope to the troubled humanity of today unless it is *continuously* made 'incarnate' in the different cultures. In this connection, Cote argues: "If incarnation is to serve as the theological basis for inculturation, it is important to view it as a *continuing* reality and not merely as the initial act whereby the Word of God assumed a human nature."[233] Just as Christ's incarnation is a permanent reality, so also should the integration of the faith into

---

[230] See Lamin Sanneh, *Translating the Message: The Missionary Impact on Culture* (Maryknoll, NY: Orbis, 1989), 32. Here, Sanneh points out that a particular people's encounter with Christ through their specific cultural context will of necessity be accompanied with some challenges. It will definitely "bring the sword of discernment" into the people's lives and "place in a redeeming light the sin of human self-sufficiency."

[231] Paul VI, *EN* 19.

[232] O'Collins, "The Incarnation: The Critical Issues," 6. See also Gerald O'Collins, *Christology: A Biblical, Historical, and Systematic Study of Jesus* (Oxford, NY: Oxford University Press, 1995), 105. See also Cote, *Re-Visioning Mission*, 77-79.

[233] Cote, *Re-Visioning Mission*, 75.

cultures and all it entails never be a once-for-all finished event. The church should rather make every effort to ensure that "the 'word' that is the Christian faith . . . [is] 'made flesh' over and over again in the life of every Christian and in the culture of every time and place."[234] It is only this way can the redemption won for humanity by Christ through the mystery of his incarnation, death, and resurrection be continuously realised in concrete terms in each cultural milieu and in individual lives of the faithful. It is by this continuous integration of the faith into the culture can the culture continuously die and rise, and thus be purified or transformed alongside the faith.[235]

From the foregoing, one can see that no genuine inculturation is possible unless it is founded on the Christ event. The Incarnate Word remains the ultimate paradigm of any genuine inculturation. During his earthly life in Palestine, he was misunderstood. He was persecuted and killed. Even after his resurrection, his message continues to be an object of controversy. Proper conception of his divinity and humanity continues till date to be an object of debate among theologians and non-theologians. We need not expect that this message will ever be fully understood and welcomed by everyone.[236] So, as the church tries to integrate its faith in Christ into the different cultures in our today's society, tensions will always come up. The dialectical conflict with cultures is sure to arise. It can never be a finished struggle. From the foregoing, one can comfortably agree with Pénoukou that "the problematics of inculturation," in every sense of it, is "essentially christocentric."[237] Inculturation succeeds or fails to the extent the church takes this seriously.

---

[234]   Groome, "Inculturation," 128.

[235]   See Dhavamony, *Christian Theology of Inculturation*, 94, 96.

[236]   Metz has, in fact, argued that, since Christians carry the memory of the suffering, death, and resurrection of Jesus Christ, which is not only revolutionary but also risky, their faith in him (which involves engagement with the context) cannot exist without tension and conflict. For this, see Boeve, *God Interrupts History*, 203.

[237]   Pénoukou, "Inculturation," 770.

CONCLUSION

It has been shown in the chapter how inculturation adequately responds to the felt need for Christian faith to address the peculiar needs and aspirations of each people in their respective cultural environments. With its emphasis on the rooting of the faith in people's cultures, it acknowledges that, for any theology to address well the issues relevant to any particular people, it must be elicited from the people and not merely imposed from outside. It is only this that will guarantee a better understanding of the demands of the faith in such a way that its practise becomes more authentic and not alienating to the Christians concerned.

Inculturation recognises that the faith encounters a culture not necessarily to introduce God where he never existed, but to make the word of God, which has been in the culture blossom all the more. In its encounter with culture, the faith never ceases to perform a critical function with regard to the culture, which, being a human reality, is never perfect. It tries to purify it of its disvalues even as it promotes the values in the culture. Just as it purifies the culture, it also undergoes its own transformation and growth. That is why the relationship between the two has been described as symbiotic and reciprocal. It is a relationship governed by mutual enrichment and dialogue, where the integrity of both are preserved.

I have demonstrated how any genuine inculturation is theologically founded on the Incarnate Word. The church's effort at inculturation is a continuation of God's identification with humanity and its redemption in the person of Christ. Only with this mystery as the base can one appreciate better the practise of inculturation, its demands and challenges, as well as its implications in the context of today's society. It is incumbent on Christians in all nations to promote inculturation of Christianity, because, being an ongoing process, it can never be said to be a *fait accompli* in any society.

Indeed, my efforts in this chapter and in the preceding ones have been devoted to examining some of the challenges that should be confronted by the church if the faith is to be genuinely lived within the different cultures of the world. In the chapter that follows, I shall specifically focus on yet another challenge that needs serious consideration in the process of inculturation in our today's society—that of religious syncretism; a challenge that is more obvious in those cultures where one religion or another has been operative for centuries before the advent of Christianity, and is still operative even today. My task is not just limited to highlighting the issues involved. I shall also try as much as possible to address them properly.

4

INCULTURATION AND CHALLENGES OF RELIGIOUS SYNCRETISM

INTRODUCTION

Vatican II is undoubtedly in favour of maximising the employment of the wisdom, philosophy and, in fact, the entire cultural riches of each people in the course of the church's evangelising mission. This much should have been clear from the preceding chapters. Nevertheless, while advocating for this, the council never fails to identify some inherent danger in the process: that of syncretism. Hence, the caution that every care be taken to avoid occasions that might favour its occurrence.[1] By this, it sends a message to the local churches that, in the process of propagation of Christian faith, the incorporation or utilisation of elements from the diverse cultures of the world in which they live does have some limits beyond which it becomes unacceptable. It also reinforces the continued concern of the church to uphold the uniqueness of Christian faith even as it encounters different

---

[1]   Vatican Council II, Decree on the Missionary Activity of the Church, *Ad Gentes*, 18 November 1965, in *Decrees of the Ecumenical Councils: Trent to Vatican II*, ed. Norman Tanner, vol. 2 (London: Sheed & Ward, 1990), no. 22. Hereafter, *AG*.

cultures and religions. Paul VI also warned against this in the years following the council.[2]

When one takes a look at the way the council employs the word, syncretism, it seems to suggest that the meaning conveyed by it is self-evident. But this is far from reality given the raging controversy among scholars concerning its referent. Some questions that needed to be addressed seem to have been glossed over by the council. These include: To what extent can the faith interact with a culture or a religious tradition within the culture without being considered religiously syncretic? Or, simply put, how can religious syncretism be concretely recognised in the process of inculturation?

Searching for answers to these questions today appears more challenging than ever, and very imperative too, given the fact that scholars are very much divided, especially in recent years, on the meaning of the term, even as the rate of contacts between different cultures and religions are on the increase. There is no general consensus on the process of religious contact that can be labelled syncretic. It is even improbable that there could ever be, since each approach is merely perspectival. Anthropologists, historians of religion, philosophers and theologians have their own sides of the story. Even among theologians, the debate has continued unabated. The contention has reached such a stage that some have variously described syncretism as a term that is very "amorphous,"[3] "problematic,"[4] "tricky,"[5] or "too ambiguous, open, and subjective."[6] Some have even suggested that it be totally dropped in scholarly discussions. For Peter Schineller, the word has reached

---

[2]   Paul VI, "Apostolic Exhortation, On Evangelization, *Evangelii Nuntiandi*, 8 December 1975," *AAS* 68 (1976): no. 65. Hereafter, *EN*.

[3]   Robert Schreiter, *Constructing Local Theologies* (Maryknoll, NY: Orbis, 1985), 146.

[4]   André Droogers and Sidney Greenfield, "Recovering and Reconstructing Syncretism" in *Reinventing Religions: Syncretism and Transformation in Africa and the Americas*, ed. Sidney Greenfield and André Droogers (Lanham, MD: Rowman & Littlefield, 2001), 27.

[5]   André Droogers, "Syncretism: The Problem of Definition, the Definition of the Problem," in *Dialogue and Syncretism: An Interdisciplinary Approach*, ed. Jerald Gort *et al.* (Grand Rapids, MI: Eerdmans, 1989), 7.

[6]   Peter Schineller, "Inculturation or Syncretism: What is the Real Issue?," *International Bulletin of Missionary Research* 16, no. 2 (1992): 52.

such a point that it has become irremediable.[7] The Swedish theologian, Helmer Ringgren, arrived at a similar conclusion in his study of the syncretic religions of the western classical antiquity. For him, to look for a precise definition of the word is uncalled for because it is not helpful as a research tool.[8]

Despite these views, there are also a great majority of scholars who argue for its retention and continued usage. The Dutch anthropologist, André Droogers, discountenanced the proposal made by some scholars to drop the term, describing it as simply unrealistic. He makes the point that "the term is so widely used that even a scholarly consensus to do away with it would not lead to a general moratorium on its use," since the phenomenon it refers to, and which arises from religious contacts is ever on the increase in today's society.[9] In theological discussions too, Robert Schreiter and Wolfhart Pannenberg, among others, have argued strongly against the proponents of its abandonment. Schreiter maintains that, to succumb to the temptation of dropping such a term with a long history "neither clears the ground for new thinking nor advances us into the thicket of contemporary theological discussion."[10] He advances three major reasons why he thinks the term needs to be kept. First, if some missiologists of the liberal type who argue for abandoning it actually do so, then, the use of it solely by the conservative ones might be a stumbling block to discussions on inculturation. Moreover, communication among missiologists will be seriously hampered. Second, to replace it with another term—say, inculturation—does not solve any problem either. Such a substitution, he argues, cannot account for some aspects of the tension between the development of theology and the dynamism of culture, which syncretism captures very vividly. Third, the word is still very relevant today, especially as we are in the age of immense and varied intercultural interactions, communications and exchange, with its implications for Christian faith

---

7   Schineller, "Inculturation or Syncretism," 50, 52.

8   Helmer Ringgren, "The Problems of Syncretism," in *Syncretism*, ed. Sven Hartman (Stockholm: Almqvist & Wiksell, 1969), 7-14.

9   Droogers, "Syncretism: The Problem of Definition," 7-8.

10   Robert Schreiter, "Defining Syncretism: An Interim Report," *International Bulletin of Missionary Research* 17, no. 2 (1993): 50.

and theology.[11] Wolfhart Pannenberg maintains that what is needed in order to deal effectively with the problems of meaning associated with syncretism is its re-evaluation.[12]

There are two major camps among those who argue for the retention of the term: those who understand it more descriptively or phenomenologically and those who use it in a more evaluative and derogatory sense. Theologians constitute the chunk of those belonging to the second group. Scholars in the first group are chiefly from the history of religions, philosophy and anthropology, who see their main task as 'liberating' the word from its evaluative, negative usage. Without completely overlooking the insights of those who argue for the abandonment of the term, it is my intention in this chapter to dialogue mostly with the scholars who believe in working with it. Part of the effort here is to critique the attempts made by some of the champions of the 'liberation' endeavour. The major point is that their efforts have not yielded much fruits in the direction desired by them because, while some of their attempts leave the word with too general a meaning, some others remain trapped in a 'crypto-evaluative tradition,' such that they end up leaving the word not much less evaluative and negative as it is within theology.

Having done that, I will try to work out a theological understanding of religious syncretism that will be of help in appreciating inculturation process. By so doing, the significance of its evaluative, theological usage will be demonstrated. I will also discuss the challenges that syncretism theologically understood poses to Christian faith, how it is unavoidable and indeed necessary in certain instances and how it also poses some obstacles to the Christian evangelisation in some others. Equally to be argued is how such obstacles can be effectively surmounted in order to give room for genuine inculturation of the faith.

---

[11]   Ibid., 50-51.

[12]   Wolfhart Pannenberg, *Basic Questions in Theology*, trans. George Kehm, vol. 2 (London: SCM, 1971), 86.

SYNCRETISM: CONTROVERSIAL AND CONTESTED

The problems associated with understanding, or rather, defining syncretism today has much to do with the complexity of its history and its conflicting etymological derivations.[13] This history cannot be reasonably bypassed if one really wants to come to grips with its meaning. An investigation into its history does reveal that it is not just a theological, but also a phenomenological problem.[14] James Moffat refers to it as a term with "a very curious record."[15] Depicting a reality, the process of which is not merely manifest within one religion but also between two or even more, it has aroused the interest of many. Thus, there have been various shifts in its meaning, just as the reality to which it refers is variously conceived by different people at different periods in history and from different scholarly perspectives. These will be examined below.

ETYMOLOGY AND HISTORY: A SYNOPSIS

The term was first used by the Greek historian, Plutarch (50 AD-120 AD), in his *Moralia*, in the chapter dealing with brotherly love, *De Fraterno amore*. In this essay, he refers to the practice of Cretans, who, despite their being often at war with one another, temporarily came together and became united when faced by an external enemy. This practice, he maintains, is referred to as syncretism (*synkretismos* in Greek). Apart from its usage by Plutarch, it did not make its appearance in any other ancient classical writing.[16] It is derived from a combination of two Greek words: the prefix, *syn* (with, together, along with), and *kretoi* (the Cretans), or *kretismos* (the Cretan behaviour).[17]

---

[13]   Anita Leopold and Jeppe Jensen, ed., *Syncretism in Religion: A Reader* (New York: Routledge, 2004), 14.

[14]   Hendrik Kraemer, *Religion and the Christian Faith* (London: Lutterworth, 1956), 392.

[15]   James Moffat, "Syncretism," *The Encyclopaedia of Religion and Ethics* 12 (1994), 155.

[16]   Moffat, "Syncretism," 155; Kraemer, *Religion and the Christian Faith*, 393.

[17]   Petra Pakkanen, *Interpreting Early Hellenistic Religions: A Study Based on the Mystery Cult of Demeter and the Cult of Isis*, Papers and Monographs of the Finnish Institute at Athens (Athens: D. Layias and E. Souvatzidakis, 1996), 86.

So, Plutarch used it to admonish his audience on the need to imitate the Cretan way of life: forming a common alliance against an external aggressor. The original referent of the word could, therefore, be said to be political, designating a welcome response of human beings to the "instinct of self-defence."[18] Instructive is the fact that in this sense it bears no negative connotation, since it merely describes a political "union of opposites."[19] Hence, the remark of Charles Stewart and Rosalind Shaw: "It is also noteworthy that the concept of syncretism begins its history with positive connotations, referring to a strategically practical, morally justified form of political allegiance—to a form of 'brotherly love.'"[20]

The term was never used again after Plutarch until fourteen centuries later, during the period of Renaissance, when it was once again employed by Erasmus of Rotterdam (1469-1536). Erasmus used it in a sense similar to that of Plutarch. He metaphorically applied it to the reconciliation, which he was advocating for, of Greek philosophy and what he termed *philosophia Christi*,[21] as well as scholars on both sides. This reconciliation (*syncretezein*), he thought, was the "good science" (*bonae litterae*) that would enable the scholars join forces to engage the barbarians.[22] In the 15th century philosophy, amidst the controversy and rivalry between Platonists and Aristotelians, some scholars who defended the harmonisation of the two systems of thought, like Cardinal Bessarion, were termed syncretists.[23]

---

[18]   Moffat, "Syncretism," 155.

[19]   Alan Tippett, "Christopaganism or Indigenous Christianity," in *Christopaganism or Indigenous Christianity?*, ed. Tetsunao Yamamori and Charles Taber (South Pasadena, CA: William Carey Library, 1975), 32.

[20]   Charles Stewart and Rosalind Shaw, ed., *Syncretism/Anti-syncretism: The Politics of Religious Synthesis* (London: Routledge, 1994), 3.

[21]   This is a philosophy that invites people to imitate Christ in their personal lives.

[22]   Leopold and Jensen, *Syncretism in Religion*, 15; Moffat, "Syncretism," 155. Erasmus identifies three classes of barbarians: those who brought to ruin the ancient civilisations; the illiterates who teach with ignorance thus making their listeners remain ignorant; those who reject good old ways and replace them with worthless new ones. See Werner Shwarz, *Principles and Problems of Biblical Translation: Some Reformation Controversies and Their Background* (Cambridge: Cambridge University Press, 1970), 97.

[23]   Moffat, "Syncretism," 155. Though his efforts failed, Bessarion tried to find a meeting point between Platonism and Aristotelianism in some kind of "Christian Neo-Platonic spirit." Kraemer, *Religion and the Christian Faith*, 393.

It was in the 17th century that syncretism became a very familiar term among theologians. During this period in Europe, some Protestant theologians, with the pioneering effort of the Lutheran theologian, George Calixtus (1586-1656), advocated for harmonisation of the diverse theological positions of Catholicism with those of different Protestant denominations. Calixtus claimed to have found in Aristotelian philosophy a rational justification for Christianity, which would eventually help to unite all Christians together. Some theologians supported such a move while others were in opposition. The debate focused on doctrinal, sacramental or liturgical unification, or otherwise, of all Christians.[24] Calixtus and his fellow supporters were disparagingly labelled syncretists by their opponents who bitterly accused them of canvassing for illegitimate mixing and muddling of conflicting religious elements. Thus, syncretism fully assumed a negative connotation, which it has retained today, especially among theologians. The circumstances surrounding the debate further resulted in the practice of etymologically associating syncretism with the Greek word, *synkerannumi*, meaning to blend or to artificially combine unrelated and incompatible ideas.[25] Describing the situation at the time, Moffat notes:

> But 'syncretism' of this kind was generally branded as a betrayal of principles or as an attempt to secure unity at the expense of truth. The 'syncretistic controversy' was a quarrel over peace, and such quarrels are not the least bitter upon earth. What the 'syncretists', in Plutarch's sense of the term called a harmony, their opponents called a 'hybrid'.[26]

From mid-nineteenth century, it became a common term in the field of history of religions. The first use of the term in this field

---

[24]   Calvinists favoured the proposal but the orthodox Lutherans and the Catholic hierarchy never welcomed it. See Charles Stewart, "Syncretism and Its Synonyms," *Diacritics* 29, no. 3 (1999): 46; Moffat, "Syncretism," 155; Leopold and Jensen *Syncretism in Religion*, 15; Charles Stewart and Rosalind Shaw, ed. *Syncretism/Anti-syncretism*, 4.

[25]   Kraemer, *Religion and the Christian Faith*, 393-394. See also Luther Martin, *Hellenistic Religions: An Introduction* (New York: Oxford University Press, 1987), 10.

[26]   Moffat, "Syncretism," 155.

probably dates back to 1853, in an anonymous review in *Fraser's Magazine for Town and Country* published in London. During the period, the term was generally used pejoratively as a mishmash of religious elements of diverse origins.[27] It was in this sense that scholars eventually applied it in their study of the ancient Roman and Hellenistic religions. The religious atmosphere in which these religions existed was described as disorderly and confused.[28] Syncretism came to be used for the mixing of different religions and combination of various deities that was ripe during the period. It is on account of this that the ancient Roman and Hellenistic period came to be considered as "the age of syncretism *par excellence*."[29] Such a practice was seen as common during the period because, for the people, as Kraemer notes, "all religions and cults, at least in principle, were acknowledged as interchangeable".[30]

As scholarly interests got more directed towards the study of religious mixtures, Christianity soon found itself being also accused of syncretism. A prominent scholar of the German *Religionsgeschichtliche Schule*, Herman Gunkel, who understands syncretism in religion as incorporation of external ideas by any religion, argues that early Christianity was also nothing less than syncretic just as the Hellenistic religions, since it cannot claim to be immune from influences from any other religion.[31]

---

[27] Carsten Colpe, "Syncretism," in *Encyclopedia of Religion* 14 (1987): 218-219.

[28] Stewart and Shaw, *Syncretism/Anti-syncretism*, 4. We recall that the term, Hellenism, was coined by the historian, Johann Gustav Droysen, in his work: *Geschichte des Hellenismus*, first published in 1836. Droysen describes Hellenistic period as roughly covering the period from 300BC to 300AD. See Luther Martin, *Syncretism, Historicism, and Cognition: A Response to Michael Pye*, in *Syncretism in Religion: A Reader*, ed. Anita Leopold and Jeppe Jensen (New York: Routledge, 2005), 286.

[29] Gresham Machen, *The Origin of Paul's Religion* (New York: Macmillan, 1925), 222. The following sources could be consulted to understand in greater detail how the Hellenistic religions functioned in the *polis* within this period: William Allan, *"Religious Syncretism: The New Gods of Greek Tragedy,"* Harvard Studies in Classical Philology 102 (2004): 113-155; Frederick Grant, *Hellenistic Religions: The Age of Syncretism* (New York: Liberal Arts, 1953); Rowland Nash, *Christianity and the Hellenistic World* (Grand Rapids, MI: Zondervan, 1984).

[30] Kraemer, *Religion and the Christian Faith*, 394.

[31] Ibid.

In the first quarter of the twentieth century, syncretism found its way into anthropological circles. Melville Herskovits pioneered this. He used it in his study of acculturation process between cultures to express the phenomenon of mixing of cultural traits and their subsequent reinterpretation.[32] Since then the discussion on the exact meaning of syncretism has been on. As regards the debate within anthropology, André Droogers and Sidney Greenfield have lamented that, had Herskovits not introduced the term into anthropology from other disciplines, but used another term coined from within anthropology, perhaps he might have spared anthropologists the controversy and the confusion that have trailed this word in today's academic research.[33]

LESS EVALUATIVE CONSIDERATION OF SYNCRETISM

Many believe that a better account of syncretism can only be given when it is studied from the phenomenological point of view. The description of syncretism from these scholars is often directed towards providing what they consider as positive and objective view of it. To support their claim to objectivity, they see syncretism merely as having to do with the dynamics of religions, and disavow its value-laden and negative usage by many theologians.

Gerardus van der Leeuw, a Dutch historian and philosopher of religion, is considered by some as the first to have dealt extensively with the concept.[34] He believes that the essential nature of syncretism can only be grasped when it is considered "as one form of the *dynamic of religions*."[35] Only thus, he argues, can one realise that all historic religions are syncretic, for they must have, in one form

---

[32]   Melville Herskovits, *Acculturation: The Study of Culture Contact* (New York: J. J. Augustin, 1938).

[33]   See André Droogers and Sidney Greenfield, *Recovering and Reconstructing Syncretism*, *Reinventing Religions: Syncretism and Transformation in Africa and the Americas*, ed. Sidney Greenfield and André Droogers (Lanham, MD: Rowman & Littlefield, 2001), 28.

[34]   Droogers, "Syncretism: The Problem of Definition," 9.

[35]   Gerardus van der Leeuw, *The Dynamics of Religions, Syncretism, Mission*, in *Syncretism in Religion: A Reader*, ed. Anita Leopold and Jeppe Jensen (New York: Routledge, 2005), 98. Emphasis in the original. See also Gerardus van

or another, undergone the creative process of incorporating within themselves elements from other religions and worldviews: "Every historic religion, therefore, is not one, but several; not of course as being the sum of different forms, but in the sense that diverse forms had approximated to its own form or amalgamated with this."[36] Thus, syncretism, he maintains, is not to be located solely within the ancient religions of Egypt and Rome or those of the Hellenistic era. Christianity and Islam are no less syncretic as these others. According to him, this is the case because Christianity combines within itself Jewish, Greek and Persian cultures, while Islam is a fusion of Judaism, Christianity and primitive religion.[37]

Van der Leeuw employs the concept of 'transposition' to explain further the phenomenon he conceives as very fundamental to the process of syncretism. He describes transposition as the variation in the meaning of various religious phenomena without altering their essential form.[38] According to him, in any borrowing of religious element by any religion from another, the essence of the borrowed element usually remains more or less the same while its significance is altered to suit the new religious context. One of the examples he uses to explain transposition within Christianity is the important changes undergone in history in the Christian understanding of the Eucharist across the different religious communities, both Protestant and Catholic. As he explains, whereas Eucharist has been retained in almost all Christian communities, its significance or meaning has undergone important changes. This is also the case, he argues, with

---

der Leeuw, *Religion in Essence and Manifestation: A Study in Phenomenology*, trans. J. E. Turner, vol. 2 (New York: Harper and Row, 1963), 609-612.

36 Van der Leeuw, *The Dynamics of Religions*, 99. He made reference to a similar observation by Joachim Wach in which Wach identifies syncretism as an indispensable element in the process of religious formation: "Every religion, therefore, has its own previous history and is to a certain extent a 'syncretism.' Then comes the time when, from being a summation, it becomes a whole and obeys its own laws." Joachim Wach, *Religionswissenschaft. Prolegomena zu ihrer wissenschaftsteoretischen Grundlegung*, Leipzig: Hinrichs, 1924, 86, cited in Van der Leeuw, *The Dynamics of Religion*, 98.

37 Ibid., 99. For Maroney, any borrowing, adoption or absorption by any religion of elements from another is syncretism. When viewed in this sense, he contends, no religion is exempt. Eric Maroney, *Religious Syncretism* (London: SCM, 2006), 6.

38 Van der Leeuw, *The Dynamics of Religions*, 99.

the Israelites' adoption and reinterpretation of "the Bedouin law of the *Decalogue*" and its subsequent re-adoption and reinterpretation by the Christians.[39] For him, syncretism is indispensable in mission, because there is always *assimilation* of new religious values, *substitution* or *isolation* of existing ones.[40]

The Dutch phenomenologist, Jacques Kamstra, though he believes that syncretism can be approached theologically, argues that it is only from the phenomenological point of view can it be studied meaningfully.[41] Locating the roots of syncretism in the human nature, he notes: "To be human is to be a syncretist."[42] Building on van der Leeuw's transposition (thus associating syncretism with the dynamics of religions), Kamstra maintains that all religions, including Christianity, are syncretic.[43] Syncretism, he asserts, results when there is "co-existence of elements foreign to each other within a specific religion, whether or not these elements originate in other religions or for example in social structures."[44] He distinguishes what he describes as syncretism 'from within' from syncretism 'from without.' The former results when elements within a particular religion continue to exist (in this religion) even though their original meanings have been lost. This brings about a sort of alienation within the religion in question, because the situation brings forth some kind of alteration in the structure of the religion. This is equally the case when something *alien* to the religion is introduced from outside, in which case syncretism 'from without' results.[45] In short, Kamstra concludes, after

---

[39]   Ibid., p. 100.

[40]   Ibid.

[41]   See Michael Pye, "Syncretism and Ambiguity," in *Syncretism in Religion: A Reader*, ed. Anita Leopold and Jeppe Jensen (New York: Routledge, 2005), 59-60. This article can also be accessed elsewhere: Michael Pye, "*Syncretism and Ambiguity*," *Numen* 81, no. 2 (1971): 83-93.

[42]   Jacques Kamstra, *Synkretisme op de Grens tussen Theologie en Godsdienstfenomenologie* (Leiden: Brill, 1970), 23, cited in PYE, *Syncretism and Ambiguity*, 60.

[43]   See Droogers, "Syncretism: The Problem of Definition," 10; Pye, "Syncretism and Ambiguity," 61; Kurt Rudolph, "Syncretism: From Theological Invective to a Concept in the Study of Religions," in *Syncretism in Religion: A Reader*, ed. Anita Leopold and Jeppe Jensen (New York: Routledge, 2005), 73.

[44]   Kamstra, *Synkretisme*, 9-10 cited in Droogers, "Syncretism: The Problem of Definition," 10.

[45]   See Pye, "Syncretism and Ambiguity," 61.

his examination of the nature of syncretism, that the basic criterion for its existence is 'alienation' initiated either from within or from without a particular religion.[46] It can happen either consciously or unconsciously.[47]

One problem that one quickly notices in Kamstra's description of the concept of syncretism, which he claims is a disavowal of its negative portrayal within theology, is his employment of the word 'alienation,' which evokes some sense of abnormality. One wonders how he could use this term and yet claim to have distanced himself enough from the value-laden understanding of syncretism. Kurt Rudolph has criticised Kamstra on this count. He accuses him of receiving through the back door what he has rejected through the front. His argument is that, though Kamstra is against examining syncretism from an evaluative viewpoint, his alienation theory, despite every appearance to the contrary, has crossed beyond the frontiers of the Study of Religion, and remains "attached to crypto-theological tradition."[48] In addition, Rudolph considers as problematic Kamstra's ontological treatment of syncretism. Locating the root of syncretism in the human nature, while at the same time using alienation as the criterion for syncretism, he notes, implies that every human person is an alienated being. He questions: alienation "by what and why?"[49]

Michael Pye has also taken Kamstra to task on his alienation theory. For him, the criterion is faulty on two counts. First, it portrays syncretism as an abnormal situation, an estrangement, and a deviation from the norm or true part, thus "is too reminiscent of prophetic religions."[50] As such, it could be said to be too narrow a criterion and to have been theologically conditioned. Second, Kamstra wrongly portrays religion as ordinarily under the threat of syncretism both from within and from without. He, therefore, concludes that Kamstra's view does not lead to a proper understanding of the nature of syncretism.[51]

---

46   Ibid., 61-62.

47   Jacques Kamstra, *Encounter or Syncretism: The Initial Growth of Japanese Buddhism* (Leiden: Brill, 1967), 9.

48   Rudolph, "Syncretism: From Theological Invective," 74.

49   Ibid.

50   Pye, "Syncretism and Ambiguity," 61.

51   Ibid., 62.

For Pye, what should rather be an appropriate criterion for syncretism is ambiguity. He develops this idea from his study of the relationship between Buddhism and Shinto, which he refers to as an obvious instance of syncretism. This ambiguity, he notes, should be construed dynamically not statically, for it is "a natural *moving* aspect" characteristic of religions.[52] Pye defines syncretism as *"the temporary ambiguous coexistence of elements from diverse religious and other contexts within a coherent religious pattern."*[53] He sees it as temporary because, according to him, religious meanings are not static, but change continuously. The process is such that whenever ambiguous meanings coexist within a religious system, a situation of tension is created, which ordinarily demands some kind of *resolution* that could be accomplished in three different ways: assimilation, fusion, or dissolution. In assimilation one meaning remains while others are eliminated. Fusion brings the meanings together producing what can be termed a new religion. Dissolution happens when the meanings drift apart.[54] This leads to another situation of syncretism. So it continues.

On the positive side, Pye has been commended by some for his analysis of syncretism as a normal dynamic process in religion. Within such a process, religious boundaries are not viewed as fixed but fluid, allowing negotiations of meanings and traditions. What have been spotted as problematic are the implications of his description of syncretism as a temporary process demanding for a resolution leading up to a more stable pattern. The problem with this is the inability to distinguish in a syncretic process what precedes each situation and what can be taken as its result.[55] Rudolph, on his own part, accuses Pye of presuming too much. According to him, Pye's criterion for syncretism is solely developed from his analysis of Japanese syncretism, which only deals with one aspect of syncretism—the *interpretatio* (the level of meaning). It is, thus, presumptuous to apply ambiguity to every instance of syncretism as it does not take into consideration the important role played by social and historical factors

---

[52] Ibid., 63-66.
[53] Ibid., 67. Emphasis in the original.
[54] Ibid., 66.
[55] Leopold and Jensen, *Syncretism in Religion*, 25.

in the production of syncretism.[56] It is based on this that he maintains that Pye's ambiguity theory cannot be sustained.

Rudolph also disagrees with van de Leeuw's transposition, as well as Kamstra's alienation. According to him, the essence of syncretism goes beyond these. Its essence lies rather in what he describes as 'interlock' of diverse religio-cultural elements in contact with each other. It is this 'interlock' that could then lead to either re-adjustment on the part of the elements concerned in order to accommodate each other, or sheer exclusion. He argues that the 'interlock' is influenced by historical, social and political factors. Rudolph distinguishes different forms in which syncretism can make its appearance: symbiosis, amalgamation, identification, metamorphosis or transformation, isolation or dissolution. In line with Pye, he contends that syncretism is temporary. The end of a particular syncretic situation leads to the beginning of another.

Rudolph further distinguishes conscious syncretism from unconscious one. The latter refers to the unreflected form of religious change within a particular religion even when its specific identity remains. This form happens mainly among the lay people and supporters of a religion, especially in their popular religious piety. The conscious type of syncretism, he states, is associated with the founders, the hierarchy or thinkers of a particular religion, who steadily rework the articles of faith and reflectively influence the movement of their respective religious traditions. Having said this, he concludes that syncretism is nothing more than a manifestation of the dynamic character of religion. It is only when so construed, he maintains, that one can appreciate the fact that every religion is syncretic, both with regard to its beginnings and its later history.[57]

No doubt, Rudolph's situating of syncretism within a wider societal context is seen as a welcome contribution to the whole debate.[58] Nevertheless, his distinction between conscious and unconscious syncretism, especially his association of the former with the founders or the hierarchy of specific religions and the latter with the followers could be problematic. It is quite unrealistic to simply characterise the lay people as not being consciously motivated towards

---

56   Rudolph, "Syncretism: From Theological Invective," 75.
57   Ibid., 79-82.
58   See Leopold and Jensen, *Syncretism in Religion*, 27.

innovations in religion, for they really exert conscious influence in religious formation and development. Moreover, it could be quite surprising that Rudolph, who accuses some scholars, like Kamstra, of having been influenced in their discussions on syncretism by Judeo-Christian tradition, may also be judged as relying on the same tradition in his own discussion. In actual fact, his distinction between the founders of religion and the laity may not be completely absolved of Judeo-Christian influence.[59]

Finally, we would wish to examine the contribution of Hendrik Vroom, who analyses syncretism from a philosophical point of view. Vroom is convinced that it is only when a belief system is analysed logically can the true nature of syncretism be unravelled. The basic characteristic of syncretism, which incorporates all others, he affirms, is logical incompatibility. It is only when two religious beliefs which are incompatible with each other co-exist within a religious system can one speak of syncretism.[60] According to Vroom, every religious tradition contains beliefs that are in some sense coherent with one another, and thereby compatible. But religions also constantly adopt incompatible ideas and beliefs from other religions and their environments.[61] Since it is logically impossible for two incompatible beliefs to co-exist within the same religious system, just as it is impossible for someone to "believe that the earth is flat *and* round at the same time, or that people live only once *and* many times,"[62] in adopting such foreign beliefs, the religious tradition often undergoes some re-interpretation. This process affects both the old beliefs within the tradition and the new ones being incorporated in such a way that the new ones are comfortably accommodated or assimilated into the tradition in question.[63] All these processes, Vroom argues, are

---

[59] Ibid., 26-27.

[60] Vroom remarks that the exclusive focus of his analysis on the belief systems of religions does not cancel out the fact that religion also has to do with practices. Rather, he believes the two are interwoven in any religious experience. In effect, then, the notion of incompatibility which he develops could as well be applied to practices as much as to beliefs. Hendrik Vroom, "Syncretism and Dialogue: A Philosophical Analysis," in *Dialogue and Syncretism: An Interdisciplinary Approach*, ed. Jerald Gort *et al*, (Grand Rapids, MI: Eerdmans, 1989), 27.

[61] Ibid., 29.

[62] Ibid., 27. Emphasis in the original.

[63] Ibid., 30-32.

involved in religious syncretism. The assimilation of these new beliefs necessarily leads to some kind of reconfiguration or adjustment in the relations between the different beliefs that make up the religious tradition. Vroom, therefore, sees syncretism as "the phenomenon of adopting or wanting to adopt beliefs which are incompatible with beliefs that are logically basic to a belief system."[64] The major issue is that the adoption of the beliefs alters "the essential experience and the central beliefs of a tradition."[65] He believes that his analysis has covered Kamstra's definition of syncretism with the notion of 'foreignness,' Pye's 'ambiguity,' as well as Droogers' definition of syncretism as "religious interpenetration, either taken for granted or subject to debate."[66]

In addition, he is of the opinion that one's approach towards syncretism depends on his or her conception of the nature of religious systems. If one sees religious belief-systems as closed entities, then incorporation of foreign ideas is easily termed syncretic. But if, on the other hand, the belief-system is understood as multi-faceted with its different parts loosely related to each other, then, one becomes more open to incorporate beliefs from others and the boundary of syncretism shifts.[67]

Granted Vroom's analysis could be very enlightening, especially his notion of incompatibility, one wonders whether anyone can do justice to the complexity of the relationship between religious beliefs (and practices) by merely analysing them in terms of their logicality. These are realities that go beyond mere logic and answer questions related to ultimate meaning of existence. What may well be logically incompatible need not be so in the existential or religious sphere. Religion is such that some beliefs that one could ordinarily see as logically incompatible are incorporated without any tension, whereas those ones assumed to be logically compatible become existentially incompatible and produce tension within the system. In essence, then, we assert that it may be over-simplistic to reduce them to a mere function of logic.

---

[64]   Ibid., 33.

[65]   Ibid., 34.

[66]   Droogers, "Syncretism: The Problem of Definition," 20-21. See Vroom, "Syncretism and Dialogue," 33.

[67]   Ibid., p. 29.

What is more, though Vroom wants to distance himself from the theological, pejorative understanding of syncretism by opting for a logical analysis, some have accused his analysis of exhibiting such pejorativeness through his notion of incompatibility. It is argued that he "must be considered anchored in theology by virtue of his relating the notion of incompatibility to syncretism."[68] This is because incompatibility, at least, has some connotation of things not agreeing in some sense. Moreover, his conviction that no one can subscribe to two logically incompatible beliefs at the same is not incontestable. Some researches in cognitive science have shown that people do hold incompatible beliefs simultaneously.[69] In some instances, the human brain retains logically incompatible beliefs, especially when they emanate from two different systems of thought. This explains why many people live comfortably with a combination of religious insights and scientific theories which might ordinarily be judged as incompatible.[70]

Some Critical Remarks

Indeed, all the authors studied so far argue against a value-laden, subjective or negative understanding of syncretism. Their attempts are directed towards offering a more descriptive and positive conception of it, which they maintain will make it a more welcome occurrence in the contact between religions and cultures. This concern of theirs is understandable, given that many a time, an anthropologist or a historian of religion claim neutrality with respect to religious beliefs. Unlike a theologian who is concerned with religious truth, authenticity and faith, these scholars, it is assumed, often study religious phenomena from a more disinterested and objective point of view.[71]

---

[68]   Leopold and Jensen, *Syncretism in Religion*, 92.

[69]   Leopold and Jensen mention two scientific researches in this regard: Paschal Boyer, *Religion Explained: The Evolutionary Origins of Religious Thought* (New York: Basic Books, 2001); Gilles Fauconier and Mark Turner, *The Way We Think: Conceptual Blending and the Mind's Hidden Complexities* (New York: Basic, 20020. See Leopold and Jensen, *Syncretism in Religion*, 92.

[70]   Ibid.

[71]   Droogers and Greenfield, *Recovering and Reconstructing Syncretism*, 31; Jacques Kamstra, "The Religion of Japan: Syncretism or Religious

Having said that, I must point out that, each of the views examined above seems to be as subjective and evaluative as the theological approach, which they disavow. Little wonder that some have noted that it is not possible to offer an objective account of syncretism.[72] Besides, some of their definitions of syncretism seem too broad. It does no real good to research if every contact in the field of religion or culture is understood to give rise to syncretism, just as most of these authors would like us to believe.[73] Clarity is necessary. If everything is syncretism, nothing is syncretism. Baird actually sees this problem when he declares:

> Now, if it is true that such borrowing and blending, and influencing on the plane of history is part of the whole historical process and is both inevitable and universal, then no real purpose is served by applying the term syncretism to such a phenomenon. Historically speaking, to say that 'Christianity' or the 'mystery religions' or 'Hinduism' are syncretistic is not to say anything that distinguishes them from anything else and is merely equivalent to admitting that each has a history and can be studied historically.[74]

Though Baird also expresses some reservations with its evaluative usage within theology, he nevertheless believes that it is only when used theologically could the term be more meaningful. Syncretism, he reasons, should be applied to "cases where two conflicting ideas or practices are brought together without the benefit of consistency."[75]

Phenomenalism," in *Dialogue and Syncretism: An Interdisciplinary Approach*, ed. Jerald Gort *et al* (Grand Rapids, MI: Eeerdmans, 1989), 137; Raimund Panikkar, *Myth, Faith and Hermeneutics* (New York: Paulist, 1979), 211-214; Raimundo Panikkar, *The Dialogical Dialogue*, in *Contemporary Approaches to the Study of Religion*, ed. Frank Whaling (Berlin: Mouton, 19840, 207-208.

72   Silvia Schroer, "Transformations of Faith: Documents of Intercultural Learning in the Bible," *Concilium*, no. 2 (1994), 3.

73   Willem Hooft, *No Other Name: The Choice between Syncretism and Christian Universalism* (London: SCM, 1963), 10-11.

74   Robert Baird, *Category Formation and History of Religions* (Hague: Mouton, 1971), 146; Robert Baird, *Syncretism and the History of Religions*, in *Syncretism in Religion: A Reader*, ed. Anita Leopold and Jeppe Jensen, ed. (New York: Routledge, 2005), 51.

75   Ibid., 52-53.

In such a situation, no harmony is produced. It is at this point that he criticises such views advanced by some scholars by which syncretism involves a process of reinterpretation, or modification of one's religious beliefs resulting in a comfortable assimilation of a previously external element. According to him, in such a situation, one should rather speak of any other thing, like 'synthesis,' or 'reconception' and not syncretism. Syncretism, on the other hand, "merely retains the conflicting elements without having successfully reconciled them."[76] He questions: "What could be objectionable in synthesising religious elements which are not in conflict? It is the willingness to maintain contradictory elements side by side that has been objectionable."[77]

TOWARDS THEOLOGICAL ARTICULATION

For many theologians, syncretism largely retains the pejorative connotation it assumed when it first appeared in theological discussions in the seventeenth century. In this wise, it represents an undesired and illegitimate mixing of religious elements of diverse origins. With regard to Christianity, it is generally believed to occur when the Christian religion incorporates elements from other religious traditions so much so that its own basic structure or identity is compromised. This view has been nurtured by the constant concern of Christian theologians to safeguard Christianity's uniqueness among other religions. [78]

For some theologians, however, syncretism is more a historical or anthropological problem than a theological one. When thus construed, they conclude that Christianity is as syncretic as any other religion.[79] A German theologian and prominent church historian, Adolf von Harnack, has expressed this view in the earliest part of the twentieth century. With reference to the complex cultural situation from which Christianity arose and how it assimilated the cultures and religious elements in those environments, Harnack comes to the conclusion that Christianity is nothing but an instance of "a special kind of syncretism,

---

[76]   Ibid., 53.

[77]   Ibid.

[78]   Schreiter, *Constructing Local Theologies*, 144; Schreiter, "Defining Syncretism," 50.

[79]   Peter Schineller, "Inculturation or Syncretism," 50.

namely the syncretism of a universal religion."[80] This syncretism, he notes, ranges from the doctrinal to the practical aspects of Christianity, and became evident when Christianity started learning and borrowing from Judaism and 'pagan' religions of antiquity:

> From the very outset it [Christianity] had been syncretistic upon pagan soil; it made its appearance, not as a gospel pure and simple, but equipped with all that Judaism had already acquired during the course of its long history, and entering forthwith upon nearly every task in which Judaism was defective. Still, it was the middle of the third century that first saw the new religion in full bloom as the syncretistic religion *par excellence*.[81]

Harnack's contention that Christianity has incorporated various elements from its surrounding environment is indeed incontestable. Nevertheless, it seems reasonable to entertain some reservations as to whether such a situation could be justifiably described as syncretism theologically understood. This is where the problem lies.

Just like Harnack, Wolfhart Pannenberg, who understands syncretism as the fusion of religious elements that were originally heterogeneous, demonstrates that most of the religious traditions, such as that of Christianity, have arisen through syncretic processes. For him, Christianity, more than any other religion, possesses the power of syncretic assimilation. It is this power, he maintains, that could probably account for its great influence in the ancient world. With it, it was able to incorporate all the religious traditions of the Mediterranean world and the rich heritage of Greek philosophy. Pannenberg maintains that the biblical figure of God is nothing but a product of syncretic process.[82]

A similar line of thought led Leonardo Boff to discredit what he refers to as the majority opinion within Catholicism which claims that Christianity, being a revealed religion, is not syncretic. According to him, this claim cannot be sustained since both the New and the Old

---

[80]   Adolf von Harnack, *The Mission and Expansion of Christianity*, 2nd ed., vol. I (New York: Williams and Norgate, 1908), 312.

[81]   Ibid., 314.

[82]   Wolfhart Pannenberg, *Basic Questions in Theology*, vol. 2 (London: SCM, 1971), 86, 87.

Testaments are results of undeniable syncretism. His main point is that syncretism is an indispensable element of Christianity, for it is only through it that the church's catholicity can be realised. He argues that, throughout its history, the church has always incorporated rites, feasts, religious expressions, teachings and heritages of other religions, reinterpreting them in the light of its own faith. These are all instances of syncretism, he contends. Boff clearly dissociates himself from any pejorative use of the word, and describes as inconsequential the alarm raised by the institutional church against syncretism as is quite evident in Vatican II. According to him, any attempt by any religion to either utilise the elements of another religion, accommodate, adapt, or translate its message using elements drawn from this other religion is nothing but syncretism.[83] He considers it as an essential part of every religion and as an expression of the principle of incarnation:

> Syncretism, then, is not necessarily evil nor does it represent a pathology of pure religion. It is a normal condition of the incarnation, expression, and objectification of a religious faith or expression. It may give rise to pathologies. Fundamentally, it emerges as a universal phenomenon constitutive of all religious expression.[84]

Though Boff argues against any pejorative view of syncretism, one discovers that, in his attempt to distinguish what he perceives as true syncretism from false one, he indicates that certain forms of syncretism are undesirable, namely the false ones. He opines that false syncretism arises within Christianity when the specific identity of the Christian faith is adulterated in the process of its contact with different religions and cultures "to such an extent that it is no longer discernible."[85] In such a situation, he argues, instead of Christianity being affirmed and converting other religions and cultures, they convert Christianity to themselves.[86] On the other hand, true Christian

---

[83]   Leonardo Boff, *Church, Charism and Power: Liberation Theology and the Institutional Church*, trans. John Diercksmeier (London: SCM, 1985), 89-91, 94.

[84]   Ibid., 93.

[85]   Ibid., 101.

[86]   Ibid., 101-102. Boff argues that, if such a thing happens between Christianity and 'pagan' religion, then, we could rightly speak of "pagan syncretism

syncretism exists when Christian faith incorporates elements from other religions and cultures while its identity remains uncorrupted, unabsorbed or uncompromised. He is of the opinion that any "true syncretism is always begun with Christian identity as its substantial nucleus."[87]

A significant dimension is added to the discussion by some theologians, like Eugene Hillman and Lamin Sanneh, who are of the view that the continued attachment of negative, pejorative sense to syncretism is often used by western scholars to forestall genuine incarnation of Christianity in the non-western cultures. While Sanneh accuses the West of very often invoking "the charges of 'syncretism' . . . against the increasing importance of African leadership in the Church,"[88] Hillman describes the attitude of the West as a manifestation of "chronic ethnocentricism of the classicist mentality," because the history of Christianity does show it to be the most concrete illustration of syncretism. Just like Boff, Hillman argues that it is even a basic condition for the concrete realisation of the church's catholicity and universality.[89]

In as much as I admit that the views of these theologians examined above have some contributions to make in our proper understanding and better evaluation of syncretism, it needs be noted that they do not lead us far. As I have noted earlier, they are more inclined towards analysing syncretism from historical or anthropological point of view than from the theological. If any borrowing of religious elements by Christianity from any other religion is syncretism, then, employing the word is, more or less useless, since nothing new has been said. To talk about syncretism would just be nothing more than stating the obvious fact that

---

with Christian connotations" and not Christian syncretism as such. Such a phenomenon, he says, is witnessed in the Brazilian Yoruba religion, where Christian elements are incorporated, assimilated and transformed in the light of the 'pagan' religious identity. This is never Christianity, he argues, and, thus, the syncretic phenomenon cannot be rightly termed Christian.

[87]   Ibid., 101.

[88]   Lamin Sanneh, *West African Christianity: The Religious Impact* (London: C. Hurst, 1983), 245. Just like Boff, he argues that syncretism is an inevitable phenomenon built upon the incarnation principle.

[89]   Eugene Hillman, *Many Paths: A Catholic Approach to Religious Pluralism* (Maryknoll, NY: Orbis, 1989), 59-60.

Christianity is concretely realised in history. Moreover, with the exception of Boff's 'false syncretism,' one gets the impression that they believe that there should not be limits to Christianity's incorporation and utilisation of foreign religious elements in the expression of its message. That is why it is worthwhile that we also discuss some other theologians who, I may say, have studied syncretism from a more theologically oriented perspective. Their insight will also add more lucidity to the discussion.

Aylward Shorter, who characterises many of the new religious movements in Africa as "crudely syncretistic," describes syncretism as unintegrated juxtaposition of elements from different religions.[90] He demonstrates that such syncretic situations arise in Christianity when one sees no reason for consciously upholding the values of the religion simply because he or she judges it as identical, and as such interchangeable, with any other religion.[91]

For some other theologians, syncretism goes deeper than just mere juxtaposition of beliefs without integration. Shreiter, for example, argues that in a syncretic situation the identity and/or the fundamental structures of the two (or at least one of the religions) are affected. That is why he defines it as "the mixing of elements of two religious systems to the point where at least one, if not both, of the systems loses basic structure or identity."[92] If this is so, it then means that syncretism is believed to have occurred in Christianity when its interaction with any other religion results in the loss or compromise of the basic structure or identity of the Christian faith. His position is quite similar to that of David Hesselgrave for whom syncretism is a situation whereby "the beliefs and practices of opposing (or at least, different) [religious] systems are modified and accommodated to each

---

90   Aylward Shorter, *African Christian Theology: Adaptation or Incarnation* (London: Chapman, 1975), 2, 13.

91   See Ibid., 15. Shorter sees this as a danger which African theologians should watch in their dialogue with the African traditional religion. He cautions that deep sense of "nationalism and African self-affirmation" might be a source of temptation in this regard.

92   Schreiter, *Constructing Local Theologies*, 144. Though Schreiter views syncretism negatively, he remains critical of the rigid stance often taken against it, so much so that it precludes any form of genuine integration of Christianity into different cultural contexts. Ibid., 145.

other in such a way that they become essentially one new system."[93] To have an 'essentially one new system' means, of course, that the previously combining or interacting systems have lost their essentiality or basic identity. To that extent, it remains a situation to be cautiously avoided.

Such a stance against syncretism is also noticed among those theologians who employ the word 'christopaganism' as a synonym for syncretism. This usage seems to put forward in a clearer light the meaning and implications of what they understand syncretism to be.[94] As a word formed from a combination of 'Christianity' and 'paganism' it portrays syncretism in Christianity as a form of muddling of Christianity and 'pagan' religion. This is evident in its employment by Charles Kraft for whom syncretism or christopaganism means a permanent "blend or mixture of Christianity with pre-Christian beliefs and practices relating to supernatural beings and powers."[95] If, however, as he argues, the blend or mixture occurs as a transitional or temporary step in the process of religious growth and development, it is not syncretism. Syncretism, he believes, can appear in two forms: The first form is a situation where the outward appearance of the blend remains Christian, whereas the deeper meanings attached to these are derived from the people's old, pre-Christian religious ideas and practices. This is the form of syncretism he refers to as christopagan syncretism. The other form, which he calls domination syncretism, results when both the Christian forms and meanings are not in any way adapted to the local situation but are all foreign. This brings about a situation where the people merely practice a foreign religion.[96]

Though Kraft's analysis could be very elucidating, especially as regards his christopagan syncretism, his domination syncretism seems to be a far cry from his definition of syncretism. There seems to be no

---

93 David Hesselgrave, *Communicating Christ Cross-Culturally* (Grand Rapids, MI: Academie, 1978), 191.

94 See, for example, Charles Kraft, *Anthropology for Christian Witness* (Maryknoll, NY: Orbis, 1996), 376-377; Louis Luzbetak, *The Church and Cultures: New Perspectives in Missiological Anthropology* (Maryknoll, NY: Orbis, 1988), 361-373; Cf. Alan Tippett, *Christopaganism or Indigenous Christianity*, in *Christopaganism or Indigenous Christianity?*, ed. Tetsunao Yamamori and Charles Taber (South Pasadena, CA: William Carey Library, 1975), 13, 17-18.

95 Kraft, *Anthropology for Christian Witness*, 376.

96 Ibid.

blending of Christianity with pre-Christian beliefs and/or practices in this second form, yet Kraft presents it as syncretism. When the forms and the meanings attached to them are both foreign to the people, from where comes the blending that could make such a situation correspond to his definition of syncretism? If he merely presents this as a pre-condition for the occurrence of syncretism as he defines it, then, it can be understandable.

It does not end at that. Another problem one could have with Kraft's analysis is that, though he seems to view syncretism pejoratively, especially when the people are settled in such a situation, his definition of syncretism does not bring out reasons why such a situation is viewed as such. To be more specific, it is not evident from his definition how the blending does affect the Christian identity or theology. If one does not bring out how offensive such a blending is to Christian theological thinking or praxis, how could one see it as undesirable from Christian theological point of view?

Moreover, he seems to presume that syncretism is an exclusive problem of newer churches witnessing evangelisation for the first time, or for whom Christianity is not yet firmly rooted. If not, why does he define it in terms of a mixture or blend with *pre-Christian* religious ideas and practices? In this connection, one might be inclined to ask: Must the blend or mixture be with *pre-Christian* religion to be syncretic? What has temporal precedence to do with making a situation syncretic or not? What if Christianity gets mixed or blended with a religion that is introduced after Christianity has already been with the people for some time? Why should such a situation not also be described as syncretic?

Equally debatable is his insistence that, for a situation to be termed syncretic, people must have settled in it; in other words, it must be a permanent phenomenon. He did not give any reasons why he introduces such a characterisation, nor can one fashion this out from his analysis. In fact, it is difficult to actually discern *from his arguments* what being permanent or not adds to the theological significance or otherwise of such a situation.

The Dutch theologian, Hendrik Kraemer, is one of the theologians whose contribution in this field is very remarkable. Kraemer believes that syncretism can be employed in two senses: conscious (genuine) and unconscious syncretism. As an unconscious reality, syncretism designates the inter-borrowing and exchange of cultural traits and religious ideas among different cultures and religions. In this sense, it is almost an inevitable effect of any real contact between cultures, and is therefore a universal human occurrence, since cultural intercourse among people is inevitable. It is "a persistent and universal phenomenon in human history. It cannot but happen, unless peoples live in entire isolation."[97] According to Kraemer, when used in this sense, which nevertheless is not the genuine application of the term, it becomes difficult to absolve any religion of being syncretic. This is because, as a consequence of their historical growth and development, all religions constantly incorporate and adapt meanings and rites of different religious origins, making them part and parcel of themselves without necessarily compromising their identity.[98] It is nothing but "a process of absorption and digestion of extraneous elements, taking place as by-product of the historical process of culture-contact."[99]

Kramer points out that, though in the unconscious sense of the word the great world religions, like Christianity and Islam, could be termed syncretic, in its conscious (and genuine) form, they are in no way to be identified as such.[100] The point he makes, which is very crucial for his contribution to the discussion, is his call for the reservation of the term, syncretism, solely for this conscious type. He believes that it is only in this form can syncretism be genuinely conceived. That being the case, the Christian mission, he insists, does not necessarily involve syncretism but "adaptation . . . a certain kind of coalescence, of symbiosis without losing identity."[101] For him, then, it is only when a religion loses its identity in the process of contact can it be genuinely termed syncretic.[102]

---

[97]   Kraemer, *Religion and the Christian Faith*, 389.
[98]   Ibid., p. 397.
[99]   Ibid.
[100]   Ibid., pp. 398-399.
[101]   Ibid., pp. 390-391.
[102]   Hendrik Kraemer, *The Christian Message in a Non-Christian World* (London: The Edinburgh House, 1938), 200-202. See also Jan van Bragt, "Multiple Religious Belonging of the Japanese People," in *Many Mansions?: Multiple Religious Belonging and Christian Identity*, ed. Catherine Cornille (Maryknoll, NY: Orbis, 2002), 7-19; Colpe, Syncretism, 222; Winston Davis, *Japanese Religion and Society* (Albany, NY: State University of New York Press, 1992), 33; Kamstra, *Encounter or Syncretism*, 470.

The American anthropologist and missiologist, Louis Luzbetak, discusses syncretism by differentiating between its anthropological and theological notions. For an anthropologist, Luzbetak submits, any form of blending of religious beliefs and practices of different origins is regarded as syncretism, since he or she is merely interested in religion and not in theology. In this sense, Christianity, Judaism, and indeed every other religion is syncretic in as much as each of them undergoes progressive borrowings or incorporation of foreign ideas into its belief system. For a theologian, Luzbetak continues, the issue is different. Syncretism receives a narrower definition: "any theologically untenable amalgam" of Christian beliefs and/or practices and those of any other religion.[103]

This definition can be said to be very theologically significant based on some grounds. First, it assesses syncretic situations based on their theological soundness or otherwise, and not merely on historical, anthropological, or any other ground. Thus, syncretism in Christianity raises the question of theological validity and plausibility, and addresses issues relating to whether the newly incorporated beliefs and practices serve the Christian theological thinking or whether they betray it. Secondly, referring to it as an amalgam already suggests that these beliefs and practices are not properly integrated but remain a mere mixture or combination; a situation where the existing system can be described as the sum of its parts. Such amalgam cannot but at the same time be theologically untenable from the Christian point of view, because it compromises the Christian identity and specificity. In effect, one hardly identifies the existing religious formation as really Christian. Judging, therefore, from the point of view of the *content* of such syncretic formations, syncretism should always be resisted. The attitude of theologians towards it should not be anything less than negative because "such amalgamations or combinations are by their very definition theologically untenable, impermissible, and therefore undesirable."[104]

In contrast to Kraft, Luzbetak believes that syncretic situations do not exclusively occur in new churches, nor does it result only from the meeting of Christianity with pre-Christian religion. It also takes place in societies which have been Christianised for centuries, but

---

[103]   Luzbetak, *The Church and Cultures: New Perspectives*, 360.
[104]   Ibid., p. 370.

which are today witnessing the process of de-Christianisation, like Europe and America: "Yes, older churches are syncretistic too, no less than the Zulu, Fijian, or Eskimo. The fact is that Western Christians absolve themselves too easily of syncretism. In fact, we can speak of a de-Christianization of Europe, which is but a syncretisation of Christianity."[105] This observation is corroborated by Claude Geffré when he writes: "The religiosity of the Western person of our times is spontaneously syncretistic."[106]

Although the above definition of syncretism from the Christian theological point of view by Luzbetak can serve as a welcome definition, I would like to offer a different one in order to incorporate other relevant aspects brought in by other scholars already discussed. Based on this, I define syncretism thus: *A theologically untenable blend of Christianity with another religion or culture or elements from this religion or culture resulting in the betrayal of the specific identity of the Christian faith.* I offer this, however, without expecting that this will settle such a question which has long defied time and scholarship, but at least, it will serve to bring about more theological clarity and as such function as a guide as we reflect along.

Having gone thus far in the investigation into the nature of syncretism, it is pertinent to examine the different forms it can take.

TYPOLOGY OF SYNCRETISM

Syncretism can appear in a variety of ways. As regards the ways it manifests itself within Christianity, two major forms can be identified, which I would wish to term—Christian-Configured Syncretism and Other-Configured Syncretism.[107] Some scholars have identified a third type, which exists in some of the new religions in Japan called *Shinko*

---

[105] Ibid., p. 366.

[106] Claude Geffré, "Double Belonging and the Originality of Christianity as a Religion," in *Many Mansions?: Multiple Religious Belonging and Christian Identity*, ed. Catherine Cornille (Maryknoll, NY: Orbis, 2002), 94. According to Geffré, what fuels this syncretism in the West is the increasing globalization with the resultant marketisation of different religious traditions, individualism and loss of credibility of the Christian tradition, especially as it has been presented by the official churches.

[107] Cf. Schreiter, *Constructing Local Theologies*, 146-147.

Shukyo.[108] It is not my wish to discuss this here. Therefore, in what follows, some light will be shed on the two major ones mentioned above.

OTHER-CONFIGURED SYNCRETISM

Within this category are those formed by the blending of Christianity with another religion in which the fundamental framework of the resultant syncretic religion is provided by the other religion. In other words, another religion absorbs Christianity in its own terms. This type of syncretism is very common in South America and Caribbean islands. It results from the amalgamation of Christianity with African traditional religions imported into the region by the former slaves. In most instances, the Christian God and some Christian saints are blended with spiritual entities of African traditional religions and worshipped or venerated, as the case may be, in accordance with forms of worship practiced in the traditional religions of Africa.[109]

What nurtured this syncretism was the forceful suppression of the religion of the slaves when Catholicism was the only officially recognised religion in the region. The African traditional religious expressions were totally forbidden. But as one would expect, they never died out. On the contrary, they continued to exist in hidden forms behind the mask of compliant Catholicism. When the people

---

[108] These are new religions in Japan that generally tend to syncretise elements from diverse religions. According to Wilhelm Schiffer, out of 375 registered religions in Japan about the year 1955, about 120 belong to the *Shinko Shukyo*. Though some authors include within this category, all those religions that sprang up from the time of Meiji Restoration (1868), majority of these religions arose shortly before, during or after the Second World War, mainly out of the peoples' dissatisfaction with the traditional religions of Shinto and Buddhism. Their leaders claim to have got the mandate to found these religions from revelations. See Wilhelm Schiffer, "New Religions in Postwar Japan," *Monumenta Nipponica* 11, no. 1 (1955): 1-14. In some of them, veneration of Jesus Christ occupies a prominent position. In fact, there is a case where a particular cult exists with one altar shared together by Jesus, Buddha and Muhammad. For this and more, see Schreiter, *Constructing Local Theologies*, 147.

[109] Ibid., 146-148. See also Luis Nicolau, "Transformations of the Sea and Thunder Vodums in the Gbe-Speaking Area and in the Bahian Jeje Candomblé," in *Africa and the Americas: Interconnections during the Slave Trade*, ed. José Curto and Renée Soulodre-La France (Trenton, NJ: Africa World 2004), 69-75.

eventually gained some sort of freedom of religious expression, various forms of mixed religions surfaced. The level of the resulting synthesis has made some scholars view them as "the epitome of syncretism."[110]

The following are some of the syncretised religions in the region: Tambor de Mina, Candomblé, Batuques, Macumbas and Umbanda. These five are mainly Afro-Brazilian. Others are: Santeria, Shango and Voodoo, which have their strongholds in Cuba, Trinidad and Haiti respectively. In 1987, Umbanda was reported to command a population of about 30 million, thereby rivalling Roman Catholicism as the largest religion in Brazil.[111] Of all these, Candomblé is perceived to be the typical. Though there are many Candomblé groups, each claiming to be a representation of the tradition of a particular ethnic group in Africa, those that claim to have (Nigerian) Yoruba ethnic roots are much more that others. Yoruba cultural traditions remain dominant in Candomblé beliefs, practices and rituals. African deities, the *orisas* (*orixás* in Portuguese), mainly of Yoruba origin, which are mostly associated with elements of nature, like water, air, fire, sun and earth, are worshipped by the members.[112] These deities, due to the perceived congruity between their functions and those of the saints of the popular Catholicism in Brazil, are amalgamated with these saints, their statues

---

[110]   Inger Sjørslev, "Possession and Syncretism: Spirits as Mediators in Modernity," in *Reinventing Religions: Syncretism and Transformation in Africa and the Americas*, ed. Sidney Greenfield and André Droogers (Lanham, MD: Rowman & Littlefield, 2001), 132.

[111]   Sidney Greenfield, "Population Growth, Industrialization and the Proliferation of Syncretized Religions in Brazil," in *Reinventing Religions: Syncretism and Transformation in Africa and the Americas*, ed. Sidney Greenfield and André Droogers (Lanham, MD: Rowman & Littlefield, 2001), 61-63; Diana Brown and Mario Bick, "Religion, Class, and Context: Continuities and Discontinuities in Brazilian Umbanda," *American Ethnologist* 14 (1987): 73-93; Albert Raboteau, *Slave Religion: The "Invisible Institution" in the Antebellum South* (New York: Oxford University Press, 1978), 16.

[112]   Roberto Motta, "Ethnicity, Purity, the Market and Syncretism in Afro-Brazilian Cults," in *Reinventing Religions: Syncretism and Transformation in Africa and the Americas*, ed. Sidney Greenfield and André Droogers (Lanham, MD: Rowman & Littlefield, 2001), 74, 76, 83. In line with Motta's observation, Voeks opines that Candomblé "is thought to represent the most orthodox expression of African magico-religion in the New World." Robert Voeks, "Sacred Leaves of Brazilian Candomblé," *Geographical Review* 80, no. 2 (1990): 118.

and holy pictures.[113] *Orisas* associated with particular saints are believed to share the same or similar essence and to perform similar roles with them. So, the people see no reason in having them mixed up in worship. Every *orisa* has a Roman Catholic saint counterpart.[114] For instance, the *orisa* for hunt in Yoruba Pantheon, *Oxossi*, becomes St. George or St. Michael, perhaps because the two Christian saints are iconographically depicted in Christian tradition as warriors (holding swords). The goddess of the sea, *Yemanjà*, turns out to be identified with Our Lady of Immaculate Conception.[115] Sometimes the two names (the specific *orisa* and the saint) are written together in a hyphenated form.[116]

Just as is typical of African traditional religions, there is a form of *do ut des* mentality pervading religious worship in Candomblé. Here, the people and the *orisas* relate as business partners with some form of agreement to do some mutual favour to each other. The adherents offer gifts and sacrifices (sometimes bloody ones) to them with the hope of gaining their blessings, patronage and benevolence.[117] The religious

---

[113] In Brazilian popular Catholicism, as different from official Catholicism, the saints and the Blessed Virgin Mary sometimes receive more reverence than God. According to Greenfield, this practice was sustained among the people because they believe the saints, as intermediaries between humans and God, would be more concerned with human affairs than the distant God. This is congruent with the Yoruba belief in which the Supreme Being, *Olodumare*, is seen as very remote and distant, and as a result, is far from often approached directly. He is believed to be reached easily through the intermediary deities, the *orisas*, who are assigned by *Olodumare* to protect and guard humans. This congruency between the nearness and intermediary functions of the Christian saints and African gods on one hand, and that between the remoteness of the God of Brazilian popular Catholicism and African Supreme Being on the other hand, contribute to their easy amalgamation. Sidney Greenfield, "The Reinterpretation of Africa: Convergence and Syncretism in Brazilian Candomblé," in *Reinventing Religions: Syncretism and Transformation in Africa and the Americas*, ed. Sidney Greenfield and André Droogers (Lanham, MD: Rowman & Littlefield, 2001), 120-122. See also Bolaji Idowu, *Olodumare: God in Yoruba Belief* (London: Longmans, 1962), 52; J. Peel, "Syncretism and Religious Change," *Comparative Studies in Society and History* 10, no. 2 (1968): 121-125; Raboteau, *Slave Religion*, 23.

[114] Motta, "Ethnicity, Purity, the Market," 74.

[115] Voeks, "Sacred Leaves," 118.

[116] Raboteau, *Slave Religion*, 24.

[117] Motta, "Ethnicity, Purity, the Market," 75.

ceremonies conducted in holy houses (*terreiros*) are coordinated by a *babalorisa*, or as is most commonly called, *paes or maes de santo* (fathers or mothers of saints). In contrast to their African progenitors, where the leader is only male, in Candomblé the office is open to both genders. Among the Yorubas of Nigeria, there is always a distinction between *babalawo*, the mediator between the spirits and humans and the traditional healer or leaf doctor (*onisegun*), but in Candomblé, these two functions become blended together, and are simultaneously performed by *babalorisa*.[118] The rites and ceremonies include a lot of drumming and dancing, healing sessions, initiation rites, ecstasy, spirit possession, and animal sacrifices. According to Roberto Motta, during the dancing sessions, fluids are emitted from the body signifying life and its transmission. He points out that the interest developed by many western researchers in recent times in studying this religious manifestation is because it has no parallel today in the western world. Describing it as the opposite of Marx Weber's rational religion, he argues that it is mainly based on emotions and intuition and do not preach salvation. The usefulness of the religion lies in its ability to aid the adherents individually in this world. They are sceptical toward political or social transformation, and thus, are at odds with liberation theology. Each congregation of Candomblé has a hierarchical structure. But there is no centralised church, for they follow congregational model of organisation.[119]

In Umbanda religion, similar traits are also observed. Some scholars are of the opinion that Umbanda arose perhaps as an attempt to purify or reinterpret some of the practices, like animal sacrifices, and other beliefs of the Candomblé, viewed as primitive and offensive.[120] Though Umbanda does not have a uniform organisation, some characteristics could be observed as basic. It combines elements of African traditional religions with Roman Catholicism and Amerindian ones. Unlike in Candomblé, the adherents believe that *orisas* or their counterpart saints are very powerful, and therefore, cannot be directly approached by humans. So, they establish a very elaborate hierarchy of spirits which separate them from direct contact with the worshippers. These spirits include, the spirits of the ancestors

---

[118]   Voeks, "Sacred Leaves," 118-120.
[119]   See Motta, "Ethnicity, Purity, the Market," 75-76.
[120]   Ibid., 76-77.

of Indians (*caboclos*) and Africans (*pretos velhos*), the spirits of dead children (*crianças*), those of powerful men and women and the prostitutes (*pombagiras* and *exus*).[121] They possess the mediums who are the leaders of the congregation. During such a period, the congregation may kneel and sign themselves with the cross as a sign of homage to the spirits. It is through the medium that solutions are then offered by the saints and the other-worldly beings to the living humans regarding practical problems of life, like getting a job, or identification of theft culprits. This way, they appear to be more involved in the people's daily problems than does the official Roman Catholicism.[122]

Some other examples of such syncretic religions where some African deities are identified with the Christian saints include, the Haitian Voodoo, where St. Anthony is identified with the trickster, *Legba*, of west African Dahomean and Yoruba origin, because the two are seen as lovers of the poor. The rainbow-serpent deity (*Damballa*) is identified with St. Patrick, while *Erzulie*, the goddess of water and riches becomes the Blessed Virgin Mary often clad in her royal garments. River Jordan of the Old Testament is also identified with some rivers in Africa. The popularity of the Haitian Voodoo is such that it thrives today even in North American cities. In New York, for instance, Voodoo imported by Haitian refugees is very vibrant.[123] In certain instances, as reported by Alfred Métraux, "prayers are addressed to 'Saint Earth,' 'Saint Thunder,' 'Saint Sun' (identified also as Saint Nicholas), and 'Saint Moon.'"[124] Their religious celebrations feature a combination of Catholic prayers and liturgy with those of the

---

[121] Denise DiPuccio, "The Magic of Umbanda in 'Gota d'água,'" *Luso-Brazilian Review* 27, no. 1 (1990): 2-3. It should be noted that ancestor worship is very central in the traditional religions of the Africans. The ancestors are believed to be the custodians of the people's cultures and traditions. As spirits, they are relied upon for help in times of trouble because they are deemed to be closer to God than humans. See W. T. Harris and Harry Sawyer, *The Springs of the Mende Belief and Conduct* (Freetown: Sierra Leone University Press, 1968), 15.

[122] Denise DiPuccio, "The Magic of Umbanda in 'Gota d'água,'" 3; Motta, "Ethnicity, Purity, the Market," 63.

[123] See Luzbetak, *The Church and Cultures: New Perspectives*, 363. See also Raboteau, *Slave Religion*, 23-25, 146-147; Alfred Métraux, *Voodoo in Haiti*, trans. Hugo Charteris, Second Edition (London: André Deutsch, 1972), 326.

[124] Ibid., 327.

African spirit, *loa*, which mediates between the people and the creator. Describing such a celebration, Métraux writes:

> Standing in the middle of their *husi* before an altar covered with candles, under a panoply of lace decorated with pictures of saints, priest or priestess recites Paters, Confiteors and Ave Marias followed by hymns to the Virgin and to the saints. The famous 'African prayer' (*prière Guinin*) which opens the most solemn ceremonies, begins with Catholic prayers and interminable invocations of the saints: the *loa* are only summoned afterwards.[125]

There is also the blessing of bread and water, which are often taken home from services to serve as magical protective objects. Their calendar bears very close similarity to that of the Roman Catholic Church. Here Christian baptismal, marriage and penitential rites assume different dimensions and significance. Regarding baptism, for instance, it is not only human beings that are baptised. Both *lao* and all objects used in the cult receive baptism, which is carried out by the priest or priestess in a manner similar to the Roman Catholic liturgy. The objects are not only sprinkled with water, but also have their respective godparents and are given baptismal names.[126]

In Maranhao, which is the second largest State in northeast Brazil, St Benedict, believed by the people to be a black, is invoked for protection by the Afro-Brazilian devotees. In *Tambor de Mina*—a syncretic religion more common in Maranhao and Para regions—St. Benedict corresponds to the sea deity, *Avekerete*. In Cuba, the god of divination, *Orunmilla*, is identified with St. Francis. This might not be unrelated to the fact that in the traditional iconographical representation of the saint, he wears a rosary, which bears some resemblance to the *opele* chain used in Yoruba *Ifa* divination.[127]

---

[125]   Ibid., 327-328.

[126]   Ibid., 328-333.

[127]   For more on these, see Sergio Ferretti, "Religious Syncretism in an Afro-Brazilian Cult House," in *Reinventing Religions: Syncretism and Transformation in Africa and the Americas*, ed. Sidney Greenfield and André Droogers (Lanham, MD: Rowman & Littlefield, 2001), 90; Raboteau, *Slave Religion*, 23-25.

Other instances of such syncretic forms could still be given. In the Jamaican Convince and Cumina religions, the basic theology of African traditional religion is operative, though the African gods no longer exist by name. In Convince, the Christian Bible and hymns are very conspicuous, but they attach much importance too to the veneration of the ancestral spirits of their African forbears, and offer animal sacrifices to them. A similar trait is also observed in the Cumina.[128] In Santeria religion, the devotees undergo baptism, but instead of using water as is common in Christian tradition, they use herbs mixed with blood. Among some black Jamaican groups, like Revival and Pocomania, one also notices the mixing of Protestant (Christian) and African beliefs and practices. The Shangoists in Trinidad synthesise their Yoruba forms of worship with the Spiritual Baptist worship, most evidently concretised in their baptismal rituals. We also notice this syncretism as very visible in the people's belief in charms and amulets. The Bible, crucifixes, blessed medals, saints' statues, stones, herbs, leaves, are simultaneously used as charms against wicked and evil forces. These cultic objects usually crowd their sacred sanctuaries.[129]

According to Greenfield, there are efforts being made today by some scholars and adherents of some of these religions to claim that their own religions are not a result of syncretism between African and Christian (mainly, Roman Catholic) beliefs and practices. This is the case with Candomblé in Brazil, which some maintain is purely and authentically African (Yoruba) and devoid of any mixture. These claims, Greenfield asserts, are made in the bid to have Candomblé better regarded and given equal official recognition on the same level as the Roman Catholic Church. These arguments notwithstanding, Greenfield insists that "recent evidence indicates that Brazilian Candomblé still cannot be accepted as an uninterrupted, authentic continuation of pure Yoruba forms."[130]

What is basic among the syncretic religions examined so far is that it is not Christianity but African traditional religions that provide the basic framework for the mixture between them and Christianity. That is why their major pattern is the alteration or configuration of the

---

128   Raboteau, *Slave Religion*, 16-17.
129   Ibid., 22-35.
130   Greenfield, "The Reinterpretation of Africa," 113-114.

previously Christian elements so that they fit into the mould provided by these other religions.

CHRISTIAN-CONFIGURED SYNCRETISM

In this kind of syncretism, Christianity is amalgamated with another religion with the former providing the background framework for the syncretic formation. The situation is such that there is a substantial and independent reinterpretation and reshaping of the basic theological insights of the Christian faith, without any recourse to the established Christian tradition.[131] Instead, such reinterpretations are coloured by the other religion or cultural tradition which Christianity has established some contacts with.

Most of the African Independent Churches springing up all over the continent of Africa fall under this category. These churches gain some popularity in the continent today partly because of the failure of the mainline churches to undergo proper integration of Christian faith into the culture of the people. It is observed that in mainline churches no proper attention is given to very strong issues within the traditional society, like ancestor veneration, witchcraft, spirit possession, healing, exorcism, and any other of such issues, which need serious spiritual, theological and pastoral consideration.[132] Because these syncretised forms of Christianity provide answers to these issues by their recourse to the traditional religion and culture with which they are syncretised, many easily identify with them. Their special asset, Edmund Ilogu argues, is their provision of easy path through which the people can move from African traditional religion to Christianity "without too much of a metamorphosis demanded on their part—and certainly not the *radical* change which orthodox form of Christianity would demand."[133] For many, these churches are a form of reaction

---

[131] Schreiter, *Constructing Local Theologies*, 147.

[132] Terence Ranger, "African Initiated Churches," *Transformation* 24, no. 2 (2007): 69. See also A. O. Nkwoka, "New Testament Research and Cultural Heritage: A Nigerian Example," *Asia Journal of Theology* 17, no. 2 (2003): 292.

[133] Edmund Ilogu, "Independent African Churches in Nigeria," *International Review of Missions* 63, no. 252 (1974): 494. The emphasis is mine. Radical in this sense would mean not only a conversion from the traditional religion, but more so, a form of uprooting of someone from his or her cultural background.

against what some of their founders expressed as racial discrimination noticed by Africans in the older churches. This informs the slogan used by some of them—"Africa for Africans."[134] Even though some of the churches may be slow to accept this, the fact is that, in the final analysis, they seem to serve as avenues by which Africans revert to the traditional religion from which they moved over to Christianity.

The number of these churches has grown astronomically in recent years. Even though some scholars have made some efforts to classify them,[135] it has not been easy to number them. In the year

---

[134] Bengt Sundkler, *Bantu Prophets in South Africa*, 2nd ed. (London: Oxford University Press, 1961), 53-54. See Ilogu, "Independent African Churches in Nigeria," 493. Ilogu observes that some of the churches see their mission also as an attempt to purify the older churches of their worldliness by laying more emphasis on such aspects, like prayer, spiritual healing, meditation, revelation, and Bible study. See also Reuben Marinda, "The Good News in Zion," *Missionalia* 28, no. 2/3 (2000): 234.

[135] Bengt Sundkler is generally regarded as having pioneered the study of these churches. His study focuses mainly on South Africa, where the majority of these churches are. He classifies them into two: Ethiopian and Zionist churches. Those who address themselves as Ethiopian churches do so because it gives them the pride of having some connections and identification with the ancient biblical tradition. In Psalm 68:31, we read: "Ethiopia shall stretch forth her arms to God." By so doing, they believe their claim of "African church," bears some stamp of antiquity. The Zionists (described by him as "syncretistic Bantu movement"), on the other hand, have their historical roots in Zion city in the American State of Illinois, and claim ideological link with mount Zion in Jerusalem. All these are geared towards establishment of authenticity via the claim of antiquity. Sundkler, *Bantu Prophets in South Africa,* 54-58. In his study of these churches in Nigeria, Ilogu divided them into two basic categories: *Aladura* and Ethiopian churches. While the Ethiopian ones are more nationalist and politically inspired, the *Aladura* appear to be more spiritualist-oriented, featuring mostly healing, speaking in tongues, and the like. Ilogu, "Independent African Churches in Nigeria," 492. Dean Gilliland provided what he calls a "fair theological classification" or "a theological typology" of these churches. He sees them as representing a continuum, at one end of which "are those churches or movements that are closest to African forms, but with an unclear Christian expression or belief. On the other end of the spectrum are those that are very close to all that traditional, often Pentecostal Christianity has taught and practiced." In line with the above, he divided them into: Indigenous eclectic, Revelational Indigenous, Secondary Evangelical-Pentecostal and Primary Evangelical-Pentecostal churches. Dean Gilliland, "How 'Christian' Are African Independent Churches?," *Missiology: An International Review* 14, no. 3 (1986): 266. See also Harold

2000, David Barrett pointed out that their membership had reached 83 million. He estimated that by 2005 the number must have been over 140 million.[136] One of the basic features of these churches is their seeming obsession with dreams and their interpretations. In African traditional religion, there is a strong belief that divinities and spirits of ancestors do communicate with the living through dreams and trances. Consequently, dreams usually have spiritual dimensions to them, which need to be explored. The dreamer does not allow its meaning to elude him or her. Instead, he or she "utilises whatever ritual or involves whomever [sic] can help him in the acting out of the demands of his dream. The dream, therefore, is not an isolated, internal, personal, private issue."[137] These churches believe so much in the interpretation of dreams featuring ancestors, God, Jesus or other spirits. Even if others do not have something to say to the living, the ancestors are believed to always have one.[138] The preachings of the prophets in these churches get greater credibility the more they claim to have received them through dreams, visions and propositional revelations. In actual fact, the mission to found these churches is often believed to have been communicated to the founders through visions.[139]

Turner, "A Typology for African Religious Movements," *Journal of Religion in Africa* 1, no. 1 (1967): 1-34; Harold Turner, "New Religious Movements and Syncretism in Tribal Cultures," in *Dialogue and Syncretism: An Interdisciplinary Approach*, ed. Jerald Gort et al. (Grand Rapids, MI: Eerdmans, 1989), 107; Wilbert Shenk, "Mission Agency and African Independent Churches," *International Review of Missions* 63, no. 252 (1974): 475.

[136] See David Barrett, George Kurian and Todd Johnson, ed., *World Christian Encyclopaedia: A Comparative Survey of Churches and Religions in the World AD 30-AD 2000*, 2nd ed., vol. 1 (New York: Oxford University Press, 2001), 13.

[137] Nelson Hayashida, *Dreams in the African Church: The Significance of Dreams and Visions among Zambian Baptists* (New York: Rodopi, 1999), 42. See also Idowu, *Olodumare*, 191. See Kofi Opoku, "Communalism and Community in the African Heritage," *International Review of Missions* 79, no. 316 (1991): 492.

[138] Ogbu Kalu, "Estranged Bedfellows?: The Demonisation of the Aladura in African Pentecostal Rhetoric," *Missionalia* 28, no. 2/3 (2000): 137; Marinda, "The Good News in Zion," 237-238.

[139] Schreiter, *Constructing Local Theologies*, 147. Cf. Terence Ranger, "'Taking on the Mission Task': African Spirituality and the Mission Churches of Manicaland in the 1930s," in *Christianity and the African Imagination: Essays in Honour of Adrian Hastings*, ed. David Maxwell and Ingrid Lawrie (Leiden: Brill, 2002), 118-119.

Miracles and healings (which usually follow the normal incantation processes of the traditional religion) are often taken as marks of authenticity of a particular church. "If miracles do not happen, they consider God to have withdrawn from that particular church."[140] In order, then, to meet the needs of their clients, some of them employ all kinds of occult means and practices. Some use the magical text—the Sixth and Seventh Books of Moses—accompanied by incantations and lighting of candles of various colours, each with its own specific function and symbolic siginificance. Some of them even tend to deify their founders, as is the case among some groups of *Aladura* churches in Nigeria. Though they believe in the scriptures, their founders are sometimes perceived as substitutes for Jesus Christ, while the place assigned to the founder's mother is often higher than that given to the Blessed Virgin Mary in the Catholic tradition.[141] In this form of syncretised religion, practised among the Kambata of Southern Ethiopia, sacrifices with Trinitarian formula are evident, as well as observation of fasts (before Easter and on the Assumption of Mary), baptismal rites, and liturgical calendar quite very close to that of Ethiopian Orthodox church. They replaced God the Father with the sky god (*Manganno*) of the indigenous Cushite religion. In their possession cult, Christ, who is perceived as a lower form of spirit, features very prominently together with St. George. Though their concept of creation, judgement, heaven and hell remain biblical, the mention of the Holy Spirit occurs in the prayers and blessings which form part of the sacrificial rites. The Holy Spirit is called Manfes Keddus as he is called among the Ethiopian Orthodox Christians. In fact, other Christian themes and elements have lost their original meanings and referents due to such syncretism.[142]

Considering what has been discussed above concerning the religious believes and practices of these groups, it is not surprising

---

[140] Marinda, "The Good News in Zion," 239. See Chris Oshun, "Healing Practices among Aladura Pentecostals: An Intercultural Study," *Missionalia* 28, no. 2/3 (2000): 243-246. Oshun argues that, for *Aladura* church, sin is the incontrovertible cause of sickness. Thus, for healing, they essentially stress the need for repentance. Since faith in God is stressed as the sole healer of sickness, other forms of healing are excluded. Ibid.

[141] Ogbu Kalu, "Estranged Bedfellows," 134-137.

[142] Ulrich Braukamper, "Aspects of Religious Syncretism in Southern Ethiopia," *Journal of Religion in Africa* 22, no. 3 (1992): 198-199.

that some scholars are in some sort of dilemma as to whether they can rightly be designated Christian or not. In the words of Dean Gilliland: "While it is unacceptable to label all these churches 'Christian,' it is just as wrong to ignore them or condemn them as non-Christian."[143]

SYNCRETISM AND DUAL (OR MULTIPLE) RELIGIOUS SYSTEMS

It is important that we make the distinction between syncretism and dual (or multiple) religious systems. This is important because many a time scholars tend to lump them together and treat them simply as syncretism.[144] Though the two manifest a similar attitude to religion, a thin line separates them one from the other. While in syncretism, elements extraneous to a particular religion get amalgamated with it or are incorporated into it, in dual (or multiple) systems, people become simultaneously or concurrently involved in two or more distinct religions lying side by side.[145]

Dual or multiple religious systems may be manifest in various ways. One of them is a situation where people practice, for instance, Christianity in its entirety as their dominant religion, but at the same time get involved in some practices and beliefs of another religion. This is common in Africa. Many claim to have converted from the traditional religion to Christianity, but in one way or another certain traditional religious beliefs contrary to the Christian faith still rule their lives at one point or another. Consequently, many a time they privately and secretly indulge in the traditional religious practices, especially in moments of crisis and sickness.[146] Many attend Masses and receive Holy Communion on Sunday morning only to consult traditional priests or healers in the evening for divination or sacrifices. This is what John Walligo describes as "dichotomy or dualism," which involves living out two distinct personalities:

---

143   Gilliland, "How 'Christian'," 266.
144   See, for instance, Anthony Asiegbu, *A Crisis of Faith and a Quest for Spirituality: An Inquiry into Some Syncretistic Practices among Some Christians in Nigeria* (Enugu: Pearl Functions, 2000), 56-98.
145   Luzbetak, *The Church and Cultures: New Perspectives*, 369.
146   Nkwoka, "New Testament Research and Cultural Heritage," 293.

During the times of joy and peace they may be able to live as true Christians, but when crises come, whether of illness, suffering misfortune, death, barrenness and so on, they easily, [ ] move back to their African personality and engage in ceremonies, rites, and worldview that have been constantly condemned by the church.[147]

While the church is very much inclined to point out the irreconcilability or the contradictory nature of such practices to the Christian faith, the people who are involved, more often than not, seem to judge the two as complementary. Some see it as an opportunity to exploit all possible avenues for communion with God.[148]

This is also noticed in the use of sacramentals. Sylvia Leith-Ross observed this trend among the Igbo Christians of Nigeria as far back as 1944. She describes how some Christians tie to their handkerchiefs a rosary together with a protective charm got from a priest of Igbo traditional religion.[149] Some other authors have written much about the prevalence of such practices among some other African Christians.[150] From his own perspective, Chukwudum Okolo argues that such people should not be regarded as Christians in the real sense of the word since, according to him, their allegiance is merely nominal. He even went as far as describing them as "half Christian, half 'pagan'; half God-worshippers, half devil worshippers, half believers in God, angels and saints and half believers in juju, fortune telling, magic, superstition, the 'abracadabra' religious rites and symbols."[151]

---

[147]   John Walligo, "Making a Church That Is Truly African," in *Inculturation: Its Meaning and Urgency*, ed. John Walligo *et al.* (Nairobi: St. Paul, 1986), 22. He attributes such a "dichotomy or dualism" to lack of proper inculturation of Christian faith in the continent, which has made Christianity to be regarded as a foreign import. Ibid.

[148]   Schreiter, *Constructing Local Theologies*, 148.

[149]   Sylvia Leith-Rose, *African Women: A Study of the Ibo of Nigeria* (London: Faber and Faber, 1944), 292-293.

[150]   See, for instance, William Bascom, "African Culture and the Missionary," *Civilization* 3 (1953): 493.

[151]   Chukwudum Okolo, "Igbo Culture and Evangelization: An Inculturation Perspective," *Bigard Theological Studies* 19, no. 1 (1999): 76. "Abracadabra" is just an onomatopoeic way of presenting the incantation that goes with some of the rituals of divination and fortune telling in African traditional religion. This form could also manifest itself in such a way that another religion is practised as a dominant religion while Christianity is practised as a subordinate religion in relation to the people's lives. This is an attitude expressed by some Buddhists

The second form of this dual (or multiple) system is where Christianity and another religion "are followed more or less equally."[152] Both of them function in an essentially independent fashion for the people, though the people concerned may officially profess to be Christians and not also the other. Mathew Schoffeleers gave an account of this kind of practice among the Nsaje people of southern Malawi.[153] This form is also noticed among the Native Americans. They feel that Christianity has contributed a lot, not only in alienating them from their culture, but also in the oppression they have suffered over the years. Therefore, they seek to recover their cherished culture and heritage by having recourse to their old traditional religion. But because they also find so many things very fashionable in Christianity in which they have been formed, they could not leave it either. So, preserving their old traditional religion alongside Christianity seems to be the only viable option.[154] They fully follow their old traditional religion as well as the newly introduced Christianity. For instance, the Aymara people in Peru and Bolivia remain fully committed to the rituals of the old Aymaran religion as well as those of Christianity. A similar practice is also noticed among the Pueblo people in the south-western United States of America. When, for instance, someone dies, a Catholic priest may be invited to perform the normal Christian funeral rites only for a traditional Tewa priest to come later to perform for the same person the funeral rites of the Aymaran religion.[155]

The third form is the one commonly referred to as double (or multiple) religious belonging. This is mostly, though not exclusively, noticed in Asia, where the idea of belonging exclusively to one religion

---

towards Christianity upon its entry into Sri Lanka. See Elisabeth Harris, "Double Belonging in Sri Lanka: Illusion or Liberating Path?," in *Many Mansions?: Multiple Religious Belonging and Christian Identity*, ed. Catherine Cornille (Maryknoll, NY: Orbis, 2002), 78.

152   Luzbetak, *The Church and Cultures: New Perspectives*, 369.

153   Mathew Schoffeleers, "Pentecostalism and Neo-Traditionalism: The Religious Polarization of a Rural District in Southern Malawi," in *Christianity and African Imagination: Essays in Honour of Adrian Hastings*, ed. David Maxwell and Ingrid Lawrie (Leiden: Brill, 2002), 233-234.

154   John Cobb, "Multiple Religious Belonging and Reconciliation," in *Many Mansions?: Multiple Religious Belonging and Christian Identity*, ed. Catherine Cornille (Maryknoll, NY: Orbis, 2002), 22.

155   Schreiter, *Constructing Local Theologies*, 148.

could be said to be foreign.[156] Here, someone professes to be a full member of two or more different religions at the same time. One of the situations that can give rise to this is where a particular religion offers practices and rituals for certain aspects of life, like those relating to death and hereafter, while another religion may limit its emphasis to healing rituals. In such a situation, someone may simultaneously belong to the two in order to fill in the gap left by either of them. This is evident in the relationship shown by some Japanese toward Shintoism and Buddhism. While they turn to Shintoism at the birth of a new child, farming rituals, New Year festivities, and other village celebrations, they turn to Buddhism for funeral rites in moments of death. Though such a practice may seem problematic for Christianity, which tends to claim exclusive or complete control over all areas of life, it is not so for these people because, for them, the two are appropriately combinable. A situation of tension may only arise in cases where the two offer similar services to their adherents. Given that the population of Japan as of 2002 was 126 million, out of which 100 million were Shinto and 95 million Buddhists, one easily observes that majority belonged to these two religions simultaneously. People do not see any contradiction in doing so, for these religions are merely of relative or instrumental importance to them. Religions, for them, are mainly relative in matters of truth claims. They are perceived as primarily concerned with practices and rituals. Questions of doctrine and formal organisation assume only secondary importance.[157]

The situation in Japan is also nurtured by the fact that Shintoism is so interwoven with the rest of the culture that it has become, in a certain sense, part of their national identity. It thus raises the question of whether one can actually become a citizen of the state without at the same time belonging to the religion in question, even after his or her embrace of another. In this kind of situation, double belonging appears inevitable. Commenting on how this functions in Japan, Bragt argues:

---

[156]   This is gradually gaining some adherents in the West, hence such expressions as "Christian-Buddhist or Buddhist-Christian," or such other combinations from people who do not want to identify exclusively with any of these religions, but feel they belong to both. See. Catherine Cornille, ed., *Many Mansions?: Multiple Religious Belonging and Christian Identity* (Maryknoll, NY: Orbis, 2002), 1-2; Bragt, "Multiple Religious Belonging of the Japanese People," 7.

[157]   Bragt, "Multiple Religious Belonging of the Japanese People," 7, 10; Cornille, *Many Mansions*, 2.

A Japanese 'belongs' to the Shinto religion by the fact of birth in Japan . . . Indeed, for the majority of the Japanese, the fact of being a Shinto does not detach itself from the fact of being Japanese, to the extent that, when asked to name the religions they know, they will mention Buddhism and Christianity, and may be Islam, Judaism, and others, but not Shintoism.[158]

To belong to a religion in the western understanding, implying that one finds his or her identity in the religion in question, does not confer the same meaning for most of the Japanese for whom "there is no perceived need for any identity besides being a Japanese and having an identifiable place in Japanese society."[159] Viewed this way, being a Shinto is generally taken for granted. There is generally no perceived problem in associating oneself completely with any other religion. Winston Davis' observation seems apt to make the issue clearer:

> Whereas in the West it was heresy (or pluralism, as it is called today) which seemed to threaten the unity of Christendom, in Japan it was monopraxis (emphasis on a single religious practice) that posed the greatest spiritual menace to the traditional integration of society.[160]

The last form of dual or multiple religious systems that is operative today is where people recognise some values inherent in many religions, show great respect for them, or even agree with some points in each of the several, without actually feeling any sense of commitment or full identification with any.[161] This kind of attitude to religion is rightly captured in 1994 by the British sociologist, Grace Davie, in the expression: "believing without belonging."[162] The "New

---

[158]   Bragt, "Multiple Religious Belonging of the Japanese People," 9.

[159]   Ibid., 10.

[160]   Davis, *Japanese Religion and Society*, 33.

[161]   Cobb, "Multiple Religious Belonging and Reconciliation," 22; Cornille, ed., *Many Mansions*, 3.

[162]   Grace Davie, *Religion in Britain since 1945: Believing without Belonging* (Oxford: Wiley-Blackwell, 1994), 93-105.

Age" movement in the West belongs to this category.[163] Describing their attitude to religion, Boeve writes: "To their hearts' content, they mix eastern meditation techniques with Christian faith symbols, incorporate ancient Celtic rituals into the sacraments, read the Hindu Bhagavadgita beside Christian classics."[164]

All things considered, one easily observes that syncretism, though very close to double or multiple religious systems, is not identical with it. But one needs to be aware that both present similar challenges to genuine inculturation.

SYNCRETISM AND INCULTURATION

The theological understanding of both inculturation and syncretism has already been extensively dealt with. But it is nothing less than worthwhile to articulate, no matter how brief, what I feel is the basic difference between them. It has been made clear enough that the content of any syncretic situation involving Christianity is theologically untenable. Since it leads to a compromise of the specific identity of Christian faith, a theologian's attitude to it should ordinarily be negative. Contrary to this, inculturation does not lead to the betrayal or loss of the identity of Christian faith. It rather points to an effort to make Christianity and its message ever more received by people within their specific cultural situations. In the process of inculturation, Christianity as well as the culture concerned undergo some changes and readjustments in accordance with the demands of both the faith and the culture. Just as the values inherent in the culture are promoted so also are those within Christian faith; just as the faith critiques the culture, so also does the culture critique the faith. It all boils down to mutuality. Both seek for the existence of each other, and not for their destruction. If, in the process, the culture loses its identity, no successful inculturation has been carried out. In the same way, the

---

[163] Cf. Wouter Hanegraaf, *New Age Religion and Western Culture: Esotericism in the Mirror of Secular Thought* (Leiden: E. J. Brill, 1996), 522.

[164] Lieven Boeve, *Between Relativizing and Dogmatizing: A Plea for an Open Concept of Tradition*; available from http://eapi.admu.edu.ph/eapr95/boeve.htm; accessed 31 March 2009.

process could be anything but inculturation if Christianity loses its identity.

Theologically speaking, therefore, one can argue that the major difference between inculturation and syncretism is that, while the latter leads to a compromise or loss of the identity of Christian faith, the former does not. Instead, it seeks to make this identity preserved through a mutually enriching dialogue with a particular culture, thus, showing the dynamic character of the faith, and making it more welcoming to the people.

One significant point that needs emphasising is that, even though the two processes can thus be differentiated, they are not that mutually exclusive. About a century ago, the Dutch theologian, Willem Hooft, posed this question: "Is therefore syncretism in some form not inevitable" in the process of evangelisation?[165] My reply to this is yes. Indeed, certain forms of syncretism may at times be unavoidable in the process of inculturation. This is when it appears as a dynamic and temporary occurrence that develops as one seeks to make the faith integrated in a particular culture. It can be manifest in the doctrinal, the liturgical or the practical forms of Christian witnessing. In such a situation, it happens as part of the growth process. Even though its content does not appear welcome by a theologian, he or she may need to exercise some patience for it may only be an intermediate phase of an "integrative process," which at a long run leads to full inculturation of the faith.[166] In this sense, then, syncretism can become an important vehicle for effective inculturation. It is in this sense that one can say that a "syncretism-free Church is an eschatological hope, not a reality."[167] Having said that, the content of a syncretic process still raises concerns for a theologian, especially if it becomes a settled reality and no longer a temporary phenomenon.

In what follows, illustrative instances will be given from the Old and the New Testaments, as well as from the history of the church,

---

[165] Hooft, *No Other Name*, 10.

[166] Luzbetak, *The Church and Cultures: New Perspectives*, 370. Cf. Turner, "New Religious Movements," 111.

[167] Ibid., 369. Luzbetak reasons that such syncretic situation might be an indication of the basic human needs and values of a particular people that demand greater attention and consideration by the church. Thus, if the church becomes positively disposed towards it, it could serve as a stepping stone in the process of proper integration of Christian faith into a particular cultural ambient.

as to what inculturation looks like. These instances may likely not be typical ones with regard to the demands of effective inculturation, especially given the circumstances of today's society, but they stand to show cases of incorporation of extraneous ideas by either Christianity or Judaism that may not be rightly termed syncretism. It is within the context of this discussion that the differences that exist between inculturation and syncretism will become much clearer. But my intention is by no means limited to this. The illustrations will also, in no small measure, deepen the understanding and appreciation of the challenges faced today by the church as it makes every effort to communicate the faith effectively in our multicultural and multi-religious society.

ILLUSTRATIONS FROM THE OLD TESTAMENT

The Old Testament, which contains the history of God's dealing with the Israelites, offers us in so many different ways powerful illustrations for understanding what is involved in the process of inculturation. We discover that within the context of Israel's history, culture played a very significant role in making their understanding of God's will and the faith they had in him possible. God's revelation of himself to the people and the process by which he made them his own was accomplished, not in spite of, but through the medium of the different cultural situations in which they found themselves at different periods in their history. He was able to communicate with them in their own peculiar situations using the cultural modes of expression that made him more clearly understood by them. In this sense, the cultural riches of the people were utilised in their response to God's offer of salvation. There could not have been any other way by which they would have known God, worshipped him, or expressed their feelings towards him if not through this vehicle.

Moreover, scripture scholars have made us much more aware today of the enormity and intensity of contacts between Israelites and other cultures and religious traditions within the context of the Old Testament, and the amount of intercultural exchange and transformation that transpired among them. That is why the Old Testament could rightly be perceived as "a crossroad of cultures or, to use another metaphor, a crucible," [168] or melting pot of cultures. Israel was able to shape its own history of faith, Joseph Ratzinger reminds us, within the context of its struggles with the different cultures and religions of the ancient Near East: those of the Egyptians, the Hittites, the Sumerians, the Babylonians, the Persians and the Greeks. Having assumed these traditions, they recomposed and transformed them such that they could very effectively be "worthy" vehicles of God's revelation to his chosen people.[169]

Some instances may help substantiate this point. Experts have often alluded to the possible influence of the Mesopotamian epic poem, *War of the gods* (*Enuma elish*), on the creation account as we find it in the Book of Genesis. There are striking parallels between the contents of the myth and the Genesis account. The first observation is the equivalence of the very first two lines of the myth, "When above the heaven had not (yet) been named, (And) below the earth had not (yet) been called by a name,"[170] to the corresponding first verse of Genesis: "In the beginning, when God created the heavens and the earth (Gn 1:1)."[171] Again, in the myth, just as it is in the Book of Genesis, primordial water was present before the act of creation. Granted that in the Book of Genesis, this watery chaos is depicted as "a mass of inanimate matter," as against its portrayal in the myth as "*living* water," related to the god, Apsu, and the goddess, Tiamat,[172] the Hebrew term used for this watery chaos in the Bible, *tehom* (the deep), bears some etymological relation to Tiamat.[173] Moreover, the

---

[168]　Paul Beauchamp, "The Role of the Old Testament in the Process of Building Local Churches," in *Bible and Inculturation*, Inculturation: Working Papers on Living Faith and Cultures, ed. Ary Crollius (Rome: Pontifical Gregorian University Press, 1983), 5.

[169]　Joseph Ratzinger, *Truth and Tolerance: Christian Belief and World Religions*, trans. Henry Taylor (San Francisco, CA: Ignatius, 2004), 70.

[170]　*Enuma elish*, Tablet, I: 1-2. We use the English translation of this poem as contained in Alexander Heidel, *The Babylonian Genesis: The Story of Creation* (Chicago, IL: The University of Chicago Press, 1963), 18-75. See also Andrew George, *The Babylonian Gilgamesh Epic: Introduction, Critical Edition and Cuneiform Texts*, vol. 1 and 2 (Oxford, NY: Oxford University Press, 2003).

[171]　Victor Hamilton, *The Book of Genesis: Chapters 1-17* (Grand Rapids, MI: Eerdmans, 1990), 104.

[172]　Heidel, *The Babylonian Genesis*, 97. Emphasis in the original.

[173]　Daniel Hillel, *The Natural History of the Bible: An Environmental Exploration of the Hebrew Scriptures* (New York: Columbia University Press, 2006), 48. Tiamat

separation of the earth and the sky and the division of waters into two: those under the earth and those above the heavens (Gn 1:6-8), also bears some similarity with the myth, especially where the powerful god, Marduk, is said to have sliced the goddess, Tiamat, in two using one part of him to make the earth and the other to make the sky.[174]

There are other parallels that can still be drawn, but an important observation to be specifically noted is that, though Israel could be said to have been influenced by such stories, they, more or less, recast and incorporated them into their monotheistic faith in Yahweh. For instance, while Marduk, who is described in the myth as "highly exalted" among the gods, surpassing "them in everything," brings order into the universe after his victory over the other lesser gods,[175] in the Genesis account, unity of God is uncompromisingly affirmed. Yahweh needed not battle with any other god before creation. Furthermore, as against the personified chaos in the myth, the chaos of Genesis was simply a depersonalised condition into which God brought some order.[176] *Gilgamesh Epic* is yet another Mesopotamian myth that possibly exerted much influence in some of the stories in the Old Testament, like that of the great flood (Gn 6: 9-8-19).[177]

There are also strong indications that Israelites borrowed some of their sacrificial rites from the Canaanites.[178] Again, in the Book of Psalms and other books of the Hebrew Scriptures, one also finds indications of Israelites' appropriation of the religious language and concepts used in the Canaanite religion into its worship of

---

is the name for the personified goddess of chaos as contained in the myth.

[174] See Tablet IV: 128-140. This parallel is pointed out by: Hillel, *The Natural History of the Bible*, 47-48; Michael Maher, *Genesis*, Old Testament Message, 2 (Wilmington, DE: Glazier, 1982), 21.

[175] See *Enuma Elish*, Tablet I: 81-104; Tab. IV-V.

[176] Hillel, *The Natural History* 49. Unlike these myths, the "Old Testament in general," argues Heidel, "refers to only one Creator and Maintainer of all things, one God who created and transcends all cosmic matter." Heidel, *The Babylonian Genesis*, 97.

[177] For the English text of this and the parallels, see Alexander Heidel, *The Gilgamesh Epic and Old Testament* (University of Chicago Press, 1963), 16-269. See also Hillel, *The Natural History*, 49-52.

[178] Roland de Vaux, *Ancient Israel: Its Life and Institutions*, trans. John McHugh (London: McGraw-Hill, 1961), 441. See also William Graham and Herbert May, *Culture and Conscience: An Archaeological Study of the New Religious Past in Ancient Palestine* (Chicago: Ill: The University of Chicago Press, 1936).

Yahweh.[179] But in doing so, the people also repudiated those aspects of the Canaanite religion and culture that threatened their allegiance to Yahweh. Thus, it was a relationship that did not merely involve acceptance and incorporation, but also "vigorous struggle with and demarcation from the culture and religion of Canaan."[180]

Attention has also been drawn by scholars to the fact that the form of the covenant between Yahweh and Israel (cf. Ex 19-24) may have been modelled after the (political) suzerainty treaties or pacts of the Hittite Empire (1450-1200 BCE), drawn between a great king and his vassal.[181] Israelites are said to have adapted what was for the Hittites a mere political covenant between men to suit its very unique religious aspirations, such that it becomes a special type of covenant between God and humans. By so doing, the covenant assumes a different

---

[179] Schroer uses Psalm 65 to illustrate this point. She shows how the psalm contains indications of Israelites' employment of old Canaanite hymns addressed to Baal, whom the Canaanites identified as the provider of rain and combater of chaos, to address Yahweh. Schroer, "Transformations of Faith," 5-7.

[180] Ibid., 4.

[181] Rita Burns, *Exodus, Leviticus, Numbers: With Excursuses on Feasts / Ritual and Typology* (Wilmington, DE: Michael Glazier, 1983), 147-148. It has been argued, however, that abundant evidences exist, which point to the fact that this form of covenant is not original with the Hittites. Its source could be traced back to Mesopotamia, from where they may have borrowed it. By the second millennium BCE, it must have been present in a number of cultures. See George Mendenhall, "Covenant Forms in Israelite Tradition," *The Biblical Archaeology* 17, no. 3 (1954): 54. For parallels between the basic structure of the Hittite covenant form and Israelite covenant form, see Meredith Kline, *The Structure of Biblical Authority* (Grand Rapids, MI: Eerdmans, 1972), 114-126; Mendenhall, "Covenant Forms in Israelite Tradition," 58-76. See also Rowland Faley, *Bonding with God: A Reflective Study of Biblical Covenant* (New York: Paulist, 1997); Tom Holmén, *Jesus and Jewish Covenant Thinking* (Leiden: Brill, 2001). Scott has also published a well-researched article detailing the present state of research on covenant theology: Scott Hahn, "Covenant in the Old and New Testaments: Some Current Research (1994-2004)," *Currents in Biblical Research* 3, no. 2 (2005): 263-292. For more on the Ancient Near Eastern texts (and pictures) that bear some parallel with the Old Testament, see James Pritchard, ed., *Ancient Near Eastern Texts Relating to the Old Testament* (Princeton, NJ: Princeton University Press), 1950; James Pritchard, ed., *The Ancient Near East in Pictures Relating to the Old Testament* (Princeton, NJ: Princeton University Press 1969).

function, meaning, and significance within their specific religious context.[182]

In addition, the Septuagint, which is a Jewish-Hellenistic production in Alexandria, can be said to be a clear example of inculturation of the Jewish faith in the diaspora Egypt. Very instructive is that the Septuagint is not a mere translation, but incorporated new theological insights, concepts and content.[183] In fact, it has been described as "an autonomous literary work organised around a new constellation of meanings within the Greek system."[184] One can take the Book of Wisdom, which appeared at this period, as a taste case. Not only did Stoic philosophical ideas find their way into it,[185] the female image of God portrayed by the personification of Wisdom (*Sophia*) also serves, in some sense, as a Jewish response to the challenge posed by the Egyptian female goddess, Isis.[186] James Reese

---

[182] Kline, *The Structure of Biblical Authority*, 49-52.

[183] Schroer, "Transformations of Faith," 7. At least, we are aware that the Septuagint contains some new books, which do not form part of the Hebrew Bible of Palestinian Judaism. These new texts, for Catholics, include: Judith, Tobit, 1 and 2 Maccabees, Ecclesiasticus, Wisdom, Baruch, some parts of Esther, and Daniel. These are called deuterocanonical books by Catholics. They very closely correspond to those books called apocrypha by the Protestants: the above named books plus the Prayer of Manasseh, the Third Book of Ezdras, (at times) Fourth Book of Ezdras, 3 and 4 Maccabees. For these, see Mathias Declor, "The Apocrypha and Pseudepigrapha of the Hellenistic Period," in *The Cambridge History of Judaism*, ed. W. Davis and Louis Finkelstein (Cambridge: Cambridge University Press, 1989), 409-410.

[184] Natalio Marcos, *The Septuagint in Context: Introduction to the Greek Version of the Bible*, trans. Wilfred Watson (Leiden: Brill, 2000), 68.

[185] The Stoic philosophical vocabulary evident in the Book include: *pronia*, providence (1: 3); *dioikein*, to order (8: 1; 12: 18; 15: 1); *stoicheia*, elements (7: 17; 19: 18); *sunechein*, to hold together (1: 17); *technitis*, fashioner (7: 22; 8: 6). Epicurean influence is also noticeable in the word, *aphtharsia*, incorruptibility. It is important too to note that it is in this book that the idea of immortality, *athanasia*, appears for the very first time in the Old Testament. See Declor, "The Apocrypha and Pseudepigrapha," 484-485.

[186] Schroer, "Transformations of Faith," 8-13. See also Silvia Schroer, *Wisdom Has Built Her House: Studies on the Figure of Sophia in the Bible*, trans. Linda Maloney and William McDonough (Collegeville, MN: The Liturgical Press, 2000). John Kloppenborg argues that profound influence exerted by the Egyptian Isis on the description of *Sophia* could be seen in *Sophia*'s assimilation into the mythical characterisation of Isis, both as a saviour and as one who

has described the presentation of *Sophia* as "a conscious effort to offset the appeal of the literature of revised Isis cult."[187] Important too is the observation that *Sophia* represents a perfect link between the philosophical tradition prevalent among the youths of Alexandria, which has a universalistic orientation, and the exclusivist attitude characteristic of the Jewish tradition. In addition, the description of Pseudo-Solomon offered the Jews a means of defining themselves against the prevailing paganism of the day by identifying with the strength, wisdom and prosperity of Solomon, who superseded even the "pagan" kings—"*sophos par excellence.*"[188]

To be sure, one sees in Israel's relationship with cultures and religious traditions other than its own the history of a people whose distinctiveness is shaped within the context of its ability to reconstruct, integrate, or assimilate within its own system the many foreign cultural and religious experiences it encountered, utilising them effectively to serve the purpose of its own religious and cultural vision.[189] This could be so because these elements were subjected to "profound transformations."[190] In this connection, Daniel Hillel writes: "Rather than adopt the religion of any of them, they integrated all those influences and gave them a new form and meaning. Their originality was manifested in the coalescence of observations and ideas and in the interpretation given them."[191] According to him, it is not fair to see it as a mere amalgam or mixture of different ideas or beliefs "but, indeed, a radically different intellectual and spiritual insight."[192] Were it to be otherwise, it may have resulted in syncretism. This is not intended to

---

enthrones, cares for and controls the affairs of the king. John Kloppenborg, "Isis and Sophia in the Book of Wisdom," *Harvard Theological Review* 75, no. 1 (1982): 67-78.

[187] James Reese, *Hellenistic Influence on the Book of Wisdom and Its Consequences* (Rome: Biblical Institute, 1970), 40.

[188] See Kloppenborg, "Isis and Sophia," 64-66.

[189] Hillel, *The Natural History*, 37. See also John Paul II, "Address to the Members of the Pontifical Biblical Commission, 26 April 1979," in *Bible and Inculturation*, Inculturation: Working Papers on Living Faith and Cultures, ed. Ary Crollius (Rome: Pontifical Gregorian University Press, 1983), xii.

[190] Efoé-Julien Pénoukou, "Inculturation," *Encyclopedia of Christian Theology* 2 (2005): 768.

[191] Hillel, *The Natural History*, 37.

[192] Ibid., 12. Cf. Colpe, "Syncretism," 220.

suggest, however, that occasions of syncretism never arose among the people. It actually did, but through the help of the prophets it was seriously and adequately checked, resisted and combated (cf. Jr 7: 8; 44: 17; Ez 8; Is 65: 1-12).[193]

EARLY CHRISTIANITY AND HISTORY OF THE CHURCH

There is no doubt that Christianity, right from the first centuries of its existence, has struggled to claim some specific identity and uniqueness among other religious alternatives. It claims to be a religion with a specific message, one based on a specific divine action in history: the perfect, definitive and full revelation of God in the person of Jesus Christ of Nazareth.[194] Though these claims are there, Christianity is also fully aware that its message cannot be completely severed from that of the Old Testament. It recognises rather that it is deeply rooted in, and connected to it and the rest of Israel's history. This is very evident in its Holy Scripture—the New Testament—which, though makes some kind of departure from the Old, nevertheless, shows a marked continuity with it. Its "newness," Francesco de Gasperis reminds us, "is in true continuity with the preceding faith of Israel, as a transfigured and transfiguring fulfilment of the Word already present in the Hebrew Scriptures."[195] Being thus linked to

---

[193] Colpe, "Syncretism," 220.

[194] Cf. Michael Amaladoss, "Inculturation: Theological Perspective," *Jeevadhara: A Journal of Christian Interpretation* 6, no. 33 (1976): 297; Gerhard Delling, *Worship in the New Testament*, trans. Percy Scott (London: Darton, Longman and Todd, 1962), 8-9; Turner, "New Religious Movements," 108.

[195] Francesco de Gasperis, "Continuity and Newness in the Faith of the Mother Church of Jerusalem," in *Bible and Inculturation*, Inculturation: Working Papers on Living Faith and Cultures, ed. Ary Crollius (Rome: Pontifical Gregorian University Press, 1983), 55. It is based on this that de Gasperis calls for a Jewish-Christian understanding of the New Testament. He argues that the New Testament could even be understood, in some sense, as Old Testament reinterpreted in the light of Jesus event. It is in this, he says, lies the unity of the two. Ibid., 56. See also Jacob Jervell, *The Theology of the Acts of the Apostles* (Cambridge: Cambridge University Press, 1996), 4-5. Jervell tries to prove in this book how Luke's Acts of the Apostles portrays the church as a continuation of Israel. He also examines how his whole theology is not only closely related to the Jewish Scriptures, but also their entire tradition.

the Old, it follows that its distinctiveness cannot be realised by being completely disengaged from the Old. This is succinctly argued by de Gasperis when he writes:

> How could Jesus, the Bridegroom, the Lamb-Temple be separated from Jerusalem, his Bride, the wife of the Lamb, the city that he has made new and newly holy? How could the City-Bride stand if her twelve gates, on which the names of the twelve tribes of the sons of Israel are inscribed, were separated from her twelve foundations, on which there are the twelve names of the twelve apostles of the Lamb?[196]

As a matter of fact, to appreciate fully the deep-rooted connection between the Jewish culture and the New Testament one needs to understand well the implications of the fact that Jesus himself was a Jew, lived a Jew and died a Jew. Besides, his immediate disciples were also Jews. Not only was his message to his disciples mediated by the Jewish cultural and religious language and concepts, the very foremost attempts to comprehend them were also made within the same context.[197] His disciples' experience of him was coloured by their Jewish heritage. Thus, their faith in him could only but be "a Jewish-Christian faith" and not otherwise.[198] Jesus only became meaningful to them not in spite of, but through their peculiar Jewish

---

[196]   de Gasperis, "Continuity and Newness," 57.

[197]   Jaroslav Pelikan, *Jesus through the Centuries: His Place in the History of Culture* (New Haven, CT: Yale University Press, 1985), 11. According to Pelikan, this is most evidently seen in the four Gospels. He contends that, though the New Testament was written in Greek, evidences of transliteration of Aramaic language (the language spoken in Palestine by the time of Jesus and the apostles) into Greek are scattered throughout the Gospels and other New Testament writings. These include, among others, the four titles of Jesus: *rabbi* (teacher), *amen, messias* (Christ), and *mar* (Lord). Included also are: Jesus' cry on the cross, "*Eloi, Eloi, lama sabachthani?*" and the word, *Hosanna*. Pelikan also argues that even the word "parable" (in Greek, *parabole*), was taken from the Septuagint, where it represents a Greek translation of the Hebrew word, *mashal*. Others are the Aramaic formulas used by Jesus in his miracles like, "*Ephphatha,*" "*Talitha cumi.*" For more on these, see Pelikan, *Jesus through the Centuries*, 11-17.

[198]   Samuel Rayan, "Flesh of India's Flesh," *Jeevadhara: A Journal of Christian Interpretation* 6, no. 33 (1976): 261.

cultural and historical matrix. In a sense, then, their relationship with the Jewish culture within the context of their new experience of Jesus was marked by continuity and discontinuity. It represents a new transforming experience which cannot be completely severed from its Jewish roots. It was indeed the level of rootedness in the Jewish culture witnessed among the early Christian community of Jerusalem that made it be initially regarded as a sect within Judaism.[199] This stands to show how cultural contexts influence religious experiences, be they beliefs or practices.

Furthermore, the existence of different Christian traditions within the wide variety of early Christian communities, as evident in the different books of the New Testament, stands to show how the singular event of Christ's life, death and resurrection could be adapted to multiple cultural contexts. In actual fact, the different books we have reflect not only a wide variety of traditions that have been handed down within particular communities, each bearing unmistakable imprints of the corresponding community's own needs, aspirations and general cultural background, but also the varied attempts to respond to them. It is very evident, for instance, that the content, style and theology of John's Gospel differ considerably from those of the synoptics.[200] It does not end there. Even among the synoptic Gospels, a whole lot of differences exist. The mere fact of temporal priority of Mark over Matthew and Luke, and the presence of Q source for the last two already make issues lie differently. Moreover, while Matthew adapts his message to the sensibilities of his Jewish addressees, the needs of Luke's gentile readers, like Theophilus (cf. Lk 1: 1-4), also exerted much influence on his own account.[201] This testifies to the determination of the early church to make the message of Christ intelligible to the different communities, be they Jewish or Greek.

---

[199] Ralph Martin, *Worship in the Early Church* (London: Marshall, Morgan and Scott, 1964), 18. See also Leonhard Goppelt, *Apostolic and Post-Apostolic Times,* trans. Robert Guelich (London: Adam and Charles Black, 1970), 26.

[200] Bruce Metzger, *The New Testament: Its Background, Growth, and Content,* Second and Enlarged ed. (Nashville, TN: Abingdon, 1989), 94-96.

[201] For further discussions on these, see Ibid., 80-94. See also George Prabhu, "The New Testament as a Model of Inculturation," Jeevadhara: A Journal of Christian Interpretation, 6, no. 33 (1976): 268-269; Teresa Okure "Inculturation: Biblical/ Theological Bases," in *32 Articles Evaluating Inculturation of Christianity in Africa,* ed. Teresa Okure and Paul van Thiel (Eldoret: AMECEA Gaba, 1990), 69.

From the foregoing, one could, therefore, observe that the significance of multi-cultural expression of the Christian faith emphasised today by the church through the theology of inculturation is not an entirely new reality. These writers reveal to us that faithfulness to the original experience of Jesus Christ, as transmitted through the different traditions can still be guaranteed without neglecting, of course, the needs of new circumstances necessitated by subsequent experiences by yet other new communities.

Therefore, the early Christian communities can be said to be truly inculturated. Even when it became clear in the eyes of the people who earlier regarded them as a sect within Judaism that they were markedly distinct from it or from any other religion, the Jewish and surrounding cultural traditions still played some significant role in their understanding and appropriation of their newly found faith. It should be noted, for instance, that even as they celebrated the Lord's Day (cf. Ap 1: 10) on the day after the Sabbath, they still followed the Jewish chronological reckoning in designating it "the first day of the week" (cf. 1 Cor 16: 2; Ac 20: 7). Furthermore, this day, which was related to the "pagan" sun god in the Greco-Roman Empire, was from then given a specifically Christian meaning. Christ now becomes the true Sun. By this, the "pagan" sun cult was imbued with Christian meaning celebrating Christ's resurrection. It was only then that the term, Sunday, starting with Justin Martyr, began to gain popularity among Christians and was eventually proclaimed as an official holiday by Emperor Constantine in the year 321.[202] Thus, Christianity not only shows some continuity with the Jewish culture, but also with those of other societies where it was subsequently introduced. One can also point out the transformation of various "pagan" festivals, like Christmas, into specifically Christian celebrations.[203] It is only

---

[202] Oscar Cullmann, *Early Christian Worship* (London: SCM, 1978), 11, 12. See Anscar Chupungco, "Inculturation," in *The New SCM Dictionary of Liturgical Worship*, ed. Paul Bradshaw (London: SCM, 2002), 225.

[203] One of the theories concerning the origin of the celebration of Christmas on 25 December has it that it was initiated by Christians in order to rival the "pagan" feast—*Natalis Solis Invicti* (the birthday of the unconquerable sun god)— originally celebrated on the same day in the Roman empire. The second one is the computation theory, which argues that the belief concerning Christ's birth on this day was arrived at after a careful calculation supported by the belief that Christ's conception coincided with his death, which is supposed to have occurred

within the context of such level of continuity with, and sensitivity to, the peculiar customs of the people that the early Christians were also able to launch a severely critical and aversive campaign towards those beliefs that were antithetical to the Christian faith.[204]

It is this pattern of sensitivity to cultural peculiarities and needs of the people that the apostles followed in order to arrive at a decision at the Council of Jerusalem (Ac 15:1-29; Gal 2: 1-10) regarding the admission of the gentiles into the church. As against the Judaisers, who wished to impose the Jewish culture of circumcision on them, it was concluded that the Jewish circumcision (the core of Jewish identity) was not necessary for the salvation of the gentiles (Ac 15: 19). After all, did Peter not argue that it was the same Spirit that was at work among the Jews and the gentiles (Ac 15: 9)? By its decision, the council avoided the uncritical imposition of the Jewish culture on others, thus, emphasising that the gospel can as well take root and be effectively expressed even in foreign cultures.[205] It becomes clear that the universal mission entrusted to the church by Christ does not necessarily entail the universalisation of the Jewish culture. Every nation has the right to be evanglised according to its own culture, thus, bringing to the fore the fact that all nations and cultures are welcome into the one community of faith without segregation.[206] Christianity, this way, constitutes "a Passover from closed Jerusalem-Jewish attitudes to the open attitudes and insights of Hellenist Christians of

---

on 25 March. For detailed account of these two theories, see Sussan Roll, *Towards the Origins of Christmas* (Kampen: Kok Pharos, 1995). See also John Baldovin, "Christmas," *Encyclopedia of Religion* 3 (2005): 1756; Sussan Roll, "Christmas and Its Cycle," *New Catholic Encyclopedia* 3 (2003): 551.

[204] Cf. Nobert Greinacher and Nobert Mette, "Christianity: A Multicultural Experiment," *Concilium*, no. 2 (1994): vii.

[205] Joseph Fitzmyer, *The Acts of the Apostles: A New Translation with Introduction and Commentary* (New York: Doubleday, 1998), 545-546; Georg Kretschmar, "The Early Church and Hellenistic Culture," *International Review of Missions* 84, no. 332/333 (1995): 37.

[206] Martin Hengel, *Acts and the History of the Earliest Christianity* (London: SCM, 1979), 116; de Gasperis, "Continuity and Newness," 59. See also Joseph Osei-Bonsu, *The Inculturation of Christianity in Africa: Antecedents and Guidelines from the New Testament and the Early Church* (Frankfurt: Peter Lang, 2005), 27-30.

Antioch,"[207] among whom Christian communities were inconceivably diverse.

Actually, the new gentile cultural context threw up new questions, new challenges and new possibilities not witnessed in the Jewish cultural milieu, and which elicited corresponding responses and approaches to the practice of the faith from the perspective of the gentile culture itself.[208] At least, this tallies very well with what the church advocates for in the process of inculturation today through its repeated warning against imposition of foreign forms of Christian expression on others in the name of evangelisation; advising rather that true integration be arrived at through an in-depth dialogue with these cultures.[209]

Paul deserves a special mention here as one in whom such dialogue is remarkably evident. Having proclaimed himself an apostle to the gentiles (Rom 11: 13; Gal 2: 8), he effectively utilised the Hellenistic cultural riches in the proclamation of the gospel. Writing in Greek, he employs the Hellenistic philosophical language to explain Christian faith. Shorter refers to a probable influence of Hellenistic mysteries on Paul's use of the Greek word, *musterion*, in the explanation of Christian baptismal initiation.[210] In fact, when Paul, in his Letter to the Philippians (4:8), calls on Christians to be open to whatever is true, just, wholesome, and excellent, Ratzinger reasons that he is likely referring to those basic elements in Stoic morality or Greco-Roman culture in general that bear some close resemblance to Christianity.[211] Some have also refered to the Pauline Areopagus speech (Ac 17: 16-34) as an appropriate illustration of this dialogue. The speech is marked by (critical) Greek philosophical argumentation and categories designed to present the mysteries of faith in such a manner that it meets his audience at their intellectual (cultural) level. Precisely, in Ac 17: 28, Paul uses expressions sometimes attributed to Epimenides of Cnossos, and makes a quote from *Phainomena*,

207   Rayan, "Flesh of India's Flesh," 261.
208   Ibid., 262. See also Fitzmyer, *The Acts of the Apostles*, 553-554.
209   See Peter Schineller, *A Handbook on Inculturation* (Mahwah, NJ: Paulist, 1990), 30.
210   Aylward Shorter, *Towards a Theology of Inculturation* (MaryKnoll, NY: Orbis, 1994), 126.
211   Joseph Ratzinger, *On the Way to Jesus Christ*, trans. Michael Miller (San Francisco, CA: Ignatius, 2005), 49.

a work composed by the Cilician poet, Aratus.[212] Other indications abound of his employment of stoic philosophy in the discourse. Even though Paul's address may not be described as having fully achieved its purpose, some have described it as an instance of inculturation.[213]

Without doubt, such dialogue is also starkly evident in the writings of the Fathers of the Church, by which they perceived earlier "pagan" traditions and cultures "as bearing some positive relationship to the revelation of Jesus Christ."[214] Consequently, even as they claimed Christianity's specificity and uniqueness, they carefully employed various elements from these other sources in presenting the Christian message, though in ways reconcilable "with the manner of living taught by divine revelation."[215] In this way, they exhibited full awareness of the fact that continuity between Christianity and a particular culture can never be complete and total.[216] They cautiously avoided any form of exchange or importation of divine figures from another religion to Christianity, which could have otherwise led to religious syncretism. It is such that, while they recognised the seed of the Word in the "pagan" philosophy, and associated Christianity with this rational process of discernment through which a human person arrives at the knowledge of the universe and the divine,[217] they still regarded Christianity as the genuine Philosophy.[218]

This underlies Justin Martyr's assertion that "whatever things were rightly said among all people are the property of us Christians."[219]

---

[212] David Williams, *New International Biblical Commentary: Acts* (Peabody, MA: Hendrickson, 1990), 301-308; Schineller, *A Handbook on Inculturation*, 127.

[213] Osei-Bonsu, *The Inculturation of Christianity in Africa*, 34. A lot of other instances could still be found among the early Christians. For these see Ibid., 34-53.

[214] Beauchamp, "The Role of the Old Testament," 2.

[215] *AG*, 22.

[216] See Patrick Ryan, "Seven Theses on Inculturation: A Response to 'Inculturation as a Face of African Theology Today,'" in *Faces of African Theology*, ed. Patrick Ryan (Nairobi: CUEA, 2003), 173.

[217] Ratzinger, *On the Way to Jesus Christ*, 72-73.

[218] This is clear in such apologists as Justin and clement. See Avery Dulles, "Can Philosophy Be Christian?," *First Things: The Journal of Religion, Culture and Public Life* (2000); available from http://www.firstthings.com/article.php3?id_article=2599; accessed 4 March 2009.

[219] Justin Martyr, *Apol.* II, 13. See Barnard Leslie trans., *St. Justin Martyr: The First and Second Apologies*, Ancient Christian Writers, vol. 56, ed. Walter Burghardt,

He specifically related Jesus, the Word of God, with the concept of *logos* associated with Middle Platonism. Christ, then, becomes the true *Logos* spoken of by these philosophers.[220] It is also in this sense that Clement of Alexandria speaks of pagan philosophy as that which prepares the way for Christ. It is the same God, he argues, that gave Christians their scriptures who also provided the Greeks with their philosophy. "The way of truth," he maintains, "is therefore one. But into it, as into a perennial river, streams flow from all sides."[221] Thus, when Plato in his *Timaeus* speaks of the three levels of divine reality in the context of his discussion of the creation of the universe, Clement understands it as a reference to the Blessed Trinity.[222] We also see a similar trend in Augustine with his deep acquaintance with neo-Platonism. He acknowledges there are truths shared in common

---

John Dillon and Dennis McManus (New York/Mahwah, NJ: Paulist, 1997), 83-84.

[220] Kretschmar, "The Early Church and Hellenistic Culture," 40. Middle Platonism is the Platonic philosophical school that began with Antiochus of Ascalon (130 BCE-68 CE) and ended with the emergence of Plotinus (204 CE-270 CE), with whom another Platonic school—Neo-Platonism—began. Though these Middle Platonists differ in many respects, there are common characteristics discernible among them: their strong emphasis on the metaphysical and religious dimensions of Plato's philosophy; their belief that Plato's ideas about the universe and divine realities could be reconciled with that of Aristotle; their conviction regarding the existence of hierarchy of spiritual beings at the head of which is the Supreme Mind (God), who, by reason of his/her transcendence, could only be reached through the intermediary ones. See *Middle Platonism: General Characteristics*; available from http://www.theologywebsite.com/history/midplato.shtml; accessed 17 April 2009. See also Jan Opsomer, *In Search of the Truth: Academic Tendencies in Middle Platonism* (Brussel: KAWLSK, 1998), 14.

[221] Clement of Alexandria, *Stromata* 1, 5. For this document, please see Alexander Roberts and James Donaldson, ed., *Ante-Nicene Fathers: Translations of the Writings of the Fathers down to AD 325*, vol. 2 (Grand Rapids, MI: Eerdmans, 1994), 299-568.

[222] Clement, *Stromata* 5, 9. We note that it is during the time of Alexandria, between the second the third centuries, that a collection of Sibylline Oracles emerged. These sayings from "pagan" prophetesses (Sibyls) were interpreted by Christians as prophesies of the coming of Christ. This explains why Sibyls have received some prominence in the tradition of Christian paintings, as one can see, for example, in the Ghent Altar Piece. For more on this, see Peter Schmidt, *The Adoration of the Lamb*, trans. Lee Preedy (Leuven: Davidsfonds, 2006), 80.

by both Christianity and neo-Platonism. It is precisely his attitude toward these pre-Christian cultures that led him to offer a messianic interpretation to Virgil's poem, the *Fourth Eclogue,* affirming that the poet undeniably refers to Christ.[223] These and more made him reach a similar conclusion as Justin did by affirming that the same reality that is now claimed to be Christian was already present in the ancient times.[224]

To be sure, one can go on examining other instances from the writings of the Fathers, but I feel that it has been sufficiently demonstrated by the discussions so far the value they placed on the surrounding cultures and how they used them to communicate the faith. But it is worth remarking that the foregoing discussion should not blur the evident fact that some aspects of such pre-Christian rationality and culture were also anti-Christian. The Fathers, no doubt, condemned them. Even those they judged worthy of the Christian faith were not just literally taken up, but were also largely reformulated.[225]

What is more, it is vital to note that during the time of the Fathers, Christianity not only related with the Greek philosophy, but also with the surrounding religious traditions of the time. There is some level of

---

[223] Augustine, *City of God,* 10, 27. For this, see Gerald Walsh and Grace Monahan trans., *Saint Augustine: The City of God, Books VIII-XVI* (Washington, DC: The Catholic University of America Press, 1952), 167. So much has been written on how neo-Platonism exerted much influence on Augustine's theological reflections. For some of these writings, see, for example, Robert Russell, "The Role of Neoplatonism in St. Augustine's *De Civitate Dei,*" in *Neoplatonism and Early Christian Thought: Essays in Honour of A. H. Armstrong,* ed. H. J. Blumenthal and R. A. Markus (London: Variorum, 1981), 160-170.

[224] Augustine, *The Retractions,* 1, 12. For this, see Mary Bogan, trans., *Saint Augustine: The Retractations* (Washington, DC: The Catholic University of America Press, 1968), 52.

[225] Ratzinger, *Truth and Tolerance,* 86. See also Rudolph Arbesmann, Emily Daly and Edwin Quain, trans., *Tertullian: Disciplinary, Moral and Ascetical Works* (Washington, DC: The Catholic University of America Press, 1959), 31-107. It is vital to note, however, that Tertullian seems to oppose in its entirety the use of philosophy by his contemporaries to explicate the Christian truth. At one point, he asks: "What indeed has Athens to do with Jerusalem? What concord is there between the Academy and the Church?" Tertullian, *On Prescriptions against the Heretics,* 7. For this, see Alexander Roberts and James Donalson, ed., *The Ante-Nicene Fathers: Translations of the Writings of the Fathers down to AD 325,* vol. 3 (Grand Rapids, MI: Eerdmans, 1993), 246.

continuity with these religions in terms of the form, the structure and places of liturgical worship, as well as the manner of spiritual life, like monasticism.[226] But the church was also able to match continuity with discontinuity such that the elements from these religions were able to serve the cause of Christian vocation and mission. That accounts for the fact that the specific identity and uniqueness of Christianity remained inviolate.

Thomas Aquinas' love for Aristotelian philosophy could very well serve as a further substantiation of the issue being pursued here. One recalls that, in the middle Ages, when interest in Aristotelianism was rekindled, Aquinas never condemned it outrightly. Though he remained critical of some of the elements of this philosophical tradition, he, nevertheless, employed it very extensively in presenting the Christian doctrine. He was able to discriminate between those aspects of Aristotelian philosophy that could serve the goal of Christian faith and those that could not. The former were effectively incorporated and utilised to make Christianity meet the intellectual culture of his day.[227] By so doing, the Christian faith was, instead of being compromised, given a new interpretation that helps safeguard its distinctive identity.

> In the language of inculturation, Thomas listened openly to the new ideas, new methods, and new culture that came with Aristotle. He evaluated them and accepted the true and the good, seeing that the same God who spoke through Jesus Christ could also speak through the writings of this pagan philosopher.[228]

The essence of any process that can be described as authentic inculturation lies in the ability to manage well the continuous tension that arises between what Geffré chooses to refer to as "rupture and continuity," or, put in another way, continuity and discontinuity, permanence/fidelity and change, in Christian faith in the course of the church's witness amidst the various cultures of the world.[229] The examination of some cases of syncretism involving Christianity has shown that syncretism usually involves significant discontinuity/

---

[226] Ratzinger, *On the Way to Jesus Christ*, 73-74.
[227] Schineller, *A Handbook on Inculturation*, 32-33.
[228] Ibid., 33.
[229] Geffré, "Double Belonging and the Originality," 97.

rupture with the gospel and the Christian tradition accompanied by easy continuity with another culture or religious tradition without the necessary discontinuity with it. On the contrary, inculturation establishes continuity with the gospel and the Christian tradition, such that even when there is discontinuity with the expression, the content, or the formulation of the faith in the light of new realities, the distinctive identity and uniqueness of the faith is not betrayed or lost.[230] Little wonder that John XXIII, while calling the attention of the Fathers of Vatican II to the need to find more appropriate ways of presenting Christian faith given the contemporary cultural realities, cautions that this should not lead to the destruction of the identity of the faith.[231] In other words, the experience of intercultural and integrative encounter involved in inculturation is directed, not towards formulation of a separate Christian identity estranged from the gospel and the Christian tradition, but towards the communication of this unique identity to suit the contextual sensibility. The identity is preserved amidst reinterpretation and reformulation while the tension between permanence and change is properly handled. Thus conceived, it cannot be said to involve a mere convergence of beliefs or reconciliation of differences.[232]

The issue is that the church should take the responsibility upon itself to study those situations that could give rise to syncretism and do its best to avoid them, even though some of them appear unavoidable. Some are necessary stages that will eventually result in authentic inculturation. Indeed, it would be presumptuous to imagine that all the

---

[230] Schreiter has worked out five criteria against which any inculturated theology (or local theology, as he chooses to describe it) should meet in order to guarantee Christian identity through continuity with the gospel and the Christian tradition. For these, see Robert Schreiter, "Local Theologies in the Local Church: Issues and Methods," in *Sourcebook for Modern Catechesis*, ed. Michael Warren (Winona, MN: St Mary's 1997), 80-82. Cf. *AG* 22; John Newman, *An Essay on the Development of Christian Doctrine* (Notre Dame, IN: Notre Dame University Press, 1989), 169-203; Aloysius Pieris, *Fire and Water: Basic Issues in Asian Buddhism and Christianity* (Maryknoll, NY: Orbis, 1996), 161.

[231] John XXIII, "Opening Address to the Second Vatican Council, 11 October 1962," in *Voices from the Council*, ed. Michael Prendergast and M.D. Ridge (Portland, Or: Pastoral, 2004), xiv-xv.

[232] Cf. Benedict XVI, *Address to the Roman Curia* (22 December 2005); available from http://www.vatican.va/holy_father/benedict_xvi/speeches/2005/december/ hf_ben_xvi_spe_2005; accessed 10 March 2009.

above instances examined from the scriptures and the history of the church just happened without some syncretic formations in one way or another at certain stages. What is needed is for the church to be aware of all these and be more careful in guiding the process so that in the end a genuine inculturation is realised.

OCCASIONS FOR SYNCRETISM AND CHURCH'S RESPONSIBILITY

There are so many situations which provide fertile grounds for the emergence of religious syncretism as far as Christianity is concerned. There is no gainsaying the fact that they pose a lot of challenges to the church. In what follows, such situations as well as the challenges they pose to the church will be discussed. Equally to be examined is how the church can manage them effectively in order that what comes out in its evangelisation work is not a multiplication of syncretised local churches, but rather the establishment of local churches that are truly inculturated.

To begin with, it is important to note that cultures, as one might expect, are very selective when they encounter each other. Being the pattern or design of living for any given society, they do not easily incorporate within themselves elements that are not compatible with the entire cultural system. This being the case, when a particular cultural expression of Christianity is first introduced into another culture, there is usually some tendency for the particular culture in question to select from Christian faith those elements that easily suit its "underlying premises, basic attitudes, and fundamental goals."[233] Should such selective process not be given the needed attention by the church, there is often the possibility that those less challenging elements of the faith, which may have greater appeal to the people are, more often than not, easily selected. Sometimes these elements are subsequently over-emphasised, or even absolutised, while the really challenging and important, but less "palatable," aspects play only veneer roles in people's lives. In such a situation,

> candles and incense may become more important than the Eucharist or the Scriptures; vows and promises, more important

---

[233] Luzbetak, *The Church and Cultures: New Perspectives*, 372.

than the Ten Commandments; the crucifix or a 'miraculous' statue, more important than Christ's death and resurrection; or a patron saint or the Virgin Mary, more important than God himself.[234]

If such a situation goes unchecked by the church, their appeal to the people becomes more and more reinforced. The most likely result is that these practices gradually move farther away from being Christian as they become increasingly directed by the underlying religious meanings derived from another religious tradition previously operative in the host culture.[235] That is why the church has a major role to play in ensuring that adequate measures are taken not to neglect those important but challenging aspects of the faith that might appear less attractive in a particular culture. This way, the "selection" is well guided and guarded for proper integration of the faith into the culture as demanded by effective inculturation.

On another note, it is normal to expect that, when Christian faith is introduced into a particular culture, the people would construe it through their own cultural "spectacle" or frame of mind. Therefore, some kind of reinterpretation becomes inevitable. If the church does not pay adequate attention to this process of reinterpretation and guide it, the people could easily identify the new with the old, thereby paving the way for syncretism.[236] This is the case with the Latin American syncretic groups, which we have examined previously. Here a Roman Catholic saint acquires significations proper to a particular African traditional deity, just because of some sort of congruity perceived between the two by the people. It is such association that eventually leads to the two being identified as one.[237] Similar situations make converts previously accustomed to the use of charms and amulets easily attach magical powers, for instance, to the sacraments, like the Eucharist, as well as the sacramentals. These issues, no doubt, pose much pastoral and theological challenge to the church. Unless they are faced squarely, Christian syncretic forms will constantly arise, not merely as transitory situations along the process of evangelisation

---

[234] Ibid., 373.
[235] Turner, "New Religious Movements," 111.
[236] Luzbetak, *The Church and Cultures: New Perspectives,* 372.
[237] Kraft, *Anthropology for Christian Witness,* 376-377.

(certain instances of which might be inevitable), but more so as settled and permanent state of affairs.

To this end, more authority needs to be given to the local churches in matters of inculturation than is presently the case. It is they who are closer to the people and are able to perceive the problems as they arise. The present practice where ecclesiastical authorities who lack such direct experience of the people and their problems pretend to dictate the pace of inculturation for the local churches will not help much. This must be re-examined and reappraised, if the church is prepared to make any serious impact in this regard.[238]

Another factor that commonly leads to syncretism is the inability of the church to provide what Luzbetak calls alternative "satisfactory Christian functional substitutes" for those unchristian elements displaced by the Christian message in its encounter with a particular culture.[239] When such substitutes are lacking, people might be tempted to slide back to their previous religious commitment (without, however, leaving Christianity entirely), in order to provide for those areas where they feel the lack exists. When these provisions are made, they are easily amalgamated with Christian faith into which they have already been introduced. This way, a syncretic mixture results. This is part of the reasons, as we have already seen, why there has been a sudden surge in recent times of syncretic independent churches all over the continent of Africa. These churches see their emergence as an opportunity to reclaim the religious functions offered them by, say, the exuberance, faith healing and exorcism characteristic of African traditional religion. These, they believe, have been unfortunately displaced by Christianity without offering suitable alternatives, except some rigid liturgical formulation fashioned by the western Christianity. The issue involved here, therefore, is not a matter of not having imposed enough liturgical rules on the people. On the contrary, it is a reaction against such "arid" legislations; a response to "a felt need

---

[238]   Joseph Mattam, "The Message of Jesus and Our Customary Theological Language: An Indian Approach to a New Language and Inculturation," *Exchange* 34, no. 3 (2005): 129. See also Sebastian Elavathingal, *Inculturation and Christian Art: An Indian Experience* (Rome: Urbaniana University Press, 1990), 264.

[239]   Luzbetak, *The Church and Cultures: New Perspectives*, 373.

for a more spontaneous outlet for religious feeling than is generally allowed in strict liturgical functions."[240]

In such a situation, naïve hostility or outright condemnation of these realities as devilish or diabolical will lead to nowhere. For Christianity to permeate these cultures thoroughly without creating such loopholes, much time and commitment is needed.[241] The church should endeavour to study carefully the functions of the people's traditional forms of religiosity before making some innovations. This will help ensure that such innovations do not only strive to serve the authenticity of Christian faith, but more importantly, to offer the people the much-needed culturally non-alienating worship of God. A situation where the church becomes "too quick to stamp Christ on local cultures or to stamp out these cultures to make room for Christ,"[242] complicates issues; a far cry from the deep integration called for by genuine inculturation.

One can identify another major cause of syncretism as the failure of the church to address questions and issues relevant to the people. "Nothing is so incredible," the American theologian, Reinhold Niebuhr reminds us, "as an answer to an unasked question."[243] If Christianity fails to meet the people were they are, the stage is set for the folk piety to evolve into syncretic religious expressions. If African Christianity, for instance, concentrates merely on highly systematised western theological speculations and is unable to address issues of, say, witchcraft, charms, belief in ancestral spirits and their enormous influence on the living, evil spirits, curses, re-incarnation, and so on, which daily suffocate the "mental space" of the people, it is simply *bound to fail*. A situation of spiritual uncertainty is created among the people. This encourages their inevitable search for solutions in their traditional religion, where they feel these issues are adequately given their deserved attention. Mixing them up with their Christian popular

---

[240] Ibid.

[241] John Paul II, "Encyclical Letter, On the Permanent Validity of the Church's Missionary Mandate, *Redemptoris Missio*, 7 December 1990," *AAS* 83 (1991): no. 52; Shorter, *African Christian Theology*, 13.

[242] Joseph O'Leary, "Towards a Buddhist Interpretation of Christian Truth," in *Many Mansions?: Multiple Religious Belonging and Christian Identity*, ed. Catherine Cornille (Maryknoll, NY: Orbis, 2002), 37.

[243] Reinhold Niebuhr, *The Nature and Destiny of Man: A Christian Interpretation*, vol. 2 (New York: Charles Scribner's Sons, 1955), 6.

piety easily becomes the next available alternative. For Luzbetak, if Christianity fails to reach the deeply felt needs of the people, it is nothing short of "elitist or culturally irrelevant." This, he opines, "will merely encourage untheological forms of popular piety, a return to pre-Christian ways, unchristian beliefs and practices borrowed from neighbouring societies, or neopaganism"[244]

Lastly, it might be important to note that unwarranted fear of syncretism and over-zealous defence of doctrinal validity remains another factor that nurtures situations that easily lead to syncretism. In point of fact, it remains to be proven how over-preoccupation with orthodoxy of doctrine would not easily result in the scuttling of ingenuity and spontaneity needed for successful inculturation. In situations where such genuine, inner, dynamic response to the faith is lacking, real conversion becomes difficult, and superficial adaptation or translation is achieved, giving room for syncretic amalgamation. It cannot be denied that inculturation involves a risk. This risk cannot be reasonably avoided. The church should be aware that, when considered from the point of view of process, in certain cases, syncretic situations are indeed inevitable, representing a necessary step towards an in-depth inculturation. Neither conversion nor inculturation is automatic. It might involve a long process which syncretic stage may form a part. Thus, in such situations, what it should do is to be patiently studying and guiding the faithful in their growth towards greater maturity of faith.

In a nutshell, one can see from the discussion so far that the issue of religious syncretism really challenges the church to study very carefully the cultures of the different people among whom it functions.[245] It is only by so doing can their deep-felt needs be properly addressed without losing the identity of Christian faith. The faith thus becomes thoroughly inculturated avoiding all unnecessary untheological amalgam or mixture.

---

[244] Luzbetak, *The Church and Cultures: New Perspectives*, 373.

[245] See Paul Hiebert, "Critical Contextualization," *Missiology* 12, no. 3 (1984): 287-296.

Conclusion

This last chapter represents, though not exclusively, an attempt to bring into clearer focus the ideas and arguments espoused in the preceding chapters. It helped to envision in a more concrete way the enormity of challenges facing the church as it tries to bear witness to the faith in specific cultural contexts. Efforts were made to examine how syncretism could constitute a serious cog in the wheel of progress of inculturation in the local churches. Apart from going through the historical development of the word, it was shown how the term is employed by researchers from different scholarly disciplines, as well as its theological usage. The point is that its usage in theology helps to promote the continued relevance of the concept. It is the theological understanding of the term achieved in the chapter that became the guide in the examination of the different forms syncretism could take as well as in distinguishing it from double religious systems and inculturation. Lastly, the different situations that could give rise to syncretism and how the church should face them squarely were examined. From the discussions, it has now become unarguably clearer that syncretism can only be properly handled in the church if the church is prepared for a deep and intense study of people's cultures, their needs and aspirations and not concentrate its energy on making mere rigid legislations and dictations from authorities. Much time and effort is needed, not only on the part of professional theologians, but also for all those involved in the pastoral work. The members of different local churches need to take the bull by the horn, because they are the ones who live these realities in their respective concrete life situations.

GENERAL CONCLUSION

From the findings in this research, the important place occupied by culture in the achievement of the church's mission has been made clearer. It has been demonstrated that the way the church conceptualises culture makes a whole lot of difference in the manner of its theological reflections and missionary praxis. This being the case, one can now better appreciate the point advanced by Luzbetak when he writes: "Nothing could be more fundamental than a proper understanding of the term [culture]. A failure to grasp the nature of culture would be a failure to grasp much of the nature of missionary work itself."[1] Since culture is the plan or the design, which directs the actual behaviour of the members of different societies, the activity of the church can only have its impact on the lives of the people if it respects and follows this pattern. I have maintained throughout the work that "there is no other way of establishing, consolidating, and perpetuating the Church in a society than through its culture."[2] Faith is always lived in a cultural milieu. Consequently, any effort to consolidate the faith without adequate reference to the cultural nature of the human person is, to say the least, unrealistic. This is the primary challenge that any genuine effort at inculturation is bound to face.

---

[1] Louis Luzbetak, *The Church and Cultures: An Applied Anthropology for the Religious Worker* (Techny, IL: Divine Word, 1970), 59. See also Louis Luzbetak, *The Church and Cultures: New Perspectives in Missiological Anthropology* (Maryknoll, NY: Orbis, 1988), 133.

[2] Ibid., 6.

It is evident that part of the reason why inculturation was not given due attention prior to Vatican II was because the church's understanding of culture by then was primarily classicist. This view of culture, as has been discussed, promoted the feeling of cultural superiority by which the western Christianity understood itself as the bearer of a universal culture according to which the lives of all other people were to be more or less patterned. This way, the hegemonic imperative that one's "particular" predominates as the "universal" became the operative principle. This, in some sense, legitimized the understanding of missionary activity to other people outside the West as involving a movement from the cultured or the civilised to the uncultured, faithless barbarians and "pagans." These other people's cultures were denigrated in favour of the western. With this classicist mindset, the church was convinced that part of its noblest actions was its conversion of the non-western "other," from his or her specific culture to the "universal" western culture presumed to be "the culture of humanity." Since others were seen to have no culture in the real sense of the word, whatever they had was perceived as unable to adequately convey the message of Christ. Western Christians thought they alone had a narrative to tell. Others were previously in the dark and it was only with their Christianity could these people behold the light. This mentality continued and was re-enforced by colonialism.

This research reveals further that this attitude created an atmosphere where the church's creeds and dogmatic statements were assumed to enjoy unchangeable essence. Consequently, theologians laboured to produce uniform theology that enjoyed both geographical and temporal universality, identical applicability and comprehensibility. It was not sufficiently realised that theological formulas claiming universal truth were often masked particularities. Little attention was given to the fact that Christian texts and practices seriously reflect the dominant cultures of their origin. Thus, the contingency of human experience and human cultural situatedness was little considered. Little wonder, then, that Christianity was, in so many cultures, labelled a foreign import which could not adequately address the people's legitimate needs and aspirations.

It is against this background that one readily appreciates the importance of an improved understanding of the nature of culture today, which an American anthropologist, Alfred Kroeber, describes as "the most significant accomplishment of anthropology in the first half of the 20th century."[3] Interestingly enough, at Vatican II, the church improved on the classicist view it had held for almost two millennia, and officially adopted a more comprehensive, descriptive and anthropological view of culture. In this sense, culture is understood as natural to all human beings in so far as it is in the human nature to strive towards self-realisation through transformation and humanisation of the universe.[4] Everyone is both an architect and object of culture. Accordingly, culture manifests a great variety following the diversity in human conditions and environments. It is in this sense that plurarity of cultures can be adequately affirmed. This ushered in the theological climate favouring the development of the theology of inculturation.

The influence of this improved understanding of culture is undeniably felt today both in theology and church's missionary commitment. Theologians have come to understand that theology is a cultural practice. Being so, its reflections are undeniably coloured by the age, the cultural forces and interests at work at any particular place and time where it takes place. The theologian cannot reflect in a vacuum. There is greater awareness of relativity of knowledge in theology because one cannot talk of propositional thinking that is culture free. Doctrinal formulations too cannot arise acontextually or ahistorically. These bear the imprints of the forces at play in the contexts of their formulations. The different Gospel narratives bear the imprint of the cultures that produced them. That is why the singular event of the life, suffering, death and resurrection of Jesus could be presented in different ways by different authors, each account betraying the cultural history of its author. Since ideas, texts, and practices arise from cultural contexts, it has become clearer that, unless these contexts are passionately studied and analysed, their intended meaning and significance may not be fully grasped. This being the case, care is taken today not to literally impose texts and theologies that emerge from different cultural situations unto others.

There is also the recognition that the word of God is already present in non-Christian cultures even before ever the good news of Christ is proclaimed to them. This fact seriously challenges the church

---

[3]   Alfred Kroeber, "Anthropology," *Scientific American* 183 (1950): 87.

[4]   Some researches in the secular sciences are even pointing toward the possibility of possession of culture by apes.

to re-examine more critically the relationship between Christian faith and different cultures. No wonder there is today greater interest in inculturation among theologians and ecclesiastical hierarchy. Part of the findings in this work is that inculturation incorporates a very suitable and viable theological model defining the proper relationship between Christian faith and specific cultures. Following the mystery of the Incarnate Word, inculturation strives to make the faith "incarnate" in different cultures so as to ensure concrete realisation of Christ's redemption in these places. Moreover, by recognising that uniform design for living is unrealistic in the world, it challenges the classicist mono-cultural view of the world, and invites all to live the mystery of Christ from within their specific cultures.

I have argued that no true unity can be achieved in the church without the legitimate diversity and pluriformity which inculturation promotes. This makes the tension between particularity and universality central in any genuine attempt at inculturation. But the particularity that inculturation promotes is not "particularity unto isolationism," but "particularity through complementarity." It is also only through such particularity can the church be truly universal in the sense that by it the faith is made to permeate each culture and locality, thus, offering the people meaning that is very fundamental to their existence and survival as human persons.

It is only when the church fails to encourage such particularity within the context of authentic inculturation that Christianity easily slides into religious syncretism. It is discovered in the course of the research that syncretism, when analysed theologically, poses a great challenge to inculturation. Unlike cases of inculturation where the encounter between Christian faith and another cultural or religious tradition makes the identity of Christianity ever more manifest within each locality, syncretism, being a theologically untenable amalgam, leads to loss of this identity. Hence, it poses a threat to the specificity of Christianity as a religion. It is my contention that this phenomenon can only be checked if the church takes seriously the fact that each locality or culture has its peculiar questions, needs, aspirations and concerns, which can only be discovered when it is given the needed attention. To achieve this, the local churches must be given more authority and responsibility to manage their own affairs than is currently the case. Only then can legitimate limit of continuity and/or discontinuity of the faith with any given culture or religious tradition be easily fostered, and the needed continuity and/or discontinuity with the established Christian tradition maintained. This alone can ensure deep encounter that is able to provide answers to questions relevant to the people, thus, reducing people's search for alternative solutions that many a time helps to promote the emergence of syncretic situations. It is in view of this that one finds seriously wanting the practice of mere imposition from the church's hierarchy of regulations that are devoid of concrete pastoral relevance. A more serious commitment is needed, the absence of which makes the whole work of evangelization seem fruitless.

As a matter of fact, it is high time the church acknowledged and faced squarely the multi-faceted nature of the challenges of effective inculturation in our today's society. Unless it does so, Christian faith will continue to fall into disrepute and may eventually run out of relevance in the lives of the majority of people. The stakes are really high that the failure of the church can hardly be excused.

SELECTED BIBLIOGRAPHY

1. ECCLESIASTICAL SOURCES

1.1. CONCILIAR DOCUMENTS

Council of Chalcedon (451). In *Decrees of the Ecumenical Councils: Nicaea I to Lateran V*, ed. Norman Tanner, vol. 1, 75-103. London: Sheed & Ward, 1990.

Council of Constantinople II (553). In *Decrees of the Ecumenical Councils: Nicaea I to Lateran V*, ed. Norman Tanner, vol. 1, 105-122. London: Sheed & Ward, 1990.

Sacred Congregation for the Divine Worship and the Discipline of the Sacraments, *Varietates Legitimae*, 29 March 1994. Available from http://www.adoremus.org/doc_inculturation.html. Accessed 23 November, 2013.

Vatican Council II. "Constitution on the Sacred Liturgy, *Sacrosanctum Concilium*," 4 December, 1963. *AAS* 56 (1964): 97-138.

Vatican Council II. "Decree on the Eastern Catholic Churches, *Orientalium Ecclesiarum*," 21 November 1964. In *Decrees of the Ecumenical Councils: Trent to Vatican II*, ed. Norman Tanner, vol. 2, 900-907. London: Sheed & Ward, 1990.

_____. "Decree on Ecumenism, *Unitatis Redintegratio*" 21 November 1965. *AAS* 57 (1965): 90-112.

_____. "Decree on the Missionary Activity of the Church, *Ad Gentes*," 18 November 1965. In *Decrees of the Ecumenical Councils: Trent to Vatican II*, ed. Norman Tanner, vol. 2, 1011-1042. London: Sheed & Ward, 1990.

_____. "Dogmatic Constitution on the Church, *Lumen Gentium*," 21 November 1964. In *Decrees of the Ecumenical Councils: Trent to Vatican II*, ed. Norman Tanner, vol. 2, 849-898. London: Sheed & Ward, 1990.

_____. "Pastoral Constitution on the Church in the World of Today, *Gaudium et Spes*," 7 December 1965. In *Decrees of the Ecumenical Councils: Trent to Vatican II*, ed. Norman Tanner, vol. 2, 1069-1135. London: Sheed & Ward, 1990.

1.2. Papal Documents

Benedict XV. "Encyclical Letter, On the Propagation of the Faith throughout the World, *Maximum Illud*," 30 November 1919. *AAS* 11 (1919): 440-455.

Francis, Apostolic Exhortation, *The Joy of the Gospel, Evangelii Gaudium*, 24 November 2013. Available from http://www.vatican.va/holy_father/francesco/apost_exhortations/documents/papa-francesco_esortazione-ap_20131124_evangelii-gaudium_en.html#Star_of_the_new_evangelization. Accessed 25 December 2013.

John Paul II. "Address to the Bishops of Nigeria," 15 February 1982. *Origins* 11, no. 37 (1982): 584-587.

_____. "Address to the First Meeting of the Pontifical Council for Culture," 18 June 1983. In *The Church and Cultures since Vatican II: The Experience of North and Latin America*, ed. Joseph Gremillion, 201-206. Notre Dame, IN: University of Notre Dame Press, 1985.

_____. "Address to the Members of the Pontifical Biblical Commission," 26 April 1979. In *Bible and Inculturation*. Inculturation: Working Papers on Living Faith and Cultures, ed. Ary Crollius, xi-xiii. Rome: Pontifical Gregorian University Press, 1983.

_____. "Address to UNESCO," 2 June 1980. *Origins* 10, no. 4 (1980): 58-64.

_____. "Apostolic Exhortation, On Catechesis, *Catechesi Tradendae*," 16 October 1979. *AAS* 71 (1979): 1277-1340.

_____. "Apostolic Exhortation, On the Church in Africa, *Ecclesia in Africa*," 14 September 1995. *AAS* 88 (1996): 5-82.

_____. "Encyclical Letter, On the Permanent Validity of the Church's Missionary Mandate, *Redemptoris Missio*," 7 December 1990. *AAS* 83 (1991): 249-390.

_____. "Encyclical Letter, On the Value and Inviolability of Human Life, *Evangelium Vitae*," 25 March 1995. *AAS* 87 (1995): 401-522.

_____. "Encyclical Letter, The Apostles of the Slavs, *Slavorum Apostoli*," 2 June 1985. *AAS* 77 (1985): 779-813.

_____. "Man's Entire Humanity Is Expressed in Culture, Address of John Paul II to UNESCO," Paris, 2 June 1980. In *The Church and Culture since Vatican II: The Experience of North and Latin America*, ed. Joseph Gremillion, 187-200. Notre Dame, IN: University of Notre Dame Press, 1985.

_____. "The African Bishop's Challenge." *Origins* 10, no. 2 (1980): 28-30.

John XXIII. "Opening Address to the Second Vatican Council," 11 October 1962. In *Voices from the Council*, ed. Michael Prendergast and M.D. Ridge, x-xviii. Portland, OR: Pastoral, 2004.

Leo XIII. "Encyclical Letter, On the Evils Affecting Modern Society: Their Causes and Remedies, *Inscrutabili*," 21 April 1878. In *The Church Speaks to the Modern World: The Social Teachings of Leo XIII*, ed. Etienne Gilson, 278-290. Garden City, NY: Image, 1954.

Nicholas V. "Bull, *Romanus Pontifex*." In *European Treaties Bearing on the History of the United States and Its Dependencies*, ed. Gardiner Davenport, 13-26. Washington, DC: Carnegie Institute of Washington, 1917.

Paul VI. "Apostolic Exhortation, On Evangelization, *Evangelii Nuntiandi*," 8 December 1975. *AAS* 68 (1976): 5-76.

Paul VI. "Apostolic Letter, *Octogesima Adveniens*," 14 May 1971. *AAS* 63 (1971): 401-441.

Pius XI. "Encyclical Letter, On Catholic Missions, *Rerum Ecclesiae*," 28 February, 1926. *AAS* 18 (1928): 65-83.

_____. "Encyclical Letter, On Reconstruction of the Social Order, *Quodragesimo Anno*," 15 May 1931. *AAS* 23 (1931): 177-228.

Pius XII. "Allocution to the Pontifical Mission Aid Societies." *AAS* 36 (1944): 207-213.

_____. "Allocution to Italian Jurists, *Ci Riesce*," 6 December 1953. *AAS* 45 (1953): 794-802.

_____. "Encyclical Letter, On the Promotion of Catholic Missions, *Evangelii Praecones*," 6 July 1951. *AAS* 43 (1951): 497-528.

1.3. Other Documents

Catechism of the Catholic Church. Revised ed. London: Chapman, 1999.

Congregation for the Propagation of the Faith, "Instruction Concerning Certain Ceremonies and the Oath about the Chinese Rites Controversy." In *100 Roman Documents Concerning the Chinese Rites Controversy (1645-1941)*, ed. Ray Noll, 88-89. San Francisco, CA: The Ricci Institute for Chinese-Western Cultural History, 1992.

The Holy Bible: Revised Standard Version. London: Catholic Truth Society, 1966.

"Statement of the Bishops of Africa." *AFER* 17, no. 1 (1975): 56-59.

2. Books

Achebe, Chinua. *Things Fall Apart*. London: Heinemann, 1981.

Amaladoss, Michael. *Making All Things New: Dialogue, Pluralism and Evangelization in Asia*. Maryknoll, NY: Orbis, 1990.

_____. *Beyond Inculturation: Can Many Be One*. Delhi: Society for Promotion of Christian Knowledge, 1998.

Aquinas, Thomas. *Summa Theologiae—Latin Text and English Translation, Introductions, Notes, Appendices and Glossaries*. Translated by Thomas Gilby. Vol. 11. Cambridge: Blackfriars, 1964.

Arbesmann, Rudolph, Emily Daly and Edwin Quain, trans. *Tertullian: Disciplinary, Moral and Ascetical Works*. Washington, DC: The Catholic University of America Press, 1959.

Arbuckle, Gerald. *Culture, Inculturation, Theologians: A Postmodern Critique*. Collegeville, MN: Liturgical, 2010.

Archer, Margaret. *Culture and Agency: The Place of Culture in Social Theory*. Revised ed. New York: Cambridge University Press, 1996.

Arnold, Matthew. *Culture and Anarchy: An Essay in Political and Social Criticism*. London: Smith and Elder, 1909.

Asiegbu, Anthony. *A Crisis of Faith and a Quest for Spirituality: An Inquiry into Some Syncretistic Practices among Some Christians in Nigeria*. Enugu: Pearl Functions, 2000.

Azevedo, Marcello. *Inculturation and the Challenges of Modernity*. Inculturation: Working Papers on Living Faith and Cultures, ed. Ary Crollius. Rome: Pontifical Gregorian University Press, 1982.

Baird, Robert. *Category Formation and History of Religions*. Hague: Mouton, 1971.

Barrett, David, George Kurian and Todd Johnson, ed. *World Christian Encyclopaedia: A Comparative Survey of Churches and Religions in the World AD 30-AD 2000*. Vol. 1. New York: Oxford University Press, 2001.

Bevans, Stephen. *Models of Contextual Theology*. Maryknoll, NY: Orbis, 1992.

_____. *Models of Contextual Theology*. Revised and Expanded ed. Maryknoll, NY: Orbis, 2002.

Blumenthal, Albert. *The Relations between Culture, Human Social Interaction, Personality and History*. Marietta, OH: Marietta College, 1938.

Blumenthal, H. J. and R. A. Markus, ed. *Neoplatonism and Early Christianity: Essays in Honour of A. H. Armstrong*. London: Variorum, 1981.

Boeve, Lieven. *God Interrupts History: Theology in a Time of Upheaval*. Translated by Brian Doyle. New York: Continuum, 2007.

_____. *Interrupting Tradition: An Essay on Christian Faith in a Postmodern Context*. Translated by Brian Doyle. Leuven: Peeters, 2003.

Boff, Leonardo. *Church, Charism and Power: Liberation Theology and the Institutional Church*. Translated by John Diercksmeier. London: SCM, 1985.

_____. *New Evangelization*. Maryknoll, NY: Orbis, 1991.

Bogan, Mary, trans. *Saint Augustine: The Retractations*. Washington, DC: The Catholic University of America Press, 1968.

Boyer, Paschal. *Religion Explained: The Evolutionary Origins of Religious Thought*. New York: Basic Books, 2001.

Brillington, Rosamund *et al*. *Culture and Society: A Sociology of Culture*. London: Macmillan, 1991.

Bühlmann, Walbert. *The Mission on Trial, Addis Ababa 1980: A Moral for the Future from the Archives of Today*. Middlegreen: St. Paul, 1978.

Burns, Rita. *Exodus, Leviticus, Numbers: With Excursuses on Feasts/ Ritual and Typology*. Wilmington, DE: Michael Glazier, 1983.

Congar, Yves. *Challenge to the Church: The Case of Archbishop Lefebvre*. Translated by Paul Inwood. London: Collins, 1977.

Cornille, Catherine, ed. *Many Mansions?: Multiple Religious Belonging and Christian Identity*. Maryknoll, NY: Orbis, 2002.

Cote, Richard. *Re-Visioning Mission: The Catholic Church and Culture in Postmodern America*. New York: Paulist, 1996.

Crowther, Samuel and J. C. Taylor. *The Gospel on the Banks of the Niger*. London: Dawsons of Pall Mall, 1869.

Cullmann, Oscar. *Early Christian Worship*. London: SCM, 1978.

Daniel, Wilson. *Anthropology*. The Humbolt Library Series. New York: Humboldt, 1885.

Davie, Grace. *Religion in Britain since 1945: Believing without Belonging*. Oxford: Wiley-Blackwell, 1994.

Davis, Winston. *Japanese Religion and Society*. Albany, NY: State University of New York Press, 1992.

Dawson, Christopher. *Religion and Culture: The Clifford Lectures Delivered at the University of Edinburg in 1947*. 2nd ed. New York: Meridan Books, 1958.

Delling, Gerhard. *Worship in the New Testament*. Translated by Percy Scott. London: Darton, Longman and Todd, 1962.

Dhavamony, Mariasusai. *Christian Theology of Inculturation*. Roma: Editrice Pontificia Universita Gregoriana, 1997.

Dorr, Donal. *Mission in Today's World*. Maryknoll, NY: Orbis, 2000.

Downs, James. *Cultures in Crisis*. Beverly Hills, CA: Glencoe, 1971.

Eagleton, Terry. *The Idea of Culture*. Oxford: Blackwell, 2003.

Edet, Rose and M. Umeagudosi, ed. *Life, Women and Culture*. Lagos: African Heritage Research, 1991.

Elavathingal, Sebastian. *Inculturation and Christian Art: An Indian Experience*. Rome: Urbaniana University Press, 1990.

Faley, Rowland. *Bonding with God: A Reflective Study of Biblical Covenant*. New York: Paulist, 1997.

Fauconnier, Gilles and Mark Turner. *The Way We Think: Conceptual Blending and the Mind's Hidden Complexities*. New York: Basic Books, 2002.

Fernandes, Angelo. *Vatican II Revisited*. Anand: Gujara Sahitya Prakash, 1997.

Ferraro, Gary and Susan Andreatta. *Cultural Anthropology: An Applied Perspective*. 8th ed. Belmont, CA: Wadsworth, 2010.

Fitzmyer, Joseph. *The Acts of the Apostles: A New Translation with Introduction and Commentary*. New York: Doubleday, 1998.

Gallagher, Michael. *Clashing Symbols: An Introduction to Faith and Culture*. 2nd ed. London: Darton, Longman and Todd, 2003.

Geertz, Clifford. *The Interpretation of Cultures: Selected Essays*. London: Hutchinson, 1975.

Gelpi, Donald. *Inculturating North American Theology: An Experiment in Foundational Method*. Atlanta, GA: Scholars, 1988.

George, Andrew. *The Babylonian Gilgamesh Epic: Introduction, Critical Edition and Cuneiform Texts*. Vol. 1 and 2. Oxford, NY: Oxford University Press, 2003.

Gilson, Etienne, ed. *The Church Speaks to the Modern World: The Social Teachings of Leo XIII*. Garden City, NY: Image, 1954.

Glaser, Barney and Anselm Strauss. *The Discovery of Grounded Theory: Strategies for Qualitative Research*. New York: Aldine, 1967.

Goppelt, Leonhard. *Apostolic and Post-Apostolic Times*. Translated by Robert Guelich. London: Adam and Charles Black, 1970.

Gort, Jerald *et al.*, ed. *Dialogue and Syncretism: An Interdisciplinary Approach*. Grand Rapids, MI: Eerdmans, 1989.

Graham, William and Herbert May. *Culture and Conscience: An Archaeological Study of the New Religious Past in Ancient Palestine*. Chicago, IL: The University of Chicago Press, 1936.

Grant, Frederick. *Hellenistic Religions: The Age of Syncretism*. New York: Liberal Arts, 1953.

Green, Peter. *Alexander the Great and the Hellenistic Age: A Short History*. London: Orion, 2008.

Greenfield, Sidney and André Droogers, ed. *Reinventing Religions: Syncretism and Transformation in Africa and the Americas*. Lanham, MD: Rowman & Littlefield, 2001.

Gremillion, Joseph, ed. *The Church and Culture since Vatican II: The Experience of North and Latin America*. Notre Dame, IN: University of Notre Dame Press, 1985.

Griswold, Wendy. *Cultures and Societies in a Changing World*. 3rd ed. Thousand Oaks, CA: Pine Forge, 2008.

Hamilton, Victor. *The Book of Genesis: Chapters 1-17*. Grand Rapids, MI: Eerdmans, 1990.

Hanegraaf, Wouter. *New Age Religion and Western Culture: Esotericism in the Mirror of Secular Thought*. Leiden: E. J. Brill, 1996.

Harnack, Adolf. *The Mission and Expansion of Christianity*. Translated by James Moffatt. Vol. I. Second, Enlarged and Revised ed. New York: Williams and Norgate, 1908.

Harris, W. T. and Harry Sawyer. *The Springs of the Mende Belief and Conduct*. Freetown: Sierra Leone University Press, 1968.

Hastings, Adrian, ed. *A World History of Christianity*. Grand Rapids, MI: Eerdmans, 1999.

_____. *One and Apostolic*. London: Darton, Longman & Todd, 1963.

Hayashida, Nelson. *Dreams in the African Church: The Significance of Dreams and Visions among Zambian Baptists*. New York: Rodopi, 1999.

Hebblethwaite, Peter. *Pope John XXIII: Shepherd of the Modern World*. Garden City, NY: Doubleday, 1985.

Heidel, Alexander. *The Babylonian Genesis: The Story of Creation*. Chicago, IL: The University of Chicago Press, 1963.

_____. *The Gilgamesh Epic and Old Testament*. Chicago, IL: University of Chicago Press, 1963.

Hengel, Martin. *Acts and the History of the Earliest Christianity*. London: SCM, 1979.

Herskovits, Melville. *Acculturation: The Study of Culture Contact*. New York: J. J. Augustin, 1938.

_____. *Man and His Works: The Science of Cultural Anthropology*. New York: Knopf, 1970.

Hesselgrave, David. *Communicating Christ Cross-Culturally*. Grand Rapids, MI: Academie, 1978.

Hill, Edmund, trans. *The Works of Saint Augustine: A Translation for the 21st Century*. Vol. 4. New York: New City, 1992.

Hillel, Daniel. *The Natural History of the Bible: An Environmental Exploration of the Hebrew Scriptures*. New York: Columbia University Press, 2006.

Hillman, Eugene. *Many Paths: A Catholic Approach to Religious Pluralism*. Maryknoll, NY: Orbis, 1989.

_____. *Toward an African Christianity*. Mahwah, NJ: Paulist, 1993.

Holmén, Tom. *Jesus and Jewish Covenant Thinking*. Leiden: Brill, 2001.

Hooft, Willem. *No Other Name: The Choice between Syncretism and Christian Universalism*. London: SCM, 1963.

Hotchkiss, Willis. *Then and Now in Kenya Colony*. New York: 1937.

Huxley, Elspeth. *The Sorcerer's Apprentice*. London: Chatto & Windus, 1949.

Idowu, Bolaji. *God in Yoruba Belief*. London: Longmans, 1962.

_____. *Olodumare: God in Yoruba Belief*. London: Longmans, Green and Co., 1962.

Irarràzaval, Diego. *Inculturation: New Dawn of the Church in Latin America*. Translated by Phillip Berrymawn. Maryknoll, NY: Orbis, 2000.

Isichei, Elizabeth. *A History of the Igbo People*. London: Macmillan, 1976.

Jervell, Jacob. *The Theology of the Acts of the Apostles*. Cambridge: Cambridge University Press, 1996.

Kalu, Ogbu, ed. *African Christianity: An African Story*. Pretoria: Department of Church History, University of Pretoria, 2005.

Kamstra, Jacques. *Encounter or Syncretism: The Initial Growth of Japanese Buddhism*. Leiden: Brill, 1967.

_____. *Synkretisme op de Grens tussen Theologie en Godsdienstfenomenologie*. Leiden: Brill, 1970.

Kenyatta, Jomo. *Facing Mount Kenya*. London: Heinemann, 1979.

Kline, Meredith. *The Structure of Biblical Authority*. Grand Rapids, MI: Eerdmans, 1972.

Komonchak, Joseph, Mary Collins and Dermot Lane, ed. *The New Dictionary of Theology*. Dublin: Gill & Macmillan, 1987.

Kraemer, Hendrick. *The Christian Message in a Non-Christian World*. London: The Edinburgh House, 1938.

_____. *Religion and the Christian Faith*. London: Lutterworth, 1956.

Kraft, Charles. *Anthropology for Christian Witness*. Maryknoll, NY: Orbis, 1996.

_____. *Christianity in Culture: A Study in Dynamic Biblical Theologizing in Cross-Cultural Perspective*. MaryKnoll, NY: Orbis 1979.

Kroeber, Alfred and Clyde Kluckhohn. *Culture: A Critical Review of Concepts and Definitions*. New York: Vintage, 1963.

Küng, Hans. *The Church*. Translated by Ray and Rosaleen Ockenden. London: Search, 1968.

_____. *The Council in Action: Theological Reflections on the Second Vatican Council*. Translated by Cecily Hastings. New York: Sheed and Ward, 1963.

Küster, Volker. *The Many Faces of Jesus Christ: Intercultural Christology*. Translated by John Bowden. London: SCM, 2001.

Leeuw, Gerardus van der. *Religion in Essence and Manifestation: A Study in Phenomenology*. Translated by J. E. Turner. Vol. 2. New York: Harper and Row, 1963.

Leith-Rose, Sylvia. *African Women: A Study of the Ibo of Nigeria*. London: Faber and Faber, 1944.

Leopold, Anita and Jeppe Jensen, ed. *Syncretism in Religion: A Reader*. New York: Routledge, 2004.

Leslie, Barnard, trans. *St. Justin Martyr: The First and Second Apologies*. Ancient Christian Writers, vol. 56, ed. Walter Burghardt, John Dillon and Dennis McManus. New York/Mahwah, NJ: Paulist, 1997.

Lightfoot, Joseph. *The Apostolic Fathers*. Grand Rapids, MI: Baker, 1987.

Lonergan, Bernard. *A Second Collection*. Edited by William Ryan and Bernard Tyrrell. London: Darton, Longman & Todd, 1974.

_____. *Method in Theology*. New York: Seabury, 1979.

Luzbetak, Louis. *The Church and Cultures: An Applied Anthropology for the Religious Worker*. Techny, IL: Divine Word, 1970.

_____. *The Church and Cultures: New Perspectives in Missiological Anthropology*. Maryknoll, NY: Orbis, 1988.

Machen, Gresham. *The Origin of Paul's Religion*. New York: Macmillan, 1925.

Magesa, Laurenti. *Anatomy of Inculturation: Transforming the Church in Africa*. Maryknoll, NY: Orbis, 2004.

Maher, Michael. *Genesis*. Old Testament Message. Vol. 2. Wilmington, DE: Glazier, 1982.

Maier, Paul. *Eusebius—The Church History: A New Translation with Commentary*. Grand Rapids, MI: Kregel, 1999.

Marcos, Natalio. *The Septuagint in Context: Introduction to the Greek Version of the Bible*. Translated by Wilfred Watson. Leiden: Brill, 2000.

Maroney, Eric. *Religious Syncretism*. London: SCM, 2006.

Martin, Luther. *Hellenistic Religions: An Introduction*. New York: Oxford University Press, 1987.

Martin, Ralph. *Worship in the Early Church*. London: Marshall, Morgan and Scott, 1964.

Mayers, Marvin. *Christianity Confronts Culture: A Strategy for Cross-Cultural Evangelism*. Grand Rapids, MI: Zondervan, 1974.

Mbefo, Luke. *The True African: Impulses for Self Affirmation*. Onitsha: Spiritan, 2001.

McCauley, Leo and Anthony Stephenson, trans. *The Fathers of the Church: A New Translation*. Vol. 64. Washington, DC: The Catholic University of America, 1970.

Meland, Bernard. *Faith and Culture*. Carbondale and Edwardsville: Southern Illionis University Press, 1953.

Mercado, Leonardo. *Inculturation and Filipino Theology*. Manila: Divine Word, 1992.

Métraux, Alfred. *Voodoo in Haiti*. Translated by Hugo Charteris. 2nd ed. London: André Deutsch, 1972.

Metzger, Bruce. *The New Testament: Its Background, Growth, and Content*. Second and Enlarged ed. Nashville, TN: Abingdon, 1989.

Mey, Peter De, Jacques Haers and Jozef Lamberts, ed. *The Mission to Proclaim and to Celebrate Christian Experience*. Leuven: Peeters, 2005.

Morris, Rudolph, trans. *The Fathers of the Church: A New Translation*. Vol. 7. Washington, DC: The Catholic University of America, 1949.

Mugambi, Jesse and Laurenti Magesa, ed. *Jesus in African Christianity: Experimentation and Diversty in African Christology*. Nairobi: Initiatives, 1989.

Nash, Rowland. *Christianity and the Hellenistic World*. Grand Rapids, MI: Zondervan, 1984.

Neckebrouck, Valeer. *Resistant Peoples: The Case of the Pastoral Maasai of East Africa*. Inculturation: Working Papers on Living Faith and Cultures, ed. Ary Crollius. Rome: Pontifical Gregorian University Press, 1993.

Nichols, Aidan. *Christendom Awake: On Reenergizing the Church in Culture*. Edinburgh: T & T Clark, 1999.

Newman, John. *An Essay on the Development of Christian Doctrine*. Notre Dame, IN: Notre Dame University Press, 1989.

Niebuhr, Reinhold. *The Nature and Destiny of Man: A Christian Interpretation*. Vol. 2. New York: Charles Scribner's Sons, 1955.

Norris, Richard, ed. *The Christological Controversy*. Philadelphia, PA: Fortress, 1980.

Nwabara, Samuel. *Iboland: A Century of Contact with Britain, 1860-1960*. London: Hodder and Stoughton, 1977.

Nwala, Uzodinma. *Igbo Philosophy*. Lagos: Lantern, 1985.

Nyerere, Julius. *Ujamaa*. London: Oxford University Press, 1974.

O'Collins, Gerald. *Incarnation: New Century Theology*. London/New York: Continuum, 2002.

_____. *Theology and Revelation*. Theology Today, ed. Edward Yarnold. Cork: Mercier, 1968.

_____. *Christology: A Biblical, Historical, and Systematic Study of Jesus*. Oxford, NY: Oxford University Press, 1995.

O'Donovan, Leo, ed. *A World of Grace: An Introduction to the Themes and Foundations of Karl Rahner's Theology*. New York: Crossroad, 1981.

O'Grady, John. *The Roman Catholic Church: Its Origin and Nature*. Mahwah, NJ: Paulist, 1997.

O'Malley, John. *Tradition and Transition: Historical Perspectives on Vatican II*. Wilmington, DE: Michael Glazier, 1989.

Omeregbe, Joseph. *A Philosophical Look at Religions*. Lagos: Joja, 1996.

Onwubiko, Oliver. *Theory and Practice of Inculturation: African Perspective*. Enugu: SNAAP, 1992.

Opsomer, Jan. *In Search of the Truth: Academic Tendencies in Middle Platonism*. Brussel: KAWLSK, 1998.

Osei-Bonsu, Joseph. *The Inculturation of Christianity in Africa: Antecedents and Guidelines from the New Testament and the Early Church*. Frankfurt: Peter Lang, 2005.

Paddila, Amado, ed. *Acculturation: Theory, Models and Some Findings*. Boulder, CO: Westview, 1980.

Pakkanen, Petra. *Interpreting Early Hellenistic Religions: A Study Based on the Mystery Cult of Demeter and the Cult of Isis*. Papers and Monographs of the Finnish Institute at Athens. Athens: D. Layias and E. Souvatzidakis, 1996.

Panikkar, Raimundo. *Myth, Faith and Hermeneutics*. New York: Paulist, 1979.

Pannenberg, Wolfhart. *Basic Questions in Theology*. Translated by George Kehm. Vol. 2. London: SCM, 1971.

Pawley, Bernard. *Looking at the Vatican II*. London: SCM, 1962.

Pelikan, Jaroslav. *Jesus through the Centuries: His Place in the History of Culture*. New Haven, CT: Yale University Press, 1985.

Phan, Peter. *Being Religious Interreligiously: Asian Perspectives on Interfaith Dialogue*. Maryknoll: Orbis, 2004.

Pieris, Aloysius. *Fire and Water: Basic Issues in Asian Buddhism and Christianity*. Maryknoll, NY: Orbis, 1996.

Poupard, Paul. *Church and Culture: Challenge and Confrontation, Inculturation and Evangelization*. Translated by John H. Miller. St. Louis, MO: Central Bureau, CCVA, 1994.

Principe, Walter. *Faith, History and Cultures: Stability and Change in Church Teachings*. The Pere Marquette Theology Lectures, no. 22. Milwaukee, WI: Marquette University Press, 1991.

Pritchard, James, ed. *Ancient Near Eastern Texts Relating to the Old Testament*. Princeton, NJ: Princeton University Press, 1950.

———. *The Ancient Near East in Pictures Relating to the Old Testament*. Princeton, NJ: Princeton University Press, 1969.

Raboteau, Albert. *Slave Religion: The "Invisible Institution" in the Antebellum South*. New York: Oxford University Press, 1978.

Rahner, Karl. *Belief Today*. Translated by Ray and Rosaleen Ockendon. New York: Sheed and Ward, 1967.

———. *Theological Investigations*. Translated by Edward Quinn. Vol. 20. London: Darton, Longman and Todd, 1981.

———. *Theological Investigations*. Translated by Kevin Smyth. Vol. 4. London: Darton, Longman and Todd, 1966.

Ratzinger, Joseph. *Truth and Tolerance: Christian Belief and World Religions*. Translated by Henry Taylor. San Francisco, CA: Ignatius, 2004.

———. *On the Way to Jesus Christ*. Translated by Michael Miller. San Francisco, CA: Ignatius, 2005.

Raush, Thomas. *Towards a Truly Catholic Church: An Ecclesiology for the Third Millennium*. Collegeville, MN: Liturgical Press, 2005.

Reese, James. *Hellenistic Influence on the Book of Wisdom and Its Consequences*. Rome: Biblical Institute, 1970.

Roberts, Alexander and James Donaldson, ed. *Ante-Nicene Fathers: Translations of the Writings of the Fathers down to AD 325*. Vol. 2. Grand Rapids, MI: Eerdmans, 1994.

———. *Ante-Nicene Fathers: Translations of the Writings of the Fathers down to AD 325*. Vol. 3. Grand Rapids, MI: Eerdmans, 1993.

Roll, Sussan. *Towards the Origins of Christmas*. Kampen: Kok Pharos, 1995.

Rowland, Tracey. *Culture and the Thomist Tradition after Vatican II*, ed. John Milbank, Catherine Pickstock and Graham Ward. London: Routledge, 2003.

Said, Edward. *Culture and Imperialism*. London: Chatto and Windus, 1993.

Sanneh, Lamin. *West African Christianity: The Religious Impact*. London: C. Hurst, 1983.

_____. *Translating the Message: The Missionary Impact on Culture.* Maryknoll, NY: Orbis, 1989.

Schillebeeckx, Edward. *Church: The Human Story of God.* Translated by John Bowden. London: SCM, 1990.

Schineller, Peter. *A Handbook on Inculturation.* Mahwah, NJ: Paulist, 1990.

Schmidt, Peter. *The Adoration of the Lamb.* Translated by Lee Preedy. Leuven: Davidsfonds, 2006.

Schreiter, Robert. *Constructing Local Theologies.* Maryknoll, NY: Orbis, 1985.

Schroer, Silvia. *Wisdom Has Built Her House: Studies on the Figure of Sophia in the Bible.* Translated by Linda Maloney and William McDonough. Collegeville, MN: The Liturgical Press, 2000.

Scruton, Roger. *Modern Culture.* London: Continuum, 2007.

Shwarz, Werner. *Principles and Problems of Biblical Translation: Some Reformation Controversies and Their Background.* Cambridge: Cambridge University Press, 1970.

Shorter, Aylward. *African Christian Theology: Adaptation or Incarnation.* London: Chapman, 1975.

_____. *Evangelization and Culture.* New York: Chapman, 1994.

_____. *Towards a Theology of Inculturation.* MaryKnoll, NY: Orbis, 1994.

Smith, Edwin. *African Ideas of God.* London: Edinburgh House, 1961.

Standaert, Nicholas. *Inculturation: The Gospel and Cultures.* Translated by Anton Bruggeman and Robert Murray. Philippines: St. Paul, 1990.

Stewart, Charles and Rosalind Shaw, ed. *Syncretism/Anti-syncretism: The Politics of Religious Synthesis.* London: Routledge, 1994.

Sullivan, Francis. *From Apostles to Bishops: The Development of Episcopacy in the Early Church.* New York: Paulist, 2001.

_____. *The Church We Believe in: One, Holy, Catholic and Apostolic.* New York: Paulist, 1988.

Sundkler, Bengt. *Bantu Prophets in South Africa.* 2nd ed. London: Oxford University Press, 1961.

Sykes, Stephen. *The Identity of Christianity.* London: SPCK, 1984.

Tanner, Kathryn. *Theories of Culture: A New Agenda for Theology.* Minneapolis, MN: Fortress, 1997.

Tanner, Norman, ed. *Decrees of the Ecumenical Councils: Nicaea I to Lateran V.* Vol. 1. London: Sheed & Ward, 1990.

_____. *Decrees of the Ecumenical Councils: Trent to Vatican II*. Vol. 2. London: Sheed & Ward, 1990.

Tempels, Placide. *Bantu Philosophy*. Translated by Colin King. Paris: Présence Africaine, 1959.

Tracy, David. *Blessed Rage for Order: The New Pluralism in Theology*. New York: Seabury, 1975.

Tylor, Edward. *Primitive Culture: Researches into the Development of Mythology, Philosophy, Religion, Language, Art, and Customs*. London: John Murray, 1871.

Udeafor, Ndubuisi. *Inculturation*. Enugu: SNAAP, 1994.

Udoidem, Inoibong. *Pope John Paul II on Inculturation*. Lanham, MD: University Press of America, 1996.

Vaux, Roland de. *Ancient Israel: Its Life and Institutions*. Translated by John McHugh. London: McGraw-Hill, 1961.

Volf, Miroslav. *After Our Own Likeness: The Church as the Image of the Trinity*. Grand Rapids, MI: Eerdmans, 1998.

Waal, Franz de. *The Ape and the Sushi Master: Cultural Reflections by a Primatologist*. New York: Basic, 2001.

Walligo, John *et al.*, ed. *Inculturation: Its Meaning and Urgency*. Nairobi: St. Paul, 1986.

Walsh, Gerald and Grace Monahan, trans., *Saint Augustine: The City of God, Books VIII-XVI*. Washington, DC: The Catholic University of America Press, 1952.

Williams, Raymond. *Keywords: A Vocabulary of Culture and Society*. London: Fontana, 1976.

3. ARTICLES

Abu-Lughod, Lila. "Writing against Culture." In *Recapturing Anthropology: Working in the Present*, edited by Richard Fox, 137-162. Santa Fe, NM: School of American Research, 1991.

Alberich, Emilio. "Is the Universal Catechism an Obstacle or a Catalyst in the Process of Inculturation?" *Concilium* 204, no. 4 (1989): 88-97.

Allan, William. "Religious Syncretism: The New Gods of Greek Tragedy." *Harvard Studies in Classical Philology* 102 (2004): 113-155.

Amaladoss, Michael. "Inculturation: Theological Perspective." *Jeevadhara: A Journal of Christian Interpretation* 6, no. 33 (1976): 293-302.

Amalorpavadass, Duraisamy. "Church and Culture." In *The New Dictionary of Theology*, ed. Joseph Komonchak, Mary Collins and Dermot Lane, 201-206. Dublin: Gill & Macmillan, 1990.

Amoah, Elizabeth, and Mercy Oduyoye. "Christ for African Women." In *With Passion and Compassion: Third World Women Doing Theology*, edited by Virginia Fabella and Mercy Oduyoye, 35-46. Maryknoll, NY: Orbis, 1988.

Anand, Subhash. "The Inculturation of the Eucharistic Liturgy." *VJTR* 57, no. 5 (1993): 269-293.

Angrosino, Michael. "The Culture Concept and the Mission of the Roman Catholic Church." *American Anthropologist* 96, no. 4 (1994): 824-823.

Arrupe, Pedro. "Catechesis and Inculturation." *Teaching All Nations* 15, no. 1 (1978): 21-24.

_____. "On Inculturation." *Acta Romana Societastis Iesu* 17, no. 1 (1978): 256-281.

Asiegbu, Martin. "Inculturation: Creating Maps of Christianity as One Understands It?" *Bigard Theological Studies* 25, no. 2 (2005): 93-110.

Baird, Robert. "Syncretism and the History of Religions." In *Syncretism in Religion: A Reader*, ed. Anita Leopold and Jeppe Jensen, 48-58. New York: Routledge, 2005.

Baker, Samuel. "The Races of the Nile Basin." In *Transactions of the Ethnological Society of London*. Vol. 5. 228-238. London: John Murray, 1867.

Balasuriya, Tissa. "Towards the Liberation of Theology in Asia." In *Asia's Struggle for Full Humanity*, ed. Virginia Fabella, 16-27. Maryknoll, NY: Orbis, 1980.

Baldovin, John. "Christmas." *Encyclopedia of Religion* 3 (2005): 1756-1757.

Bascom, William. "African Culture and the Missionary." *Civilization* 3 (1953): 491-502.

Bashford, James. "Adaptation of Modern Christianity to the People of the Orient." *American Journal of Theology* 17, no. 3 (1913): 389-394.

Baum, Gregory. "The Church against Itself." *Concilium* 204 (1989): xiii-xv.

Beauchamp, Paul. "The Role of the Old Testament in the Process of Building Local Churches." In *Bible and Inculturation*. Inculturation:

Working Papers on Living Faith and Cultures, ed. Ary Crollius, 1-16. Rome: Pontifical Gregorian University Press, 1983.

Bediako, Kwame. "Culture." In *New Dictionary of Theology*, ed. Sindair Ferguson and David Wright, 183-184. England: Inter-varsity, 1988.

Bernardin, Joseph. "Comment on 'Theology of Liberation' Document." *AFER* 26, no. 6 (1984): 373-374.

Berry, John. "Acculturation as Varieties of Adaptation." In *Acculturation: Theory, Models and Some Findings*, ed. Amado Padilla, 9-25. Boulder, CO: Westview, 1980.

Bianchi, Eugene. "John XXIII, Vatican II, and American Catholicism." *Annals of the American Academy of Political and Social Science* 387 (1970): 30-40.

Biernatzki, William. "Symbol and Root Paradigm: The Locus of Effective Inculturation." In *Effective Inculturation and Ethnic Identity*. Inculturation: Working Papers on Living Faith and Cultures, ed. Ary Crollius, 49-68. Rome: Pontifical Gregorian University Press, 1987.

Blomjous, Joseph. "Development in Mission Thinking and Practice 1950-1980: Inculturation and Interculturation." *AFER* 22, no. 6 (1980): 393-398.

Blükert, Kjell. "The Church as Mosaic: Catholicity in a Pluralistic Context." *International Journal for the Study of the Christian Church* 6, no. 2 (2006): 166-179.

Boeve, Lieven. "*Gaudium et Spes* and the Crisis of Modernity: The End of the Dialogue with the World." In *Vatican II and Its Legacy*. BETL, no. 166, ed. Mathijs Lamberigts and Leo Kenis, 83-93. Leuven: Leuven University Press, 2002.

Borofsky, Robert. "Introduction." *American Anthropologist* 103, no. 2 (2001): 432-435.

Boxer, Charles. "A Note on Portuguese Missionary Methods in the East: Sixteenth to Eighteenth Centuries." In *Christianity and Missions, 1450-1800*, ed. James Cummins, 77-90. Aldershot: Variorum, 1997.

Bragt, Jan van. "Multiple Religious Belonging of the Japanese People." In *Many Mansions?: Multiple Religious Belonging and Christian Identity*, ed. Catherine Cornille, 7-19. Maryknoll, NY: Orbis, 2002.

Braukamper, Ulrich. "Aspects of Religious Syncretism in Southern Ethiopia." *Journal of Religion in Africa* 22, no. 3 (1992): 194-207.

Brown, Diana and Mario Bick. "Religion, Class, and Context: Continuities and Discontinuities in Brazilian Umbanda." *American Ethnologist* 14 (1987): 73-93.

Cady, Linell. "Loosening the Category that Binds: Modern 'Religion' and the Promise of Cultural Studies." In *Converging on Culture: Theologians in Dialogue with Cultural Analysis and Criticism*, ed. Delwin Brown, Sheila Davaney and Kathryn Tanner, 17-40. Oxford, NY: Oxford University Press, 2001.

Carrier, Hervé. "The Church Meeting Cultures: Convergences and Perspectives." In *The Church and Culture since Vatican II: The Experience in North and Latin America*, ed. Joseph Gremillion, 140-152. Notre Dame, IN: University of Notre Dame Press, 1985.

_____. "The Contribution of the Council to Culture." In *Vatican II: Assessment and Perspectives Twenty-Five Years after (1962-1987)*, ed. René Latourelle, vol. 3, 442-465. New York/ Mahwah, NJ: Paulist, 1989.

_____. "Understanding Culture: The Ultimate Challenge of the World-Church." In *The Church and Culture since Vatican II: The Experience of North and Latin America*, ed. Joseph Gremillion, 13-30. Notre Dame, IN: University of Notre Dame Press, 1985.

Chibuko, Patrick. "The Structures of Rituals: Rules and Creativity." In *The Mission to Proclaim and to Celebrate Christian Existence*, ed. Peter De Mey, Jacques Haers and Jozef Lamberts, 292-306. Leuven: Peeters, 2005.

Chupungco, Anscar. "Inculturation." In *The New SCM Dictionary of Liturgy and Worship*, ed. Paul Bradshow, 244-251. London: SCM, 2002.

Clarke, Peter. "The Methods and Ideology of the Holy Ghost Fathers in Eastern Nigeria 1885-1905." *Journal of Religion in Africa* 6, no 2 (1974): 81-108.

Cobb, John. "Multiple Religious Belonging and Reconciliation." In *Many Mansions?: Multiple Religious Belonging and Christian Identity*, ed. Catherine Cornille, 20-28. Maryknoll, NY: Orbis, 2002.

Coleman John. "Vatican II as a Social Movement." In *The Belgian Contribution to the Council*. BETL, no. 216, ed. Doris Donnelly *et al*, 5-28. Leuven: Peeters, 2008.

Collet, Giancarlo. "From Theological Vandalism to Theological Romanticism? Questions about a Multicultural Identity of Christianity." *Concilium*, no. 2 (1994): 25-37.

Collins, Paul. "The Praxis of Inculturation for Mission: Roberto de Nobili's Example and Legacy." *Ecclesiology* 3, no. 3 (2007): 323-342.

Colpe, Carsten. "Syncretism." *Encyclopedia of Religion* 14 (1987): 218-227.

Crollius, Ary. "Inculturation: Newness and Ongoing Process." In *Inculturation: Its Meaning and Urgency*, ed. John Walligo *et al.*, 31-45. Nairobi: St. Paul, 1986.

_____. "Presentation." In *Cultural Change and Liberation in a Christian Perspective*, ed. Arij Crollius, ix-xi. Rome: Gregorian University Press, 1987.

_____. "The Meaning of Culture in Theological Anthropology." In *Inculturation: Its Meaning and Urgency*, ed. John Walligo *et al.*, 47-65. Nairobi: St. Paul, 1986.

_____. "What Is So New about Inculturation? A Concept and Its Implications." *Gregorianum* 59 (1979): 721-738.

Davaney, Sheila. "Theology and the Turn to Cultural Analysis." In *Converging on Culture: Theologians in Dialogue with Cultural Analysis*, ed. Delwin Brown, Sheila Davaney and Kathryn Tanner, 3-16. Oxford, NY: Oxford University Press, 2001.

Declor, Mathias. "The Apocrypha and Pseudepigrapha of the Hellenistic Period." In *The Cambridge History of Judaism*, ed. Winston Davis and Louis Finkelstein, vol. 2, 409-503. Cambridge: Cambridge University Press, 1989.

De Gasperis, Francesco. "Continuity and Newness in the Faith of the Mother Church of Jerusalem." In *Bible and Inculturation*. Inculturation: Working Papers on Living Faith and Cultures, ed. Ary Crollius, 17-69. Rome: Pontifical Gregorian University Press, 1983.

De Laguna, Grace. "Cultural Relativism and Science." *The Philosophical Review* 51, no. 2 (1942): 141-166.

DiPuccio, Denise. "The Magic of Umbanda in 'Gota d'água,'" *Luso-Brazilian Review* 27, no. 1 (1990): 1-10.

Droogers, André. "Syncretism: The Problem of Definition, the Definition of the Problem." In *Dialogue and Syncretism: An Interdisciplinary Approach*, ed. Jerald Gort *et al.*, 7-25. Grand Rapids, MI: Eerdmans, 1989.

Droogers, André and Sidney Greenfield. "Recovering and Reconstructing Syncretism." In *Reinventing Religions: Syncretism and Transformation in Africa and the Americas*, ed. Sidney Greenfield and André Droogers, 21-42. Lanham, MD: Rowman & Littlefield, 2001.

Dulles, Avery. "The Church is Catholic." In *The Many Marks of the Church*, ed. Williams Madges and Michael Daley, 43-47. New London, Conn: Twenty Third, 2006.

Fabella, Virginia. "Inculturation." In *Dictionary of Third World Theologies*, ed. Virginia Fabella and Rasiah Sugirtharajah, 104-106. Maryknoll: Orbis, 2000.

Fashole, Luke. "What is African Christian Theology." *AFER* 16, no. 4 (1974): 383-388.

Ferretti, Sergio. "Religious Syncretism in an Afro-Brazilian Cult House." In *Reinventing Religions: Syncretism and Transformation in Africa and the Americas*, ed. Sidney Greenfield and André Droogers, 87-97. Lanham, MD: Rowman & Littlefield, 2001.

Frykenberg, Robert. "Christians in India: A Historical Overview of Their Complex Origins." In *Christians and Missionaries in India: Cross-Cultural Communication since 1500*, ed. Robert Frykenberg and Alaine Low, 33-61. Grand Rapids, MI: Eerdmans, 2003.

Gallagher, Michael. "Inculturation: Some Theological Perspectives." *International Review of Mission* 85, no. 337 (1996): 173-180.

Galvin, John. "The Invitation of Grace." In *A World of Grace: An Introduction to the Themes and Foundations of Karl Rahner's Theology*, ed. Leo O'Donovan, 64-75. New York: Crossroad, 1981.

Gassmann, Günther. "The Church Is a Communion of Churches." In *The Catholicity of the Reformation*, ed. Carl Braaten and Robert Jenson, 93-105. Grand Rapids, MI: Eerdmans, 1996.

Geffré, Claude. "Double Belonging and the Originality of Christianity as a Religion." In *Many Mansions?: Multiple Religious Belonging and Christian Identity*, ed. Catherine Cornille, 93-105. Maryknoll, NY: Orbis, 2002.

Gilliland, Dean. "How 'Christian' Are African Independent Churches?" *Missiology: An International Review* 14, no. 3 (1986): 259-272.

Greenfield, Sidney. "Population Growth, Industrialization and the Proliferation of Syncretized Religions in Brazil." In *Reinventing Religions: Syncretism and Transformation in Africa and the Americas*, ed. Sidney Greenfield and André Droogers, 55-70. Lanham, MD: Rowman & Littlefield, 2001.

_____. "The Reinterpretation of Africa: Convergence and Syncretism in Brazilian Candomblé." In *Reinventing Religions: Syncretism and*

Transformation in Africa and Americas, ed. Sidney Greenfield and André Droogers, 113-129. Lanham, MD: Rowman & Littlefield, 2001.

Greinacher, Nobert and Nobert Mette. "Christianity: A Multicultural Experiment." *Concilium*, no. 2 (1994): vii-x.

Grenham, Thomas. "Interculturation: Exploring Changing Religious, Cultural, and Faith Identities in an African Context." *Pacifica* 14, no. 2 (2001): 191-206.

Groome, Thomas. "Inculturation: How to Proceed in a Pastoral Context." *Concilium*, no. 2 (1994): 120-133.

Hahn, Scott. "Covenant in the Old and New Testaments: Some Current Research (1994-2004)." *Currents in Biblical Research* 3, no. 2 (2005): 263-292.

Haleblian, Krikor. "The Problem of Contextualization." *Missiology: An International Review* 11, no. 1 (1983): 95-111.

Hamilton, Victor. *The Book of Genesis: Chapters 1-17*. Grand Rapids, MI: Eerdmans, 1990.

Häring, Hermann. "Experiences with the 'Short-Formula' of the Faith." *Concilium* 204, no. 4 (1989): 61-75.

Harris, Elisabeth. "Double Belonging in Sri Lanka: Illusion or Liberating Path?" In *Many Mansions?: Multiple Religious Belonging and Christian Identity*, ed. Catherine Cornille, 76-92. Maryknoll, NY: Orbis, 2002.

Hastings, Adrian. "150-550." In *A World History of the Church*, ed. Adrian Hastings, 25-65. Grand Rapids, MI: Eerdmans, 1999.

Herder, Johann. "Ideas towards a Philosophy of the History of Man." In *Theories of History*, ed. Patrick Gardiner, 34-51. Glencoe, IL: The Free Press, 1959.

Hewlett, Martinez. "Evolution: Evolutionism." *Encyclopedia of Religion* 5 (2005): 2913-2917.

Hiebert, Paul. "Critical Contextualization." *Missiology* 12, no. 3 (1984): 287-296.

_____. "The Gospel in Our Culture: Methods of Social and Cultural Analysis." In *The Church between Gospel and Culture: The Emerging Mission in North America*, ed. George Hunsberger and Craig Van Gelder, 139-157. Grand Rapids, MI: Eerdmans, 1996.

Hillman, Eugene. "Good News for Every Nation via Inculturation." *Louvain Studies* 25, no. 4 (2000): 336-347.

_____. "Inculturation." In *The New Dictionary of Theology*, ed. Joseph Komonchak, Mary Collins and Dermot Lane, 510-513. Dublin: Gill & Macmillan, 1987.

_____. "Missionary Approach to African Cultures." In *32 Articles Evaluating Inculturation of Christianity in Africa*, ed. Teresa Okure and Paul van Thiel, 148-162. Eldoret: AMECEA Gaba, 1990.

Hinga, Teresa. "Jesus Christ and the Liberation of Women in Africa." In *Feminist Theology from the Third World Perspective*, ed. Ursula King, 261-268. Maryknoll, NY: Orbis, 1994.

Ilogu, Edmund. "Independent African Churches in Nigeria." *International Review of Missions* 63, no. 252 (1974): 492-498.

Isichei, Elizabeth. "Seven Varieties of Ambiguity: Some Patterns of Igbo Response to Christian Missions." *Journal of Religion in Africa* 3, no. 3 (1970): 209-227.

Jaeger, Gertrude and Philip Selznick. "A Normative Theory of Culture." *American Sociological Review* 29, no. 5 (1964): 653-669.

Kalilombe, Patrick. "Doing Theology at the Grassroots: A Challenge for Professional Theologians." *AFER* 27, no. 3 (1985): 148-161.

Kalu, Ogbu. "Estranged Bedfellows?: The Demonisation of the Aladura in African Pentecostal Rhetoric." *Missionalia* 28, no. 2/3 (2000): 121-142.

Kamstra, Jacques. "The Religion of Japan: Syncretism or Religious Phenomenalism." In *Dialogue and Syncretism: An Interdisciplinary Approach*, ed. Jerald Gort *et al.*, 134-145. Grand Rapids, MI: Eerdmans, 1989.

Kane, Mort. "African Liturgy and the Papal Visit to Zaire." *AFER* 26, no. 4 (1984): 246-247.

Kanyoro, Musini. "Called to One Hope: The Gospel in Diverse Cultures." In *Called to One Hope: The Gospel in Diverse Cultures*, ed. Christopher Duraisingh, 96-110. Geneva: WCC, 1998.

Kasper, Walter. "The Theological Anthropology of *Gaudium et Spes*." *Communio* 23 (1996): 129-140.

Kelly, J. N. D. "'Catholic and Apostolic' in the Early Centuries," *One in Christ* 7, no. 3 (1970): 274-287.

Kloppenborg, John. "Isis and Sophia in the Book of Wisdom." *Harvard Theological Review* 75, no. 1 (1982): 57-84.

Kretschmar, Georg. "The Early Church and Hellenistic Culture." *International Review of Missions* 84, no. 332/333 (1995): 33-46.

Kroeber, Alfred. "Anthropology." *Scientific American* 183 (1950): 87-94.

Lamberigts, Mathijs. "*Gaudium et Spes*: A Council in Dialogue with the World." In *Scrutinizing the Signs of the Times in the Light of the Gospel*. BETL, no. 208, ed. John Verstraeten, 17-40. Leuven: Leuven University Press, 2007.

Lamberigts, Mathijs and Leo Dedreck. "The Role of Cardinal Léon-Joseph Suenens at Vatican II." In *The Belgian Contribution to the Second Vatican Council*. BETL, no. 216, ed. Doris Donnelly *et al*, 61-217. Leuven: Peeters, 2008.

Lambert, Bernard. "*Gaudium et Spes* and the Travail of Today's Ecclesial Conception." In *The Church and Culture since Vatican II: The Experience of North and Latin America*, ed. Joseph Gremillion, 31-52. Notre Dame, IN: University of Notre Dame Press, 1985.

Leeuw, Gerardus van der. "The Dynamics of Religions. Syncretism. Mission." In *Syncretism in Religion: A Reader*, ed. Anita Leopold and Jeppe Jensen, 98-102. New York: Routledge, 2005.

Levering, Mathew. "Pastoral Perspectives on the Church in the Modern World." In *Vatican II: Renewal within Tradition*, ed. Mathew Lamb and Mathew Levering, 165-183. Oxford: Oxford University Press, 2008.

Liddy, T. "Catholic." In *Encyclopedic Dictionary of Religion*, ed. Paul Meagher and Thomas O'Brien, 669-670. Philadelphia, PA: Sisters of St Joseph, 1979.

Lobkowicz, Nicholas. "Christianity and Culture." *The Review of Politics* 53, no. 2 (1991): 373-389.

Lohmann, Roger. "Culture." *Encyclopedia of Religion* 3 (2005): 2086-2090.

Magesa, Laurenti. "Instruction on the 'Theology of Liberation:' A Comment." *AFER* 27, no. 1 (1984): 3-8.

Malinowski, Bronislaw. "Review of Six Essays on Culture by Albert Blumenthal." *American Sociological Review* 4, no. 4 (1939): 588-592.

Marinda, Reuben. "The Good News in Zion." *Missionalia* 28, no. 2/3 (2000): 233-241.

Martin, Luther. "Syncretism, Historicism, and Cognition: A Response to Michael Pye." In *Syncretism in Religion: A Reader*, ed. Anita Leopold and Jeppe Jensen, 286-294. New York: Routledge, 2005.

Mattam, Joseph. "The Message of Jesus and Our Customary Theological Language: An Indian Approach to a New Language and Inculturation." *Exchange* 34, no. 3 (2005): 116-134.

Mbefo, Luke. "Tensions between Christianity and African Traditional Religion: The Igbo Case." In *Yearbook of Contextual Theologies*, vol. 93, 117-132. Frankfurt: Verlag, 1994.

McGrath, Marcos. "The Impact of *Gaudium et Spes*: Medellin, Puebla, and Pastoral Creativity." In *The Church and Culture since Vatican II: The Experience of North and Latin America*, ed. Joseph Gremillion, 61-73. Notre Dame, IN: Notre Dame University Press, 1985.

McKenna, S. J. "Pelagius and Pelagianism." *New Catholic Encyclopedia* 11 (1967): 60-63.

Meagher, Paul. "Catholicity." In *Encyclopedic Dictionary of Religion*, ed. Paul Meagher and Thomas O'Brien, 677-678. Philadelphia, PA: Sisters of St Joseph, 1979.

Mendenhall, George. "Covenant Forms in Israelite Tradition." *The Biblical Archaeology* 17, no. 3 (1954): 50-76.

Merigan, Terrence. "What's in a Word? Revelation and Tradition in Vatican II and Contemporary Theology." In *Vatican II and Its Legacy*. BETL, no. 166, ed. Mathijs Lamberigts and Leo Kenis, 59-83. Leuven: Leuven University Press, 2002.

Metz, Johann-Baptist. "Unity and Diversity: Problems and Prospects for Inculturation." *Concilium* 204, no. 4 (1989): 79-87.

Moffat, James. "Syncretism." *The Encyclopaedia of Religion and Ethics* 12 (1994): 155-157.

Motta, Roberto. "Ethnicity, Purity, the Market and Syncretism in Afro-Brazilian Cults." In *Reinventing Religions: Syncretism and Transformation in Africa and the Americas*, ed. Sidney Greenfield and André Droogers, 71-85. Lanham, MD: Rowman & Littlefield, 2001.

Mugambi, Jesse. "Christological Paradigms in African Christianity." In *African Christianity: Experimentation and Diversity in African Christology*, ed. Jesse Mugambi, 136-161. Nairobi: Initiatives, 1989.

Murphy, Francis. "Vatican Politics: Structure and Function." *World Politics* 26, no. 4 (1974): 542-559.

Nauwens, Leo. "Clash between Globalization and Local Cultures." In *Liberation Theologies on Shifting Grounds: A Clash of Socio-Economic and Cultural Paradigms*. BETL, no. 135, ed. Georges De Schrijver, 272-283. Leuven: Leuven University Press, 1998.

Nebechukwu, Augustine. "Third World Theology and the Recovery of African Identity." *Journal of Inculturation Theology* 2, no. 1 (1995): 17-27.

Nicolau, Luis. "Transformations of the Sea and Thunder Vodums in the Gbe-Speaking Area and in the Bahian Jeje Candomblé." In *Africa and the Americas: Interconnections during the Slave Trade*, ed. José Curto and Renée Soulodre-La France, 69-94. Trenton, NJ: Africa World, 2004.

Njoku, Chukwudi. "The Missionary Factor in African Christianity, 1884-1914." In *African Christianity*, ed. Ogbu Kalu, 218-255. Pretoria: Department of Church History, University of Pretoria, 2005.

Nkéramihigo, Théoneste. "Inculturation and the Specificity of Christian Message." In *Inculturation: Its Meaning and Urgency*, ed. John Walligo *et al.*, 67-74. Nairobi: St. Paul, 1986.

Nkwoka, A. O. "New Testament Research and Cultural Heritage: A Nigerian Example." *Asia Journal of Theology* 17, no. 2 (2003): 287-300.

Ochsner, Knud. "Church, School and the Clash of Cultures: Examples from North-West Tanzania." *Journal of Religion in Africa* 4, no. 2 (1971): 97-118.

O'Collins, Gerald. "The Incarnation: The Critical Issues." In *The Incarnation: An Interdisciplinary Symposium on the Incarnation of the Son of God*, ed. Stephen Davis, Daniel Kendall and Gerald O'Collins, 1-27. Oxford, NY: Oxford University Press, 2002.

O'Daly, Gerard. "Augustine on the Measurement of Time: Some Comparisons with Aristotelian and Stoic Texts." In *Neoplatonism and Early Christian Thought: Essays in Honour of A. H. Armstrong*, ed. H. J. Blumenthal and R. A. Markus, 171-179. London: Variorum, 1981.

Okolo, Chukwudum. "Igbo Culture and Evangelization: An Inculturation Perspective." *Bigard Theological Studies* 19, no. 1 (1999): 70-87.

Okure, Teresa. "Inculturation: Biblical/Theological Basis." In *32 Articles Evaluating Inculturation of Christianity in Africa*, ed. Teresa Okure and Paul van Thiel, 54-88. Eldoret: AMECEA Gaba, 1990.

O'Leary, Joseph. "Towards a Buddhist Interpretation of Christian Truth." In *Many Mansions?: Multiple Religious Belonging and Christian Identity*, ed. Catherine Cornille, 29-43. Maryknoll, NY: Orbis, 2002.

O'Meara, Thomas. "A History of Grace." In *A World of Grace: An Introduction to the Themes and Foundations of Karl Rahner's Theology*, ed. Leo O'Donovan, 76-91. New York: Crossroad, 1981.

Ong, Walter. "T. S. Eliot and Today's Ecumenism." *Religion and Literature* 21, no. 2 (1989): 1-17.

Opoku, Kofi. "Communalism and Community in the African Heritage." *International Review of Missions* 79, no. 316 (1991): 487-492

Oshun, Chris. "Healing Practices among Aladura Pentecostals: An Intercultural Study." *Missionalia* 28, no. 2/3 (2000): 242-252.

Otunga, Maurice. "African Cultures and Life-Centered Catechesis." *Teaching All Nations* 15, no. 1 (1978): 25-27.

Outler, Albert. "After-Thought of a Protestant Observer of Vatican II." In *The Church and Culture since Vatican II: The Experience of North and Latin America*, ed. Joseph Gremillion, 153-155. Notre Dame, IN: University of Notre Dame Press, 1985.

Panikkar, Raimundo. "The Dialogical Dialogue." In *Contemporary Approaches to the Study of Religion*, ed. Frank Whaling, 201-221. Berlin: Mouton, 1984.

Peel, J. "Syncretism and Religious Change." *Comparative Studies in Society and History* 10, no. 2 (1968): 121-141.

Pénoukou, Efoé-Julien. "Inculturation." *Encyclopedia of Christian Theology* 2 (2005): 767-771.

Pottmeyer, Herman. "A New Phase in the Reception of Vatican II: Twenty Years of Interpretation of the Council." In *The Reception of Vatican II*, ed. Guiseppe Alberigo, Jean-Pierre Jossua and Joseph Komonchak, 27-43. Washington, DC: University of America Press, 1987.

Prabhu, George. "The New Testament as a Model of Inculturation." *Jeevadhara: A Journal of Christian Interpretation* 6, no. 33 (1976): 268-282.

Pye, Michael. "Syncretism and Ambiguity." In *Syncretism in Religion: A Reader*, ed. Anita Leopold and Jeppe Jensen, 59-67. New York: Routledge, 2005.

_____. "Syncretism and Ambiguity." *Numen* 81, no. 2 (1971): 83-93.

Quesnell, Quentin. "Grace." In *The New Dictionary of Theology,* ed. Joseph Komonchak, Mary Collins and Dermot Lane, 437-450. Dublin: Gill & Macmillan, 1987.

Ranger, Terence. "'Taking on the Mission Task': African Spirituality and the Mission Churches of Manicaland in the 1930s." In *Christianity and the African Imagination: Essays in Honour of Adrian Hastings*, ed. David Maxwell and Ingrid Lawrie, 93-126. Leiden: Brill, 2002.

_____. "African Initiated Churches." *Transformation* 24, no. 2 (2007): 65-71.

Rayan, Samuel. "Flesh of India's Flesh." *Jeevadhara: A Journal of Christian Interpretation* 6, no. 33 (1976): 259-267.

"Results of the SEDOS Seminar on the Future of Mission, Rome, March 1981." *SEDOS*, no. 7 (1981): 118-136.

Riccardi, Andrea. "The Tumultous Opening Days of the Council." In *History of Vatican II: The Formation of the Council's Identity, First Period and Intersession, October 1962-September 1963*, ed. Guiseppe Alberigo and Joseph Komonchak, vol. 2, 1-67. Leuven: Peeters, 1997.

Ringgren, Helmer. "The Problems of Syncretism." In *Syncretism*, ed. Sven Hartman, 7-14. Stockholm: Almqvist & Wiksell, 1969.

Rodseth, Lars. "Another Passage to Pragmatism." *American Anthropologist* 103, no. 2 (2001): 440-442.

Roll, Sussan. "Christmas and Its Cycle." *New Catholic Encyclopedia* 3 (2003): 551-557.

Rottländer, Peter. "One World: Opportunity or Threat for the Global Church?" *Concilium* 204, no. 4 (1989): 107-117.

Rudolph, Kurt. "Syncretism: From Theological Invective to a Concept in the Study of Religions." In *Syncretism in Religion: A Reader*, ed. Anita Leopold and Jeppe Jensen, 68-85. New York: Routledge, 2005.

Russell, Robert. "The Role of Neoplatonism in St. Augustine's *De Civitate Dei*." In *Neoplatonism and Early Christian Thought: Essays in Honour of A. H. Armstrong*, ed. H. J. Blumenthal and R. A. Markus, 160-170. London: Variorum, 1981.

Ryan, Patrick. "Seven Theses on Inculturation: A Response to 'Inculturation as a Face of African Theology Today.'" In *Faces of African Theology*, ed. Patrick Ryan, 170-181. Nairobi: CUEA, 2003.

Schiffer, Wilhelm. "New Religions in Postwar Japan." *Monumenta Nipponica* 11, no. 1 (1955): 1-14.

Schineller, Peter. "Inculturation or Syncretism: What is the Real Issue?" *International Bulletin of Missionary Research* 16, no. 2 (1992): 50-53.

_____. "Inculturation as the Pilgrimage to Catholicity." *Concilium* 204, no. 4 (1989): 98-106.

_____. "Inculturation: Why So Slow?" *Journal of Inculturation Theology* 4, no. 2 (1997): 131-140.

_____. "Ten summary Statements on the Meaning, Challenge and Significance of Inculturation as Applied to the Church and Society of Jesus in the United States, in Light of the Global Process of Modernization." In *On Being the Church in a Modern Society*. Inculturation: Working Papers on Living Faith and Cultures, ed. Ary Crollius, 53-83. Rome: Pontifical Gregorian University Press, 1983.

Schmidt, Paul. "Some Criticisms of Cultural Relativism." *The Journal of Philosophy* 52, no. 25 (1955): 780-791.

Schoffeleers, Mathew. "Pentecostalism and Neo-Traditionalism: The Religious Polarization of a Rural District in Southern Malawi." In *Christianity and African Imagination: Essays in Honour of Adrian Hastings*, ed. David Maxwell and Ingrid Lawrie, 225-270. Leiden: Brill, 2002.

Schreiter, Robert. "Defining Syncretism: An Interim Report." *International Bulletin of Missionary Research* 17, no. 2 (1993): 50-53.

_____. "Faith and Cultures: Challenges to a World Church." *Theological Studies* 50 (1989): 744-760.

_____. "Inculturation or Identification with Culture." *Concilium*, no. 2 (1994): 15-24.

_____. "Local Theologies in the Local Church: Issues and Methods." In *Sourcebook for Modern Catechesis*, ed. Michael Warren, 69-84. Winona, MN: St Mary's, 1997.

Schrijver, Georges De. "*Gaudium et Spes* on the Church's Dialogue with Contemporary Society and Culture: A Seedbed for the Divergent Options Adopted in Medellin, Puebla, and Santo Domingo." In *Vatican II and Its Legacy*. BETL, no. 166, ed. Mathijs Lamberigts and Leo Kenis, 289-324. Leuven: Leuven University Press, 2002.

Schroer, Silvia. "Transformations of Faith: Documents of Intercultural Learning in the Bible." *Concilium*, no. 2 (1994): 3-14.

Shenk, Wilbert. "Mission Agency and African Independent Churches." *International Review of Missions* 63, no. 252 (1974): 475-491.

_____. "Missionary Encounter with Culture." *International Bulletin of Missionary Research* 15, no. 3 (1991): 104-109.

Shorter, Aylward. "Inculturation: The Premise of Universality." In *A Universal Faith?: Peoples, Cultures, Religions, and the Christ*, ed. Catherine Cornille and Valeer Neckebrouck, 1-19. Louvain: Peeters, 1992.

Shweder, Richard. "Rethinking the Object of Anthropology and Ending up Where Kroeber and Kluckhohn Began." *American Anthropologist* 103, no. 2 (2001): 437-440.

Sjørslev, Inger. "Possession and Syncretism: Spirits as Mediators in Modernity." In *Reinventing Religions: Syncretism and Transformation in Africa and the Americas*, ed. Sidney Greenfield and André Droogers, 131-144. Lanham, MD: Rowman & Littlefield, 2001.

Small, Meredith. "Do Animals Have Culture?: An Eminent Primatologist Challenges Long-held Convictions about What Makes Humans Distinct." *Scientific American*, July 2001, 92-93.

Smith, Simon. "The Vatican Document on Liberation Theology." *AFER* 26, no. 6 (1984): 372-373.

Smith, Theresa. "The Church of the Immaculate Conception: Inculturation and Identity among the Anishnaabeg of Manitoulin Island." *American Indian Quarterly* 20, no. 4 (1996): 515-526.

Stewart, Charles. "Syncretism and Its Synonyms." *Diacritics* 29, no. 3 (1999): 40-62.

Stolzenberg, Nomi. "What We Talk about When We Talk about Culture." *American Anthropologist* 103, no. 2 (2001): 442-444.

Stringer, Martin. "Rethinking Animism: Thoughts from the Infancy of Our Discipline." *The Journal of Royal Anthropology Institute* 5, no. 4 (1999): 541-555.

Teske, Raymond and Bardin Nelson. "Acculturation and Assimilation: A Clarification." *American Ethnologist* 1, no. 2 (1974): 351-367.

Tetlow, Joseph. "The Inculturation of Catholicism in the United States." In *On Being Church in a Modern Society*. Inculturation: Working Papers on Living Faith and Cultures, ed. Ary Crollius, 15-50. Rome: Pontifical Gregorian University Press, 1983.

Thiel, John. "Pluralism in Theological Truth." *Concilium*, no. 6 (1994): 56-69.

Thils, Gustav and R. Kress. "Catholicity." *New Catholic Encyclopedia* 3 (2003): 339-340.

Thurston, Herbert. "Catholic." *The Catholic Encyclopedia* 3 (1980): 449-452.

Tippett, Alan. "Christopaganism or Indigenous Christianity." In *Christopaganism or Indigenous Christianity?*, ed. Tetsunao Yamamori and Charles Taber, 13-34. South Pasadena, CA: William Carey Library, 1975.

Tracy, David. "World Church or World Catechism: The Problem of Eurocentrism." *Concilium* 204, no. 4 (1989): 28-37.

Troeltsch, Ernst. "The Place of Christianity among the World Religions." In *Attitudes toward Other Religions*, ed. Owen Thomas, 73-91. New York: Harper & Row, 1969.

Tucci, Roberto. "The Proper Development of Culture." In *Commentary on the Documents of Vatican II: Pastoral Constitution on the Church in the Modern World*, ed. Herbert Vorgrimler, vol. 2, 246-287. New York: Herder & Herder, 1969.

Turbanti, Giovanni. "The Attitude of the Church to the Modern World at and after Vatican II." *Concilium*, no. 6 (1992): 87-96.

Turner, Harold. "A Typology for African Religious Movements." *Journal of Religion in Africa* 1, no. 1 (1967): 1-34.

_____. "New Religious Movements and Syncretism in Tribal Cultures." In *Dialogue and Syncretism: An Interdisciplinary Approach*, ed. Jerald Gort *et al.*, 105-113. Grand Rapids, MI: Eerdmans, 1989.

Ubah, Christopher. "Religious Change among the Igbo during the Colonial Period." *Journal of Religion in Africa* 18, no. 1 (1988): 71-91.

Ukpong, Justin. "African Inculturation Theology." *Voices from the Third World* 9, no. 4 (1986): 20-31.

_____. "Christology and Inculturation: A New Testament Perspective." In *Paths of African Theology*, ed. Rosino Gibellini, 40-61. Maryknoll, NY: Orbis, 1994.

_____. "Contextualization: A Historical Survey." *AFER* 29, no. 5 (1987): 278-286.

Umorem, Uduakobong. "Socio-Cultural Anthropology and the Methodology of Inculturation in Africa." *Journal of Inculturation Theology* 2, no. 1 (1995): 5-16.

Voeks, Robert. "Sacred Leaves of Brazilian Candomble." *Geographical Review* 80, no. 2 (1990): 118-131.

Vroom, Hendrik. "Syncretism and Dialogue: A Philosophical Analysis." In *Dialogue and Syncretism: An Interdisciplinary Approach*, ed. Jerald Gort *et al.*, 26-35. Grand Rapids, MI: Eerdmans, 1989.

Walligo, John. "Making a Church That Is Truly African." In *Inculturation: Its Meaning and Urgency*, ed. John Walligo *et al.*, 11-30. Nairobi: St. Paul, 1986.

Weise, Leopold von. "Review of Six Essays on Culture by Albert Blumenthal." *American Sociological Review* 4, no. 4 (1939): 592-594.

Werbick, Jürgen. "Can the Universal Catechism Help Overcome the Crisis in Handing on the Faith?" *Concilium* 204, no. 4 (1989): 50-60.

Wilde, Melissa. "How Culture Mattered at Vatican II: Collegiality Triumphs Authority in the Council's Social Movement Organizations." *American Sociological Review* 69, no. 4 (2004): 576-602.

Williams, M. E. "Catholic." *New Catholic Encyclopedia* 3 (2003): 275-276

Yakubu, Victor. "Contextual Theology: A Basic Need within the Church in Africa Today." *AFER* 38, no. 3 (1996): 130-147.

Zuern, Theodore. "The Preservation of Native Identity in the Process of Inculturation, as Experienced in American Indian Cultures." In *On Being the Church in a Modern Society. Inculturation: Working Papers on Living Faith and Cultures*, ed. Ary Crollius, 1-11. Rome: Pontifical Gregorian University Press, 1983.

4. Internet Sources

Benedict XVI. *Address to the Roman Curia* 22 December 2005. Available from http://www.vatican.va/holy_father/benedict_xvi/speeches/2005/december/hf_ben_xvi spe_2005. Accessed 10 March 2009.

Boeve, Lieven. *Between Relativizing and Dogmatizing: A Plea for an Open Concept of Tradition*. Available from http://eapi.admu.edu.ph/eapr95/boeve.htm. Accessed 31 March 2009.

Congregation for the Doctrine of the Faith. *Instruction on Certain Aspects of the "Theology of Liberation," Libertatis Nuntius*, 6 August 1984. Available from http://www.vatican.va/roman_curia/congregations/cfaith/documents/rc_con_cfaith_doc-19840806_theology-liberation_en.html. Accessed 11 April 2008.

Dulles, Avery. "Can Philosophy Be Christian?" *First Things: The Journal of Religion, Culture and Public Life* (2000). Available from http://www.firstthings.com/article.php3?id_article=2599. Accessed 4 March 2009.

http://www.ewtn.com/library/PAPALDOC/P12CIRI.HTM. Accessed 20 March 2009.

John Paul II. *Discourse to the Plenary Assembly of the Pontifical Council for Culture*, 18 January 1983. Available from http://www.vatican.va/holy_father/john_paul_ii/speeches/1996/documents/

hf_jp—ii_spe_18011983_address-to-pc-culture_en.html. Accessed 13 April 2009.

Middle Platonism: General Characteristics. Available from http://www.theologywebsite.com/history/midplato.shtml. Accessed 17 April 2009.

INDEX

Printed in the United States
By Bookmasters